LEAVING THE WIRE

—

An Infantryman's Iraq

David P. Ervin

Bookbaby Publishing | Portland, Oregon

LEAVING THE WIRE: AN INFANTRYMAN'S IRAQ

Cover Design by Tyler Young Guzman and Tif Holmes

Print ISBN: 978-1-68222-960-6
eBook ISBN: 9781483509440
BookBaby Publishing
Portland, OR

davidervinauthor.com

To the Soldiers of Echo Troop

Acknowledgements

A book may be written by its author, but it is made possible through the support of many. I must extend my heartfelt gratitude to the men of Echo Troop, 2-11 Armored Cavalry Regiment and the families of our fallen brothers. Without their enthusiastic support for my decision to tell this story, it wouldn't have been told. Mark Steppe and Tyler Young Guzman helped me recover many memories. Both of them, along with Tyler's wife Brandy, offered their friendship and support during some tough times. Brandy proofread a draft as well. Chaz Ervin read through drafts of the manuscript and offered invaluable insight and suggestions. April (Muncy) Taylor read a manuscript and, more importantly, offered me the kind of support only a true and dear friend could. Tammy Nutter and Leslie Lombardy each read drafts and offered their own useful perspectives.

Karen Rinaldi kept me hopeful through the tour itself and provided me with the many letters I sent her. Seth Lombardy kept me moving forward through the artistic process in immeasurable ways. Joseph Pierstorff reminded me of what this project was about at times. Many others helped in ways large and small, and all deserve credit for keeping me motivated and inspired to tell this story; Janet Cruise, Chuck Ervin, Lance Evin, Amy McCambridge Steppe, Gary Jarrell, Rhonda King Cooper, Robert Villers, Amy Long, John McConihay, Karie Martin, Sara Gianola, Emily Nenni, Rebecca Summers, Tom Lyons, and Caitlin Carrigan are among the many. There are more, and to each I am deeply grateful. I hope this story does their support the justice it deserves.

Preface

What's contained within the following pages is nothing more or less than a war story. In certain regards it may be useful to history even if its scope is limited to that of a participant. If the Iraq War is anything, it is difficult to understand. The circumstances that surround that conflict are unmatched in their complexity and ambiguity, and as such are, and will continue to be, the subject of many contentious historical works. When I arrived there at the beginning of 2005, the campaign had already turned into a fight against a multi-faceted insurgency and a struggle to promote and stabilize the nascent Iraqi government. There were no front lines, no easily distinguishable enemies, no clear victories or defeats, no vast numbers of causalities. In that way, it differs from most other wars in our country's history. But it was still a war. It was still a violent clash of opposing forces regardless of the form it took. What that war was like for a US combatant is the subject of this book.

Throughout my year there as an infantryman I experienced the essence of the conflict. Grunts in Iraq had no other task but the relentless search for enemies and the provision of security and support for an ambivalent, if not hostile, population. We raided houses of suspected insurgents, set up ambushes to catch them at their deadly work, patrolled endlessly to deny them a safe haven, and lived among the people to show them our dedication to their safety. We were shot at, bombed, mortared, and rocketed. We killed and maimed, and we suffered our own losses. Our adversaries were sophisticated in their own way and highly effective in their employment of guerilla tactics against us and of terrorism against their neighbors. This took place in an environment that was absolutely foreign and notably harsh for us young Americans. It was an intense physical and mental experience, and one which I remember very well.

A common shortcoming of memoirs in terms of their usefulness to history is that human memory is problematic. Over time, details fade away and the edges of the broader outlines of any given period of time become dulled. Throughout this book I have been true to my memory and taken measures to ensure its accuracy. I have kept in touch with many of my brothers-in-arms, and their memories aided me greatly. My letters home, numerous photographs and videos from the tour, and my own notes recorded shortly after returning have helped as well. It is certainly not everything I remember, but what I thought was most important is a part of this story. While much of the dialogue is generalized, and some of the names are changed, my creative license extends no further. Most of the memories from that time and place are intense; the impression they leave is indelible. Still, we each remember things differently sometimes, and individual experiences varied even between the men of my platoon.

The other failing attributed to memoirs is that they are self-serving. A writer of his own story will, at times, render a rosy version of events, employ enough hindsight, or bash the actions and decisions of others to explain away any personal shortcomings. I have not done so here. Besides my own conduct, I do not put others' actions under scrutiny. If anything, I have bared it all in these pages on a personal level. Often I did things and thought in ways for which I am not particularly proud in hindsight, but they are recorded here. Omitting them would diminish the credibility of this story and deprive the reader of essential components in understanding the character of this war. Furthermore, it is the task of historians to analyze the events and ask questions about them. It is the role of the people who lived through them to record what it was like to do so. I have not included any hindsight; my reflections are those which occurred at the time and serve to provide the reader a sense of what was going through our minds as we experienced the war.

This book is just that. It provides answers the question posed to many combat veterans; "what was it like?" It is not easily answered. Often there's just no frame of reference around which to shape that response. In another sense, it's simply too painful a story to tell. Someone must reply, though, and this book is my answer. It is still my own answer. I cannot tell the story of the millions of my comrades who went to Iraq with the same authority that I can my own. But, if by providing a deeply personal and brutally honest version of events as I saw them I can answer that question– at least in part – then this work will have achieved its goal.

David P. Ervin
Morgantown, 2013

Glossary of Acronyms

AAFES – Army Air Force Exchange Services

ACR – Armored Cavalry Regiment

ACU – Army Combat Uniform

AO – Area of Operations, also called "sector"

APC – Armored Personnel Carrier

ASR – Alternate Supply Route

BC – Bradley Commander

CLS – Combat Lifesaver

CP(#) – Checkpoint

CP – Command Post

COB – Civilians on the Battlefield

DCU – Desert Combat Uniform

EFP – Explosively Formed Projectile

EOD – Explosive Ordnance Disposal

FOB – Forward Operating Base

HHT – Headquarters and Headquarters Troop

IA – Iraqi Army

IBA – Interceptor Body Armor

IP – Iraqi Police

ISF – Iraqi Security Forces (comprised of Iraqi Army and Iraqi Police)

ISU – Integrated Sight Unit

LSA – Logistical Support Area

MAC – Military Airlift Command

MiTT – Military Transition Team

MOUT – Military Operations Urban Terrain

MSR – Main Supply Route

MWR – Morale, Welfare, Recreation
NCO – Non-commissioned Officer
NTC – National Training Center
NVG – Night Vision Goggles
OIF – Operation Iraqi Freedom
OP – Observation Post
OPFOR – Opposing Forces
OPSEC – Operational Security
OSV – Opposing Forces Surrogate Vehicle
PCIs and PCCs – Pre-combat inspections and pre-combat checks
PMCS – Preventative Maintenance Checks and Services
PSYOPs – Psychological Operations
PT – Physical Training
PX – Post Exchange
QRF – Quick Reaction Force
SAW – Squad Automatic Weapon
SF – Special Forces
SOP – Standard Operating Procedure
TC – Truck or Track Commander
TCP – Tactical Checkpoint
TRP – Target Reference Point
VBIED – Vehicle-borne improvised explosive device

Many aspects of my early life pointed me in the direction of the military service. My first word was even "GI Joe." I could begin this story with my childhood in the suburbs of Charleston, West Virginia, where I devoured military history and was active in the Boy Scouts. Or I could begin by telling you that my senior year in high school coincided with September 11, 2001. That event made up my mind that I would enlist in the Army and choose the infantry as my occupation, knowing that I'd go to war one day. Perhaps I could begin in Fort Benning, Georgia, where I became a soldier. But the truth is that many of us took similar paths for different reasons. Where this story really starts is in the desert of southern California. That's where I learned what it meant to be an infantryman and what life in the Army was like. It's where I made friends that I could call brothers. Eventually, it was the place where I trained for war. Not at first, though.

Fort Irwin, California, situated on a thousand square miles of Mojave Desert just outside of Barstow, was the National Training Center (NTC) for the Army's combat units. Going to a rotation at NTC was a simulation of the entire deployment process to include moving equipment and vehicles to the training area, large-scale war games, and live-fire exercises. I arrived there in November 2002 and was assigned to 1st platoon, Echo Troop, 2nd Squadron of the 11th Armored Cavalry Regiment (ACR). It was our role to play the bad guys, or opposing forces (OPFOR), during the war games, so it was a unique duty assignment. We weren't considered an operational combat unit. We wore different uniforms, our vehicles had no weapons systems, and we lacked a full complement of modern weapons and equipment. In short, nothing about our unit was designed to deploy to a war zone.

For the most part, fulfilling the 11th's primary mission undermined our focus on real-world preparation as combat soldiers. Even so, there were things to learn. The biggest lesson was my introduction to the mechanized infantry. A lot of the Army's infantry operates and rides into battle on Bradley Fighting Vehicles. But the bad guys don't use Bradleys, so the 11th had none. Instead, Echo Troop had about twenty M113 Armored Personnel Carrier (APC) chassis modified to look like old Soviet vehicles, complete with painted pipes for cannons. These curiously configured armored vehicles, "Opposing Forces Surrogate Vehicles" (OSVs), only existed at Fort Irwin. I won't go into detail, but I did manage to learn a lot about the world of 'tracks.' That's what we called any infantry fighting vehicle. (Think of a miniature tank designed to carry infantry soldiers in the back.) Besides driving and riding in it, we changed the tank treads, fixed the shocks, and performed a mind-numbing amount of other mechanical work on that thing. I spent more time in my track, either working on it or living in it, than anywhere else at Irwin.

Being junior in rank in any mechanized unit usually meant that you'd be a driver. Next up the totem pole was the gunner, and then a squad leader or team leader was the track commander (TC). This rank-structured crew was the same in tanks or Humvees. Driving an armored vehicle, even a modified version of an M113 APC like we had, was quite an experience. There were tons of steel being propelled through the desert by my foot on the pedal. It was big, loud, and powerful, and the M113s were babies compared the Bradleys we were outfitted with later.

Luckily, I had a great squad leader to show me the ropes

when I first arrived named Peter D'Andrea. He was a short Italian guy several years older than me. He was a sergeant at the time, and had been to a few other duty assignments already. He knew the mechanized infantry well. He was dedicated to his soldiers' professional growth and well-being, and I became a better soldier because of it regardless of our unit's unique mission. He also happened to be hilarious, so his joking around always brightened up our work. He was good to drive for, too, even in the hairiest of situations. I learned that quickly in the driver's hatch of an OSV.

One of the most memorable aspects of my OPFOR experience was night driving. When the hatch was closed in an APC or Bradley, the driver had to look out of a bank of periscopes to see. There were some blind spots. A driver couldn't see anything at all on the right side, and even seeing directly in front was difficult. So it was a good thing that you were plugged into an intercom system and could speak with the TC and gunner, the former of which rode halfway out of the turret so he could see all around. For night driving, the driver mounted a night vision periscope onto the top of the closed hatch. This periscope limited your field of vision to a circle six inches in diameter. Within that circle was a green, blurry view of the outside without any depth perception. Since night vision technology amplifies ambient light (moonlight for instance) the darker it was in the desert, the less a driver could see. Sometimes a driver was completely blind. SGT D'Andrea used to have me close my eyes, and then he dictated exactly what I had to do to navigate the terrain.

"SGT D'Andrea, I can't see shit out of my night sight."

"Yeah? Real bad? Like can you see the road?"

"Not really, I can barely see the vehicle in front of me."

"Okay close your eyes." The first time he asked me to do this I couldn't quite believe it. He explained to me why we did this, though. If I couldn't see well enough to drive, my eyes and my night sight ceased to be of value. The TC always had the most modern night vision devices. Furthermore, he was on top of the vehicle and could see all around. All we did was eliminate the most unreliable factor in the operation of the vehicle: my eyes.

"Okay, Ervin, left a little bit. Straight. Speed up a little. Right a hair. Okay, back left you went too far." I listened and followed directions. I wasn't the only driver that did this, either. It was really strange the first time, but I got used to it. Some of us even preferred hearing the directions over looking through our night sight. It really was a lot easier.

Whether or not it was a training exercise didn't matter very much when driving a multi-ton armored vehicle in the pitch black. It was still scary. Rollovers were a common enough occurrence that rollover drills became a part of routine training. The prescribed manner by which a vehicle crew responded to a rollover was as follows: whoever sensed the rollover yelled "Rollover!" until everyone echoed it. The driver was supposed to kill the fuel to the engine (there was a kill-switch) and hang on. The gunner and TC were to get down into the turret if they were out and close the hatches if they had time. Then everyone reported in to the TC to establish that they weren't mangled or otherwise incapacitated. After all, thirty tons of steel rolling over can be bumpy for a crew.

"Driver okay."

"Gunner okay."

"This is Reaper One-Six India [our call-sign] we are green to go." In military parlance, the words 'green' and 'go' were both ways to say you're okay. The repetition of these drills served the purpose of instilling that knowledge in our heads regardless of the sincerity we put into the exercises. Sometimes we didn't do them at all, but even hearing about it reminded you of the procedure. That went for a lot of things in the Army. Even though we were OPFOR, we were still American soldiers. We could learn and gain experience even from the games we played for the benefit of the rest of the Army. Driving as much as I did, there were plenty of times when we almost toppled over or had a track slip off of a ledge. Those kinds of puckering memories didn't go away, but as they accumulated so did my confidence. I became comfortable around mechanized forces, although I respected the dangerous aspects of it. I had ample exposure to it all if nothing else.

The 11th performed ten monthly rotations a year. We usually spent at least two weeks out of each of these months out in the 'Box', as we called the training area. Our schedule was highly predictable by Army standards. We'd all come in one day to the motorpool and pack gear and supplies into our vehicles. Then we drove the vehicles out into the training area and stashed them. We rode a truck back to the base and spent a night in the rear enjoying the comforts of civilization. The next day we would depart again to our desert motorpool and prepare for the next morning's engagement with the unit on rotation. We'd conduct these maneuvers for a while, and then do a recovery process which included cleaning and performing maintenance on our equipment and vehicles. It amounted to about two-and-a-half weeks in the field, then a few days of recovery. Then they'd let us off for a three-day and four-day weekend to wrap up the month. Ten times a year.

Sometimes our role in the rotation would vary from this routine. For instance, on rare occasions, and much to our enjoyment actually, the training exercises required us to go out as dismounted infantrymen. You wouldn't think that digging foxholes or lugging around machine guns could ever be considered fun. It was exhausting and its very own world of pain. But to me, at least, it was a much better way to spend the time than sweating inside of a driver's hatch in one of those vehicles. This was also a little livelier for us since we got to shoot blank rounds out of our weapons. For that matter, we took our individual weapons out to the field for these exercises. I vividly remember actually having fun on those missions.

Despite our primary focus on performing the functions of OPFOR, we did find the time to train as regular grunts. Our physical training (PT) was challenging. We were expected to perform well on PT tests since our job was highly physical. This meant doing five-mile runs or more, sometimes in gas masks, and a wide array of other conditioning routines like endless sets of push-ups and sit-ups. We went to rifle and machine gun ranges regularly. Once a year we performed a live-fire exercise at the platoon level which required us to maneuver towards and attack a mock position. I remember being on a machine gun team for my first one, carrying a thousand rounds for a light machine gun and its tripod in addition to my own gear and ammo. I'll never forget the feel of all that weight. I had to be helped up each time we had to move. Every year we also participated in Expert Infantryman Badge (EIB) training.

The EIB was hard to earn. It consisted of a wide range of testing on infantry tasks; first aid, communications, Nuclear, Biological, and Chemical (NBC) warfare skills, grenade throwing, calling in artillery, assembly, disassembly, and correcting malfunctions on every weapon in our repertoire, range estimation, movement techniques under fire, camouflage, map reading, and many others. There were forty individual tasks a soldier had to complete perfectly in all. Only two failures were allowed, but if you failed one task twice you were disqualified. As prerequisites, a soldier had to perform well enough on a PT test, qualify Expert with an M16 rifle or M4 carbine, and complete a twelve-mile forced march with nearly sixty pounds of gear in three hours. The second time I tested for EIB, I actually passed out somewhere after the eleventh mile of the road march from heat exhaustion. I never earned mine, but participating in that training regimen every year was a learning experience nonetheless.

And, of course, our leaders taught us things in our down time. SGT D'Andrea had me prepare endlessly for Soldier of the Month and Soldier of the Quarter boards, for instance. It was basically a process of learning the book knowledge of the Army, which took a lot of memorization. He drilled me pretty endlessly. If I couldn't remember answers to questions I paid in push-ups. When it came time to appear before the board, it was actually a dress rehearsal for the promotion boards for sergeant and above. In dress uniform, a soldier appeared before a panel of all the Troop first sergeants and the command sergeant major of the squadron. They inspected your uniform closely and asked a wide range of questions. A soldier's composure, appearance, and knowledge were factored into the scoring system, and the best soldier won. I received the honor only once, but would see a board again.

In addition to board preparation, SGT D'Andrea taught me how to do the paperwork of an NCO as a very junior soldier. Out in the field, he instructed me on the use of the GPS systems and technical details about our equipment and how to use it. He taught battle drills, or standard reactions to numerous types of engagements infantrymen may encounter. Beyond that, he told me a lot about regular units; how they trained, what their standards were, the type of discipline instilled, and other things. Many times I learned a lot just by listening to his stories.

I also got to know a lot of people as well. For all the cliché talk of America's being a melting pot, the Army entirely fits the bill. Even in a combat profession every walk of life was represented. I met people – literally – from all over the country. Some were college educated, some were poor kids, but most, I think, joined for a combination of an adventure and patriotism. We did more than meet, of course. We worked together and endured the hardships par for the course in the profession of arms.

The bonds that men form in the military are the stuff of legends, and rightly so. It's quite something. You see, the Army's particularly conducive to this. Take a bunch of young men away from similar lifestyles, immerse them in the unique, challenging, and rather unforgiving environment that active duty Army is, and they're bound to befriend one another. That's exactly how it went with me. When I arrived at Fort Irwin in November 2002, fresh out of Fort Benning, I made friends in the first billet I had. Everyone went to a central location on the base to be assigned to individual units and organizations there. The 11th's influx of new infantry soldiers contained, that month, one particularly remarkable guy. We were assigned to 1st platoon together. He's somewhat of a legend among those of us Echo Troopers that knew him.

Kevin Prince is someone who's exceedingly difficult to describe. To me, his personality was too big to capture here in words. An Ohio native, he looked the part of any average guy, with nothing really remarkable about his appearance. Average height, slender build, and light brown hair, he spoke almost always with a sarcastic tone. He carried himself with a nonchalant dignity. He was gifted with a massive wit and was intelligent in every application of the word. He had a keen sense for people and a brilliant capacity for intellectual conversation or even gambling; it was really whatever he put his mind to. He was the type of guy who could recommend that I read *The Prince* or *Dante's Inferno* and three minutes later have a group of us rolling with laughter.

He had an innate ability to be crass, yet funny about it. I always expected that the rigid rank structure and discipline of the Army would spell doom for him if he kept it up. He was sort of a smart-ass, after all, and proud of it. In the earliest days of my knowing him at work he was pretty reserved. He and I were smart enough to stay quiet being so new. But as time went on, and we became more proficient at our jobs and more relaxed with our team leaders and squad leaders, he began to open up a lot more. When this started to happen I was surprised by how well he pulled it off. Essentially, he was too funny for anyone to want to stop him. Everyone, usually regardless of rank, was too busy laughing their guts out at his wisecracks to ever think of doing such a thing as reprimanding him. I think the perfect example was when a man named SGT Henderson had the unfortunate task to be Kevin's team leader.

Prince had an uncanny way of giving his superiors hell without being insubordinate. SGT Henderson was on the overweight side and had a tendency to say awkward things. In a general sort of way Prince would make fun of these things constantly, always careful not to be outright belligerent. As SGT Henderson's driver out in the box, he came up with a code word with his gunner, and would hit bumps as hard as he could to give Henderson a rough ride; at one point he even bruised his ribs. SGT Henderson would make Prince do plenty of push-ups and the like as punishment, but he was in good shape so it didn't faze him in the least. Most of the time, Prince out-smarted those around him, and could make fun of someone without their even realizing what was happening. He kept us laughing all the time.

Besides those more memorable aspects about Kevin, he became my best friend. We came to the Army and our unit at the same time and for the most part thought the same things of it. We both believed the Army would improve our lives, but that it wasn't something we wanted to do long-term. We did our best to be good soldiers in the meantime, more for ourselves and our peers than for career advancement. We drank together and talked of our lives back home, to which we both longed to return. We shared books and movies, nights out on the town, and lazy days in our barracks. We talked about our difficulties at work and in our lives. He was pretty much a brother to me, but he wasn't the only one.

There was also Mark Steppe. He was in many ways a study in contrast to Kevin, although the three of us got along well. He was a southern California guy. Shaved head, piercing blue eyes, slender but powerful physique, and covered in tattoos, he looked the part of a death metal connoisseur. He'd started out at Fort Hood, Texas, and was assigned to Fort Irwin from South Korea. The latter was a notoriously hardcore unit both in its discipline and training regimen as well as its night life. He excelled at both, but some thought he overdid the night life. We shared a barracks room his first night in Echo. I recall lying down to read that night around ten or so, our 0630 PT being the next morning. He was changing to go out.

"Where are you going man?" I asked. It wasn't really a normal time to be going out on weeknight, even for us.

"I'm going out, have to investigate the nightlife around here," he replied with a devious smile. I remember thinking that he'd be sorely disappointed. He was. There wasn't much to Fort Irwin itself; an enlisted club, an officer's club, a convenience store, grocery store, post exchange (PX), a few restaurants, and a movie theater that played older movies. That was about it. Of course, once I got to know Steppe, it didn't matter much that there wasn't any craziness going on at the base. He would find a way to create it. The man was certainly a drinker, like most of us, but he really, really reveled in it. Part of the reason we all came to find out he was so tough was watching him drink copious amounts of liquor the night before a really long PT run. He still outran us. He never, ever, fell out of a run, road march, or anything. He was a tank. And as crazy as he was, he was a really good infantry soldier.

He was a hardcore guy. For our live-fire exercises he was picked to be a machine gunner. The M240B crew-served light machine gun was the biggest weapon we had on that exercise, and he made it clear that he wanted it. As an ammo bearer and assistant gunner I got to lug the extra ammunition, tripod, and spare barrels up a mountain with him during the exercise. He was laughing the whole way up, despite the fact (or because of it) that we were loaded down and straining like animals to reach the top. He loved anything we did that required a bit of savage strength and caused pain. In a lot of ways, he was the epitome of what the infantry should be; mean, dedicated, unstoppable, and highly motivated. He was a good friend, too. We visited his house nearby often where his parents made us feel at home. He cared about is friends, and he always had your back.

There were many others I came to know. Faucher, who received the inevitable nickname "Fucker," was a former member of a Ranger battalion and had been in the Iraq invasion. He was a wiry white guy from a military family, and was a military history buff like me. Like Prince, he was hilarious, but his humor had less of an edge. It was more of a slap-stick style of joking around. He knew the job of an infantryman very well, having been in one of the most elite units in the Army, and didn't much like being in the OPFOR. Then there was Chris Logsdon from Indiana. He was a hard drinker like all of us and an intense guy. He was easy to get along with, and we had a lot of fun. There were many more. All of these men were highly intelligent and capable soldiers. I was glad that I had such a group of friends, and they became my family in many ways.

With these friends, and the sense many of us shared that we would miss the war, life was good. For my part, I had to put up with the Army long enough to get out and use my college benefits. We had a lot to do in the meantime. We lived three hours away from Los Angeles one way and three hours from Las Vegas the other. We enjoyed these locations as any young military men would, flush with money and ready to play hard after working harder. We had enough off-time to have somewhat of a social life and even hobbies. Work wasn't terrible, either. I had some good opportunities presented to me. For example, since my PT test scores were high and I wasn't exactly a moron, I was offered the chance to go to Army Sniper School. I attended and passed squadron's two week long prerequisite course and was awaiting orders that would send me to the school. It was one of the Army's most challenging training courses, and I was excited. My leaders had a good idea that I wouldn't re-enlist, but they wanted to give me the opportunity regardless. The prerequisite course was fun, anyway, even if the orders never came through. Soon, however, I'd have a chance to do a lot more than that, and it would be thrilling in its own way.

By the spring of 2004 I was close to having served two-thirds of my enlistment. With only a little more than a year left, I was content with the knowledge that I'd leave the Army from Fort Irwin and go on to obtain an education. Since I and most of my friends enjoyed the rank of Specialist, we tended to get lighter duties than those below us, although not always. It looked as if I'd while away the rest of my enlistment hanging out with my friends in the desert playing Civilians on the Battlefield (COBs). This was the new twist to the OPFOR mission intended to reflect the conditions of Iraq and Afghanistan. Instead of being bad guys in armored vehicles, now we'd just be people in a fictitious town. We even grew facial hair and wore jeans and long-sleeved shirts out there. There were rarely weapons, no vehicles, and lots of barbecuing and playing cards out there. When the units training would pass through our town we'd play whatever role we had to that day, be it unruly mob, benign spectators, or insurgents. With the exception of the things like preparing for Army schools and our own training, things were going to be easy.

One windy, chilly, April day, Echo was qualifying with our rifles on one of the base's ranges. Our training had recently stepped up on account of some revelations regarding service in the OPFOR and re-enlistment. (No one was re-enlisting on account of not feeling prepared for a real unit. The answer to this was to spend a lot more time training). A cease-fire call came from the range tower and spread along the firing line. It turned out that we had to return to 2-11's parade area for an emergency formation called by the squadron commander.

As much effort as it takes to get men, ammunition, and weapons out to a range, it wasn't something lightly cancelled at the last minute. Furthermore, since I'd been in Echo we'd never heard of an emergency formation. Everyone knew what was up immediately. Some of us were excited as we got on trucks and headed back towards our parade area. Fully armed and equipped with helmets and battle rattle, riding in the open backs of deuce-and-a-half trucks through main post, it was easy to get caught up in the moment. It seemed like we were going to war. Not everyone was excited. I recall some grim looks as well, especially from those who had been to Iraq or Afghanistan already. They knew what we didn't, and it took all the excitement out of it for them.

As the nearly seven-hundred of us formed up in the parade area, there was a palpable buzz in the air as 2-11's squadron commander, LTC William Simril, stepped out to tell us why he'd called the formation.

Yes, we were going to Iraq, and would do so just outside of six months. Of course, there was lot to do in the meantime, but he was sure his troopers were up to the task. There was doubtless going to be a stop-loss order announced soon. I can't remember the exact words he used, but those two I do. No one in the 11th was to be discharged from the Army, assigned to another unit, or sent to any Army training outside of Fort Irwin from that point until a few months after we returned from Iraq. My easy last year in the Army with a chance to go to Sniper School got erased with one phrase actually: "extended for the convenience of the government." In the end it was convenient for them to have me serve an additional nine months beyond my three-year enlistment. It was worse for others. Some were due out of the Army in a month or so when that order came out. I treated it matter -of -factly, as there wasn't anything I could do about it anyway.

One soldier in particular was only a few days shy of leaving the Army when the order came down, Mark Maida. He was an average sized white guy from Wisconsin. He was the life of every party, loved to goof off in a good natured sort of way, and was an all-around amiable guy. He didn't contest the stop-loss although he had already cleaned and turned in his equipment, and had been serving in a cushy job awaiting his departure. He didn't flinch in choosing to deploy with us to Iraq, and he was given a choice. He preferred to be with his friends for the big show. It was an admirable, honorable thing to do, and we all respected him for it.

Beyond the immediate knowledge that my plans had changed, I can't recall how I felt when I first learned I was going to Iraq. As the situation developed so did my thoughts at our new prospects, but upon hearing the words setting all this about my memory is blank. I know I wasn't ambivalent about it by any means. Perhaps, as with learning anything momentous, there was simply too much to comprehend at the moment to feel much of anything but surprise. SGT D'Andrea had left for the 3rd Infantry Division recently, and I do remember wishing he was going with us. Regardless, after that day life in the 11th took on a fever pitch, and later we would be thankful for the time to think and feel.

The task facing us was nothing less than enormous. Any other unit in the Army prepares for this eventuality perpetually. That's why they came to NTC: to fine tune the skills everyone needed to make such a thing go smoothly. Not us. As I've mentioned, there wasn't much about the 11th engendered towards that role; not its organization, equipment, vehicles, or the main focus of its training. The 11th hadn't been in combat since the Vietnam War. It was odd that we were picked to go, actually, given all that the OPFOR was. I suppose we had certain things going for us, though. To name a few, we worked well together, were highly adaptable soldiers, and also inured to a harsh desert environment. We still had to do our OPFOR missions for a while. As if the job ahead of us wasn't enough to demand our full resources, we didn't stop doing COB rotations until about two months before we left. We stayed busy and things changed rapidly.

One of the first orders of business was the reorganization of our unit. We were re-designated as Task Force (TF) 2-11 because we were attached to the 155th Brigade of Mississippi National Guard for the deployment. TF 2-11, "Eaglehorse," operated virtually independently, but that's who we fell under. The TF was composed of Headquarters and Headquarters Troop (HHT), Echo Troop, Alpha Troop, Delta Troop, Hotel Company, and later Charlie Company from the 155th. Alpha and Delta Troops were Armor, meaning they were equipped with Abrams tanks. The infantry companies had Bradleys. HHT was comprised of the command group and all the support personnel; mortars, scouts, communications, medics, logistics, and personnel specialists.

Echo Troop (troop just being another term for a company in the cavalry), "the Reapers," was comprised of headquarters platoon and three combat platoons. HQ platoon had our company level support personnel like mechanics and supply specialists. Describing one of the combat platoons' structure in detail describes the rest.

The platoon is built around four squads. 1st and 2nd squads contained crews to man four Bradleys. 1st squad contained the platoon leader's Bradley plus his wingman, and 2nd squad had the platoon sergeant's Bradley plus his wingman. 3rd and 4th dismount squads each consisted of two fire teams plus their respective squad leaders. Each Bradley had a fire team riding in the back: 1st squad carried 3rd squad in its Bradleys, 2nd squad carried 4th squad in theirs. In this way the four Bradleys and two dismount squads of the platoon could be split in half. We called 1st and 3rd squads "Alpha section" and 2nd and 4th squads

"Bravo section." We were never full strength. At most, a fire team contained three men including its leader instead of the nominal four.

The platoon is sort of staffed around its weapons systems, including the Bradleys. The Bradley itself is formidable, even the second-hand, obsolete M2A1s we had. It was armored well enough to handle all but tank rounds or direct hits from artillery. It could move quickly and smoothly with its six-hundred horsepower engine and wide tracks. In its turret was a 25mm Bushmaster Chain gun cannon. It fired two types of ammunition; armor piercing (AP) or high explosive (HE) projectiles. There was a coaxial, 7.62mm machine gun. On top was a TOW missile, essentially a wire guided anti-tank weapon. The gunner aimed with the use of a target reticle system (ISU) with daytime or thermal imaging sights and dual joysticks. He punched up what ammo he wanted at what rate of fire, dialed in the range, and squeezed the triggers. The Bradley Commander (BC) could also shoot all of the weapons as well from his side of the turret, although he couldn't manipulate the magnification or imaging of the ISU.

In the back were the dismounts. Even our short-staffed versions were formidable. Team leaders carried grenade launchers on their M4 carbine, which was a shorter version of the M16. One of their men carried the M249 squad automatic weapon (SAW), a small machine gun. It was the lone rifleman who usually got to carry everything else the squad needed like a radio, first aid bag, etc. It was the Bradleys' job to get these guys into a good place to attack the objective, and provide covering fire while they maneuvered towards it. It was all straight out of the field manuals, or at least our closest approximation.

For a lot of us this was way of doing things was entirely new. Besides the OPFOR soldiers who hadn't been assigned anywhere else, men new to the unit from light infantry divisions like the

82nd and 101st, although experienced infantrymen, were also new to Bradleys and mechanized infantry. While operating like a mechanized infantry platoon could be considered by some to be basic knowledge for a grunt, it's hard to master if your past two years in the Army had little to do with it, like Prince and I. Nonetheless, we all had to learn. Our company commander, platoon leaders, first sergeant and platoon sergeants eventually placed us in all of the assignments I've described. Faucher, now a sergeant, became a team leader in 4th squad. Since I'd at least been in track for a while I was assigned as gunner in Alpha section's second track. Logsdon was to be my driver. I was confident in his abilities. Steppe was gunner for the platoon leader since he'd had fairly extensive experience in the turret in Korea, and Kevin was a SAW gunner in 4th squad. We had to wait a while on the Bradleys to get down to the real training.

We got some new men, too. My Bradley Commander (BC) was SSG Mounlasy, or "Moon." He was an interesting man. He was of Laotian decent and had been a Buddhist monk while he lived in San Diego. He was slightly older than the rest of us, very quiet, but pretty strict. He really didn't joke around much. He knew the Bradley and its weapons systems extremely well having attended an advanced school. Steppe's driver was SPC Stephen Wantz. He was a stocky white guy from upstate New York. He had an odd sense of humor that struck some as awkward at times, but he was a good guy. Eventually we got a new platoon sergeant, SFC Green. SFC Green stood out as an NCO who really looked out for the men in his platoon. He wasn't a hard-ass even though he trained us hard. He joked around with us often. He opened up his home to us in the months preceding our deployment so we could all get acquainted, have home-cooked meals, and have fun. He took the job seriously and worked us hard, but he was cool about it.

There was more to do on an individual basis as well. I got

appointed by SFC Green to be the platoon's arms room representative. That meant I'd oversee the distribution of all the weapons and sensitive gear to every member of the platoon, record their serial numbers, and address any maintenance issues. This suited my skills pretty well, and I got to unpack all of our new toys as they arrived. Being that we'd be in Iraq soon, the Army didn't spare any financial burdens. Each guy in the Troop got state-of-the-art night vision goggles (NVGs), infrared attachments (IR) for their weapons (only visible with NVGs on, they were basically a laser pointer for a weapon), and other optics to make shooting easier. We received Surefire flashlights to attach to weapons and a host of other small items. Each fire team also got a short-barreled Mossberg shotgun. I got to handle it all first, and for a grunt that was a pretty big deal. A lot of us had to learn how to use the stuff, since walking around with NVGs was a lot like night driving. It took practice. Additionally, all the optics and new weapons had to be zeroed on a range.

Carrying all of this stuff was another matter. It can only be listed, because it was a lot. By the time we deployed this was the minimum we'd carry when dismounted: a new Kevlar helmet, Interceptor Body Armor (IBA) made of Kevlar with bulletproof ceramic plates, goggles or sunglasses, individual weapon, at least three-hundred rounds of ammo for rifleman, much more for the SAW gunners, HE, parachute flares and smoke rounds for grenade launchers, NVGs, extra batteries, gloves, first aid kit, two or three liter camelback, flashlight, knife, zip-strips for prisoners, pens and paper, cheat sheets for medical evacuations and radio frequencies, and that was on top of the long-sleeved, Desert Combat Uniform (DCU) and boots. Throw in as many cigarettes and snuff or snacks that you needed, and it added up to about forty or fifty pounds. It tended to weigh mostly on your neck and shoulders; ultimately your back. While getting used to this new stuff, I had another job to learn.

The first Bradleys arrived from Mississippi around June or July of 2004. As new as having Bradleys was, the vehicles themselves were old. They were some of the first models ever built and were rather obsolete compared to what other units had. There were rust spots, and the tracks themselves were in particularly bad shape. It's what we had. Becoming a Bradley gunner from scratch took some work. The main cannon was an intricate weapon, and each of its components weighed a third of my body weight at the time. I had to learn to disassemble and reassemble its basic parts and put it into the turret in operational order under a certain amount of time. I always likened this particular task to wrestling a grandfather clock into a refrigerator from within the refrigerator. There was a system to it, though, and through hours of practice guided by SSG Moon and Steppe I was able to get it down pretty well. The Bradley crews spent most of the working days learning all about the Bradley, its technical aspects, maintenance procedures, and other means of familiarization. We also underwent a turret simulation program to train us on the controls. The dismounts drilled endlessly on clearing buildings and the like.

Of course, part of getting to know a Bradley was using its weapons systems and driving it. As a part of a larger training regimen for the platoon called Table XII, all of our crews had to participate in and pass a gunnery course; in other words, we were tested on how well we worked together and operated our equipment. We'd drive the vehicle up to designated firing positions and fire live ammunition at pop-up targets ranging in distances from a hundred meters for the coax targets and three thousand meters for the main cannon. Some of the targets moved, and some of the engagements had us moving as well. Our crew managed to do pretty well; we executed ninety percent of our engagements perfectly. Considering that Logsdon and I were new to Bradleys, during some of the engagements we wore gas masks, and for the week that gunnery lasted the crews averaged only a few hours of sleep a night, it was challenging. An added annoyance was the receipt of the third of our anthrax vaccinations that week. Most of us had flu-like symptoms as a result.

After the Bradleys had their go with the live ammo and the dismounts completed their own exercises, the next week it was each platoon's turn to qualify as a unit. For the last exercise of Table XII, the Bradleys and dismounts operate together with live ammunition during a night and daytime engagement. This was where things really got hairy. Four Bradleys were moving and shooting up to a certain point on the range where they dropped their dismounts. Then the Bradleys shot suppressing fire at any targets that appeared while all of our dismounts maneuvered towards their objective, in this case a building. More than a few times, the Bradleys were shooting over their heads. I only had split seconds and a very narrow field of view in my target reticle to make sure I shot safely. I remember it well.

K-chunk, K-chunk, K-chunk! was all I heard in my helmet/headset inside the turret. It was pitch black outside. Through my ISU reticle, I watched the 25mm rounds blazing towards my target in the red and black thermal vision. In between three-round bursts I switched to low magnification to locate our dismounts and the Bradleys around us that were also firing. The radio crackled with excited voices calling out their positions or whatever they were doing. In these frantic few seconds I'd already found another target, announced it to my BC, selected the proper ammo and range, and was poised to shoot again. It was thrilling, dangerous, and nerve-wracking. It was decidedly not like a video game. For the dismounts it was even more intense.

Once the ramp dropped they ran out of the Bradley into the darkness. The gunners all around them kept up the fire with their main cannons. Simulating moving under fire, the dismounts 'bounded' to their objective. Bounding was another term for running a few paces and flopping down on the ground for cover. They hit hard, too, considering the weight each was lugging. Meanwhile, hot plastic shards from the AP rounds racing overhead rained down on them. They didn't mind. I asked a few of them afterwards, "That was fucking awesome," and a huge smile was usually the response. Just as they got to their building, the Bradleys shifted fire a safe distance to let them get to work. Their building had targets inside that they shot and fragged with grenades. When the crews got word from the dismounts that the area was secure we moved up to meet them, everyone popped a squat, and they told us what we'd done well or badly in what was called an After Action Report (AAR). It was basically a debriefing. I can't remember the details, nor do they matter. 1st platoon passed the exercise in teamwork and technical proficiency and was deemed qualified.

For the final part of our training, the 155th came to NTC in November 2004 to do a rotation with 2-11. It was ironic that for so long we'd gone out there as OPFOR, and now we'd face them in our own training exercise. They didn't sugar-coat it just because we could see our barracks rooms from the Box's staging area. We spent Thanksgiving out there, men and women (by now we did have a couple of female soldiers attached to the task force) who had families included. A lot of the wives and children came down to say hello and pass food over the fence. I remember distinctly thinking how bad it must have been to keep us there despite being so close to our homes. We only had a month or so left in the states. But training was training.

We spent a month out there all told, and the whole time without a shower. The whole Troop slept on cots in a circus sized tent out in the Box. November in the High Mojave Desert was cold, and the wind never stopped. Maybe that was best since it kept our smell down; somewhat at least. We essentially simulated a deployment to Iraq. Close to our little base in the Box was a fictitious town constructed with connex containers and boxcars stacked upon one another, complete with windows and doors cut out. It was populated with soldiers posing as COBs along with actual Arab-speaking American contractors to create a variety of scenarios. Inside this town, every day and night, we would conduct various operations; cordon and searches, raids, or normal patrols. My own part in these missions almost always consisted of a lot of time in the turret 'scanning,' or moving the turret and its sights all around the town to provide security for the dismounts.

The kinds of missions they had us training for in this town were hardcore. Among other things, riots were a frequent feature. One mission called for the entire Troop to go in on foot, loaded for bear, for a quick raid. We hopped down off the trucks and got into our pre-designated formation to approach the target building. The whole town erupted. Shouting and cursing, an angry mob descended upon us. The NCOs were yelling at us to form a shoulder-to-shoulder line and maintain contact, but above all, to, "Watch those fucking rooftops! Watch those fucking rooftops!" The noise was pretty incredible; I couldn't hear anything on my handheld radio. Shots rang out. As good grunts we returned fire, well, shot blanks, immediately in the direction of the shooting and got to cover near surrounding buildings. The crowd dispersed and scurried indoors. Then the Troop assaulted the whole place to clear out the bad guys and detain anyone suspicious. We crashed through doors only to find a few old men and rubbish. The 'enemy' had evaporated.

Not all of the scenarios we trained in were so large scale. Nevertheless, all of them shared the common element that they reinforced aggression and tested our endurance. Our platoon was on the go constantly, and the action of the training never let

23

up. By the end of the rotation, the populace of our fictitious town was completely turned against us, and it was more or less a pitched battle. The real lessons of the training were cohesion under duress (even without live bullets zipping overhead) and an immersion into the conditions of a deployment as the Army's senior leadership saw it at the time. Our rotation, after all, was concurrent with the siege of Fallujah by US Marines in November 2004. Our training was thus action-oriented, and it ultimately gave us the impression that we were expected to see some heavy fighting in Iraq.

We all got to know one another quite well living in such close quarters. Whenever we were all together, there was always a lot of joking and playing around despite the circumstances. We conversed with one another and traded books and good things to eat. We got bored enough to do some ridiculous things, too. One guy ate a five-pound can of peaches on a dare, and Steppe drank something like fifteen little cartons of strawberry milk. The sicker they became the funnier it all got. That's how it went. We just entertained one another as best we could. It was one way in which we could make the hard times pass a little easier, and the same thing continued when we got to Iraq. Hardship really did seem to bond us together.

However, I was preoccupied. The reorganization and the stop-loss had the combined effect to make a lot of us eligible for promotion. Since I had more than a year left in the Army now, my superiors saw fit to send me to the promotion board for sergeant. I'd done well and had all the prerequisites to get the promotion if I had the recommendations I needed. I did.

On a pre-dawn, highly informal promotion ceremony attended by the whole, filthy, complement of Echo Troop in our tent, I got pinned with the three chevrons of a sergeant. I'd been twenty-one years old for a month-and-a-half when I was given the additional responsibility of leading men into combat that

December. Granted, my only charge was my Bradley driver, and he never gave me anything to worry about, but that could change quickly. Above all, I had the rank now where people would depend on my decisions in life-or-death situations. Although I couldn't recall how it felt upon first hearing that we were going overseas, the thoughts incurred with this knowledge were more poignant. I was purely terrified.

I questioned my level of knowledge, above all. I didn't feel as if I had been trained enough to know everything there was to know about our jobs. Many things were relatively new to me, and the anxiety created by the feeling of having to learn it all so quickly was memorable. I wondered if I would make the right decisions when the time came, if I had what it took to earn the respect of my men, and if I could truly lead by setting an example for them to follow. Another aspect was that other soldiers had been in the Army longer than I had. I remember it being odd that Steppe wasn't promoted before I was, since I knew for a fact he knew the Bradleys and the dismount side of the job better than I did. Still, a lot of the leaders in the platoon had confidence my leadership skills. That, at least, was reassuring.

Our last several months at Irwin flew by. As a unit we'd been working at breakneck speed preparing and training for months. But December had a sense of finality to it. Our vehicles and some of our equipment were already on a ship bound for Kuwait, and the Task Force had already deployed people to prepare for our arrival overseas. The tasks at hand now were different and a little grimmer. We wrote our wills, updated life insurance policies, made arrangements to put our belongings in storage, and received the last round of shots including smallpox; a sort of scary one because you actually had a spot of smallpox on your arm that could get you sick if you touched it. We took training classes in improvised explosive devices (IEDs) and cultural familiarization. We wore the desert combat uniforms (DCUs) we'd wear overseas. I set up a system whereby my mother would receive the news if anything happened to me and pass it along to everyone I knew, including my girlfriend Karen back in West Virginia. Oddly, though, there was also more free time on our hands, and it was then that things like stress really showed.

We all drank excessively even in the best of times, yet I remember staying more inebriated than usual during December. By this time, thing had taken a more intense edge, though. There were more fights with guys from other units, for one, and there was a tendency for the revelry to take on a more somber tone. We talked about places like Fallujah and Najaf. They'd hinted to us by now that we were destined for Mahmoudiya, a pretty hardcore insurgent stronghold south of Baghdad. We did our best to have fun, but it wasn't always easy. In reality, we were all wondering which of us wasn't coming back, and we hadn't thought about it much until then. There were other things troubling me, too.

Maybe it was my new rank, or maybe all the fear and stress we were living under, that led Prince and me to withdraw from one another. It wasn't that he was jealous that I'd been promoted. I think my rank represented, to him, my caving into the Army ways that we had both sort of spurned. I could only speculate, and doing so didn't change the fact that by the time we deployed, although we hadn't had a falling out per se, Kevin and I were barely speaking. I remained really close with Steppe. I was also befriended by a relative newcomer to 1st platoon by way of the 82nd Airborne Division after a tour with them in Iraq.

SGT John M. Smith was his real name, he used to joke. It was. He also went by "Smitty" and an even more unique "Pudge." The latter came from his stature, perhaps all of five-and-a-half feet tall but incredibly stout. He wasn't afraid to admit that he was a tad overweight, too. He was easy going, but took his job as a dismount team leader in the back of my Bradley deadly seriously. I did see him berate a guy after the live-fire. I can't remember the details, but Smitty was pissed, apparently from a close call on account of the private. He came from North Carolina, although he lacked an accent. If he could have been classified as belonging to any type of people outside of the Army it would be hippies, buzz cut and all. The first time I met him he was underneath a Bradley in the motorpool, and the only thing I could see of him was one arm. That arm was covered from top to bottom in tattoos of the characters from *Where the Wild Things Are.*

We had a lot in common with our similar interests in music and movies. We drank together often. Like with Steppe, I learned a lot from him. He was a team leader in 3rd squad and had already been to war. He wasn't particularly thrilled to be going to Iraq with us. However, he lent me his time in teaching me some facets of his job. Over a few beers we used to discuss how best to deploy a squad to patrol a certain area he'd point out on a map, or we'd have a discussion on some of the do's and don't's of being an NCO. He was one of the few guys, also, who could tell us what it was like in Iraq. He never volunteered too much, but I got the impression that the place was a cesspool and its people weren't exactly friendly. Nor did he have a good time of it. That much was apparent.

Beneath the surface of that entire month for me was genuine fear and stress besides my misgivings about being a leader. Among the flood in my mind there was fear, anxiety, and an uncertainty about what was going to happen. A year was a long time, especially looking back on all that had happened in the preceding six months. Looking forward, it seemed like an eternity to me. I wondered who wouldn't make it or if I was going to be killed or wounded. Losing a limb was my biggest fear. There were plenty of others. What would we see? What would I have to do? How bad would it get? My impression at the time was that whatever happened was going to be intense. Probably the same as so many of us, I felt incredibly wound-up, only just as ready to cringe as to spring into action. It was a frightening feeling. Now, it wasn't an outside chance anymore, no abstract thought of what being in combat was going to be like. Now it was inevitable. I would face it in a short amount of time.

In a letter I wrote to my brother shortly after I'd arrived in Kuwait, I told him something that sheds a lot of light on another aspect of my thinking at the time. I wrote to him that I'd sat beside Smitty on the plane because he was a good friend. At the same time, I was trying to detach myself from everyone so that it wouldn't hurt so badly if I lost them. I was attempting to desensitize myself from everything. It was a survival mechanism; nothing that I'd been taught or had learned from another source. It was real instinct. None of us ever talked about this phenomenon. It could very well have been what Prince was experiencing, or any number of us for that matter. Although our drunks had recently taken on a somber, even melancholy tone, and we'd discussed casualties, no one ever really talked about what they'd feel or what they'd do if it happened. We did our best to bury those thoughts and focus on the tasks at hand.

In the darkness of the morning of January 7, 2005, I carried my rucksack and duffel bag, alone, to the parade area where the 659 troopers and fifty officers that composed TF 2-11's main body converged. For us, Operation Iraq Freedom III had officially begun. We drew our weapons, NVGs, bayonets, GPS devices, and all the other regalia out of the arms room and waited around for the buses that would take us to the plane bound for Kuwait. There, we would meet up with our vehicles and move north into Iraq. It was a long, long wait for those buses. Family members lingered around for as long as they could, not knowing when the next time they'd see their soldier would be, if at all. I wasn't scared at this point anymore, or even particularly nervous. I was just ready to get it over with. We had another stop before we'd be expected to put our training to use, though, so it would be a while.

3

We deployed to the Middle East in style. The main body of TF 2-11 rode in a Boeing 747 from just outside of Victorville, CA to Kuwait City by way of Germany. It was a long trip, and a surreal one. There we were in a civilian aircraft with pretty flight attendants, only we had rifles and NVGs under our seats. Somehow *The Notebook* ended up being our in-flight movie. Stranger still was that there wasn't much complaining about the selection. It was a comfortable flight. The senior NCOs and officers let the lower enlisted men rotate out of business and first class seats. The flight crew, all volunteers for Military Airlift Command (MAC) flights, treated us very well. But for all that, the destination still loomed large in my mind. I couldn't focus on reading a book, watching a movie, or anything else. I don't remember sleeping much, either. I more or less waited it out and talked with Smitty.

During our descent into Kuwait City the gravity of the journey I'd just made hit me hard. The Persian Gulf was visible outside the window, and as we approached the runway I realized that the curiously shaped holes all around the airport were craters from the Gulf War in 1991. The plane taxied to the US military area of the airport, we un-stowed our gear, and went down the steps, single file, to where I first stepped foot on the Asian continent. It wasn't as memorable as taking the last step off of US soil, but it seemed momentous all the same. We filed past a group of soldiers on their way out. Their uniforms were dingy, and they looked worn out. No one had to point out that they were leaving after a tour; they looked the part. Reaching an assembly area behind a hangar, we waited for a while on our ride out into the desert. I stood and gawked as if I was a tourist. The control tower of the Kuwait City airport had featured prominently in pictures of the buildup before the invasion, and it really felt like I was a part of something big.

With armed Humvees escorting us down the highway, buses driven by Kuwaitis took us to Camp Beuhring. There wasn't much to see on the way. The bus curtains were closed for security reasons, and the sky was darkening anyway. The only real view out the window was an utterly featureless desert, although I noted many expensive cars sharing the highway with us. We were on the bus for maybe two hours. Camp Beuhring was one of several camps set up throughout the Kuwait desert, each of which temporarily housed units on their way into Iraq. In logistical terms, a unit was able to perform the myriad of tasks necessary to prepare for combat there; everything from unpacking our Bradleys and readying them for operation to conducting last-minute training and acquiring extra equipment. As for our acclimation to the Middle East, there were a few things about our new environment and way of living that actually wouldn't change much during my entire tour.

The universally recognizable element of every bigger American base I saw was contracting at work. I'll put it out there: I relished having these things, even though I knew full well the government was paying dearly for it. There were shower trailers with individual stalls and hot water, and although we were relegated to using port-o-johns they were always kept scrupulously clean. The dining facilities were surprisingly great. There was good food and as much of it as you wanted. There was a weekly crab leg and steak dinner even in Iraq. Nor did they shirk on the fresh fruits and vegetables and other goodies at the well-rounded salad and dessert bars. Any kind of drink you wanted was available via fountain, can, or bottle, right down to a variety of non-alcoholic beer. (There is zero tolerance for alcohol in the Middle East; hypothetically, the US forces there had no alcohol or pornography.) The Army and Air Force Exchange Services (AAFES) ran a PX stocked with anything you'd find in a generalized store back home; from food and movies to snuff and cigarettes. They also carried some field gear and plenty of junk souvenirs.

Another common feature of these ready-made bases was the use of foreign labor. The people that ran the laundry service were from Albania or somewhere in the Balkans, the cooks in the dining facilities and the men who cleaned the latrines from places like Bangladesh or India. Local merchants were allowed onto US bases (even in Iraq) to set up small shops. From them we could cheaply obtain pirated copies of movies concurrent with their theatrical release back home. To keep us in touch with home and keep up morale, there were also facilities for telephones and computers with internet connection. It never seemed as if there were enough to make using them very easy, but if you had the time you could get through the line and make a twenty-minute call home. One tent served as a Morale, Welfare, and Recreation (MWR) center. It was stocked with free books and coffee, had movies playing, and cards and other games were handy. Sometimes there was even real furniture. Lastly, there were gyms, volleyball courts, and other distractions aimed at keeping us physically fit. But we weren't tourists, and our work started immediately upon our arrival.

Our job there was simple: get the vehicles, weapons, and ourselves ready to cross the berm into Iraq. That entailed a few things. The Humvees and other trucks that we'd shipped over without armor had to be upgraded. It was hardly an accurate description of the process since the armoring of these vehicles consisted of nothing more than welding sheets of steel to the doors and sides. The windshields and windows were replaced with bulletproof glass. It looked ridiculous and inspired zero confidence. Some of the doors to the Humvees had to be latched shut with pieces of wire. It was slip-shod at best, and if it weren't potentially deadly it would have been laughable. I was thankful for my Bradley, to say the least. The only modifications those received were a mount welded onto the top of the turret for an extra machine gun and the installation of wooden bench seats in the back. The benches were an improvement over the un-wieldy troop seat configuration of the early model Bradleys we had.

Once we had things situated enough, the entire Troop drove out into the Kuwaiti desert nearby to zero our weapons. From the Bradley's main gun to the IR devices on the rifles, and even some test rounds for the shotguns, everything was tested out and sighted in as well as we could manage. The gunners invited dismount team leaders into the turret to teach them how to fire the Bradley's weapons systems. It was the only bit of cross-train-ing we had done in the turret and really didn't amount to much besides getting to shoot a few rounds for familiarization. We spent an entire day and night out there, and the ammunition was plentiful. For one of the first times in my military career, the only rule on the range was to shoot in a certain direction. We shot as much as we wanted from any weapon we had. I can't say it was a bad time.

You'd think that we'd have known by this point exactly where in Iraq we were headed, and exactly when we would de-part Kuwait. Not quite. Whether because of operational security (OPSEC) concerns or some other reason, we had only the va-guest sense of when we'd leave. Our destination was revealed to us only when we acquired the maps we'd need for the convoy through all of southern Iraq. As a gunner, I had to plot the coor-dinates in our vehicles' GPS device and organize and annotate the maps. That is how I learned that we were destined for Forward Operating Base (FOB) Kalsu in Babil Province, about twenty-five miles south of Baghdad on the main road north-south road in Iraq, Main Supply Route (MSR) Tampa.

Our tanks and Bradleys were going to ride on flatbed trucks driven by contracted Arab drivers. This was to save wear and tear on the tracks, although the logic behind employing the Arab drivers as opposed to Army personnel escaped me. We were supposed to maintain security the whole way up, actively scanning around with fully loaded weapons. The dismounts would fly by C-130 to an airbase inside Iraq, and then take helicopters into Kalsu. The FOB was really just an encampment from which we would conduct operations. It was a relatively secure home in the war zone and outside its wire was unsecured territory. As we would learn, though, the confines of its perimeter weren't always safe. It would be our home for the duration, though, and we were anxious to get there.

We had to wait a while, of course. The ammo issue was a few days before we left. All the dismounts met up with the crews in the motorpool; not to help the crews, necessarily, but so they could issue the whole Troop its ammo at once. They helped anyway, each dismount team aiding the Bradley crews that gave them a ride. The ammo trucks didn't arrive until evening was falling, so it was mostly done in the cold and dark. The 25mm rounds came in plastic boxes of twenty-five or so, and they were quite heavy. We unloaded hundreds of those cases. While the dismounts hauled the stuff to the opened ramps of the Bradleys, the crews were inside scrambling to link the rounds together and weave them into the turret's ammo boxes. Loading the 25mm was an ordeal. I was in a dimly lit turret with a ratchet (a Bradley gunner's best friend) cranking the rounds through the feeder chutes and up into the action of the gun. There was no room to work, and the phrase 'Bradley bite' derived from the many small wounds incurred while trying to connect those feed chutes onto the action of the gun with ammo in them, or having your hand slip off of a ratchet and bang against a cold metal surface. It was heavy, yet intricate work done with fingertips numbed by the cold. Gloves made the detailed work impossible.

The extra cases of 25mm had to be stowed under floorboards in the troop compartment or wherever they'd fit inside the Bradley. Then there were the tubes that TOW missiles came in and the bullets for the coax machine gun. The latter were easier to deal with since we could just drop them into slots made for them on the turret's equipment basket. Then we had to load our own nine or ten magazines for our rifles. Of course the dismounts were already done with theirs, and of course they were in the way. That's how it usually went. What wasn't the normal way of doing things at all was our Bradley's final load-out. There are two ready boxes which feed the main gun: one holds seventy-five AP rounds, the other 225 HE rounds. Somehow Echo got almost nothing but depleted uranium tipped AP rounds. There were barely enough HE rounds to load in the smaller box. The master gunner in the platoon, SSG Moon, was perplexed, and the gunners weren't happy. We needed HE given that there weren't going to be any engagements with armor. Instead, cars, buildings, and people were all we would be up against. Like everything else, though, we had to make it work.

It wasn't but two-and-a-half weeks into being in Kuwait until the vehicle crews were ordered to stand by their vehicles and get ready for the trip into Iraq. We had to report in as being at readiness condition (REDCON) two within a few hours, which meant ready to roll in fewer than twenty minutes or so. The different REDCON numbers signified the state of readiness, one being the highest of four. I made a couple of nervous phone calls home to relay the news that I was leaving Kuwait very soon. Of course I couldn't say when exactly, even if I had known. My voice probably betrayed some fear and anxiety, for at this point I could feel it. We were going. The Bradley crews, including the platoon sergeant and lieutenant, said our 'see you laters' to the dismounts, who were happy to be flying into country, and waited by our Bradleys for the trucks and convoy escorts to arrive.

The weather up this point hadn't been remarkable, but the afternoon we took up stations down in the motorpool it was. First, it was cold. During the day the temperatures warmed up to a comfortable level, but nights and mornings were frosty. That day, though, a dust storm had blown up. These Middle Eastern dust storms blotted out the sun, keeping it cold all day, and cast an unearthly pallor to everything. It looked like a paler version of Mars. The fine sand and dust blew everywhere, so we kept our faces and eyes covered up for the most part. (There was a reason why soldiers have goggles.) It reminded me of the weather during the invasion of 2003 that I'd seen on the news. To me, it had the same feeling wrapped up in it was well. It might have been the sense of impending violence. Whatever it was, it seemed big.

In the evening, the flatbed trucks and the convoy escorts arrived. We quickly loaded tanks and Bradleys onto the trailers and gathered for the escort commander's briefing. It was my first real one of the war. We wrote down the radio frequencies we'd use and the order in which we'd travel. It was confirmed that we would be operational in our vehicles while chained to the flatbed trailers, guns ready. As for the intelligence portion, I remember it well. All of us do, because it seemed unnecessarily dramatic.

We were informed that overpasses on our route, MSR Tampa, were dangerous. We were told to watch out for insurgents dropping grenades on the tops of passing vehicles. That was understandable. Their commander next said that upon crossing the border we could expect that children would be lying in the road to block our movement. They made it clear that we weren't stopping for anything, and that they'd be run over if they didn't move. Whether or not they were screwing with us we'll never know. It was a bit much to stomach even then, primed as I felt for the worst. Nevertheless, Steppe lit upon the idea of gathering rocks to throw at these kids in the hopes of getting them out of the way without having to shoot at them.

Our company commander, CPT Ralph Harting, held a smaller briefing for us. I didn't know him really well considering he outranked me so much. He was fairly reserved, but I could always tell he was deadly serious about our work. He was a big man, built like a football player, a West Point graduate, and carried himself with all the professionalism and earnestness that one would expect from an officer. He kept his remarks to a minimum. He expected that we'd do our jobs well, and that the NCOs would ensure our readiness as a unit. Finally, he wanted us to stay alert. As for that advice, I can tell you that it wasn't exactly needed. We'd been on standby for a few days already.

The arrival of the trucks for the convoy and our loading up hit me hard. This was it! I had a keen sense of the historic, or at least what I thought was historic for me, and I wondered if I'd be able to write about it one day. It was all pretty big to me. That night, we departed Beuhring in a column that must have stretched nearly a mile, bound for NAVSTAR, the last stop for fuel in Kuwait before crossing the border. SSG Moon had gone to sleep in the troop compartment, leaving Logsdon and I alone on our intercom system. Our conversation was subdued. For the most part the engine wasn't running, and it was eerily quiet. Even to be moving inside that behemoth without the sound of the engine was unnerving.

We didn't have to be awake then, yet we were. It was too cold to keep my head out of the hatch to watch the terrain move past with NVGs, and the lights along the highway washed them out anyway. I looked out of the periscopes. I remember thinking that a lot of people had taken this road before, going all the way back to 1991. I was just one of thousands. Logsdon and I talked about how SSG Moon used to be a Buddhist monk, how I was a Protestant, and he was a Catholic. We figured we were being watched over pretty well as a crew, having a good variety of the spiritual bases covered. It was an uneventful trip, and the strain on my nerves caught up to me eventually. Once we arrived at our destination for the night and our conversation had petered out, I took my sleeping bag outside and laid down on the flatbed in front of the Bradley. It was pretty cold, but it was better than being cramped up in the Bradley.

"SGT Ervin, you going to get up today?" I awoke with a start. CPT Harting was glaring at me. Everyone around me was up and moving around. Embarrassed, I was glad that he kept walking down the line checking on all rest of the men. I guess it was the effect of all the excitement in the preceding days, but I had slept an exhausted sleep for about twelve hours. We were well into the morning when I stashed my gear and got ready to go. I felt like hell. I was groggy, cranky, and in a dark mood. I didn't feel like playing that day. It was times like those that would become more frequent as the tour dragged on. For the moment, though, we had to make our crawl through southern Iraq to get to Kalsu, situated just east of the Euphrates on MSR Tampa. At our pace it would take a few days.

You'd think that crossing the border into Iraq and travelling its main highway north, into the heart of the country, would be a thrilling adventure. It was hardly that. There were no kids at the border crossing, or even any people. There was only a forlorn crossing manned by Kuwaiti soldiers and mud huts surrounded by squalor on the other side. I was in the gunner's seat scanning around the terrain with the vigilance of a new soldier. We'd been trained to look for IEDs or objects which could contain them, things like piles of garbage, derelict vehicles, or even dead animals. Each time we approached an overpass we closed all of the hatches to protect us from insurgent grenades. Watchfulness was our *modus operandi*, but it really didn't last long. After a few hours of monotonous desert rolling through your sights, the thrill is all gone. No, you're not amped up all the time just because you're in a war zone. After the first day, we didn't bother with the hatches, just kept them shut. By the second day it didn't matter to scan around the empty desert of southern Iraq anymore. We were in the middle of the column anyway. I got bored there just as easily as anywhere else, although it was still surprising to find myself fighting complacency within the first few days of entering a war zone.

Nevertheless, we covered a lot of ground and experienced some more firsts. We passed through two major Coalition bases, first Logistical Support Area (LSA) Scania, where we stayed the first night in Iraq, then Cedar II, just an outpost with a fueling station on Tampa. They were heavily fortified. One way this was done was by using things called Hesco bastions (or baskets). It was nothing more than a foldable, four-by-four wire and fabric basket filled with earth. Entire perimeters were made out of these things, and they were used extensively all through Iraq. We also saw a lot of convoys heading south. At one point, a large contingent of Italian troops passed us that were pulling out of the country entirely. Even more frequent were the endless convoys of oil tankers heading south escorted by US troops in Humvees. I'd never thought much of the politics of this whole deal until then, but this wouldn't be a faithful recollection if I didn't mention that the sight struck me as a bit strange. Conspiratorial or not, the US was getting Iraqi oil down to the ports.

There was sightseeing of sorts. We passed the Ziggurat of Ur. I was able to get a decent view of it through the ISU. It looked like a pile of rocks in the middle of the desert. There were beggars on the side of the road. We'd toss them MREs and water sometimes. They were sorry sights. Even though the women were covered in black from head to toe you could tell they were emaciated. The landscape changed as we made our way north into the river valleys, becoming greener, yet far from lush. It may have been a trick of my mind, but my entire time in Iraq I had the feeling that everything looked dingy and had a sinister, dark pallor to it. The sky had lost its stark blue from Kuwait and was replaced by a filmy, brownish-grey haze. The date and palm trees which could have ornamented the bleak, flat panorama seemed out of place. After all, instead of a pretty sky above them I could usually catch a glimpse of pairs of Apache helicopters flying low and fast on patrols. Thick clouds of black smoke from burning oil wells spotted the horizon as well. Once we crossed the Euphrates River we were in the famous agricultural land of the Fertile Crescent. If by nothing else, you knew it from the smell. To those of us that have been there, Iraq's smell was unique in a terrible sort of way.

It'll take a bit to describe the odor that offended our noses and left an indelible impression on us, but the first element of it was shit. It was every conceivable form of it yet none; its own brand of reek. It was sort of reminiscent of sewage, but of the decomposing and fermenting kind. There was also the smell of a polluted river, which most of us could at least fathom. Throughout the country, though, was a foulness that you couldn't escape. Even the dirt had that awful, rotting Iraq smell. Our convoy was during winter, so the colder temperatures dulled the stench. Later, in the cities and open air markets where animals were being butchered beside filthy, stagnant canals in the heat of summer, well, it got much worse. It always smelled terrible there. It was only different by degrees.

The smell of third world filth didn't come from nowhere.

Most Americans have never experienced a truly devastated, third-world country. The entire place was rotten and collapsing. There weren't any Iraqi cars or trucks on the road that weren't ten years old or more. In fact, there wasn't anything new there at all due to the economic sanctions which had been in place for years. Their buildings were all dilapidated, and some of the dwellings were constructed of little more than mud bricks, sticks, and plastic sheeting. Everything was constructed shoddily, quickly, and with questionable materials. Their power lines were a confused tangle of wires. Their alleys overflowed with sewage and rubbish. Perhaps this general rot of their entire infrastructure added to the smell. Maybe it was the fact that the fields we drove by had been irrigated, farmed, and fertilized for thousands of years. In any event, the sights and smells of that place were entirely foreign to most of us and none too pleasant. After that convoy I knew what the definition of a third-world country entailed.

It took us two-and-a- half days to reach Kalsu, and we arrived around dark, in utter chaos it would seem. Our convoy pulled off of the MSR and onto Kalsu's access road approaching the gate. We were stopped there for quite a while. Everyone was up in their turrets gawking around. It was primarily a Marine Corps base up to that point. There was a young Marine in the guard tower at the gate manning a heavy machine gun. The chin strap of his helmet was unfastened. He looked bedraggled and dirty. He looked like he'd had it; not defeated, just done. He was looking around waiting on someone to tell him what to do about the giant column that had just pulled up to the gate. Eventually, the convoy crawled through the maze of concrete barriers at the gate, into the perimeter, and lined up for another wait. A few 1st platoon dismounts found us there and brought news. We were temporarily housed in more circus tents, but the food was just as good as in Kuwait. This chow hall had already been hit by a couple of mortar rounds, though. They also told us about a helicopter crash which killed thirty-one Marines. It was by far the largest amount of people killed in Iraq at one time, and the news was rather disturbing.

Once again, there was so much going on I didn't have a reaction to any of it. I was just busy. We had to park our Bradleys, and Kalsu was under a blackout. After dark there was no light allowed on the FOB: no un-cuffed cigarettes, no flashlights, no floodlights, or anything could help you through that darkness. We only had chemlites (popularly known as 'glow sticks') for guiding the Bradley drivers. I'd never experienced pitch black, inky darkness like that. Without the moon you couldn't see but a few feet in front of you. I just followed in the path of the shadowy hulk of the Bradley in front of me. Actually, I didn't walk. It was more of a trudge through a morass. It had rained recently, and there was nothing like Iraqi mud. It was thick, sticky stuff owing to is silt content, and it added weight to your boots and clung to everything it touched. I was covered up to my knees by the time I'd guided the Bradley down to our new motorpool.

And then we got one of them stuck, not in the mud, but in a folded Hesco basket. The wire of the basket had wrapped around the vehicle's sprocket and tracks. This wasn't stuff easily cut or bent. We had a time of it. I plunged right in with wire cutters, thankful that we'd broken the blackout rule to do so. By the time it was freed, I was covered in Kalsu mud and stunk like it, too. Exhausted and thoroughly unimpressed with my new home thus far, I crawled into the Bradley for the night. SSG Moon and I stayed awake for a little while smoking cigarettes. It was good to be in our base, no matter how bad it seemed, and the thought of getting my own cot in a tent was an exciting prospect. At that point so were the showers, for already the smell had crept into uniforms and gear. We slept in the Bradley that first night there. Trying to find our tents on a base we'd never seen in daylight was just out of the question. I fell asleep quickly, and woke up just as fast.

Whump...Whump...Whump. There were dull explosions. I looked at SSG Moon.

"What the fuck was that?" I asked.

"Is that incoming?" Logsdon shouted from his driver's seat.

SSG Moon reached up and shut the top hatch of the troop compartment through which we'd been ventilating our cigarette smoke. We all looked at each other in disbelief. That first time was just surreal and hard to believe. It was the exact moment in time that had tortured and piqued my imagination since joining the Army. It was more dramatic in my contemplations, not the dull thump of indirect fire. There was no immediate terror followed by the moment of truth which defined hero and coward. There was nothing of the sort. In fact, I even smiled. The waiting was over, and it didn't turn out to be so bad. It was a few thuds proceeded by a realization that I'd just experienced indirect fire. It wasn't even scary. It just seemed odd. The Marines' Cobra attack helicopters scrambled and circled a patch of terrain just outside the FOB looking for those who had shot the mortar rounds. We powered up radios, switched on walkie-talkies, and got a head count of the platoon to pass up through the chain of command. This was standard operating procedure (SOP) for indirect fire attacks: physically locate the men and equipment in your charge and report their status up the chain of command. Everyone was okay. No one was shaken up or cowering. Instead, a lot of us were excitedly chattering about our first incoming. That it was pretty interesting seemed to be the only thought on my mind.

Our mission there began to piece itself together. In complete honesty, none of us up to this point had anything more than a general sense of what our jobs would be here. We knew, so far, that we'd be taking over operations from a Marine infantry battalion there, and that Kalsu was just one of the FOBs from which we'd operate. The other was just outside a city named Iskandariyah close by. It eventually came out that we would conduct 'right-seat-rides' with the Marines. Essentially, we'd team up on patrols so they could show us the ropes of the sector, how they operated on their patrols, and specific areas of interest and tactics which we'd find valuable later. This was SOP in Iraq when units switched out at the end of their tour. There was never a sit down with a map showing our sector that I experienced. I was surprised at our relative lack of knowledge.

The Marines envied our Bradleys and the safety they afforded us from IEDs, not to mention the firepower. (We envied their seven-month combat tour.) But it was impossible to do right seat rides in them for a couple of reasons. One, passengers and crews couldn't communicate when a Bradley was moving, and the passengers just couldn't see well out of the troop compartment. Another reason was the terrain of our area of operations (AO). The main roads, like MSR Tampa and alternate supply route (ASR) Cleveland (they were all named after cities that had football teams) were paved, and somewhat ideal for armored vehicles. Most other roads in our very large sector were dirt, and usually on top of an embankment separating irrigated fields: canal roads. Some of them must have been thousands of years old (literally), and it was questionable whether most of them would support the weight of a Bradley, not to mention the very, very small margin of error involved in driving over them. With a sheer drop-off and a watery landing, it wouldn't do well for the road to crumble away or a track to come off the edge. It could be disastrous. It was certainly nothing like the desert terrain we'd mastered back at Fort Irwin.

So we began making use of Humvees. Luckily, none of the vehicles that were refitted in Kuwait were going to be used on patrols. They'd conveyed some of the unit north during the convoy, but afterwards were relegated to laundry runs on the FOB. Of course the real up-armored Humvees didn't inspire much confidence, either. In early 2005, the up-armor kit added bullet-proof glass for the windows and windshields, heavily armored doors, and a boosted engine to handle the extra weight. Everything else was normal actually. If there happened to be a hole in the metal floor at your feet, you could see the road pass underneath. The sloped trunk compartment was made of fiberglass, as was the barrier between this cargo space and the passenger area. The machine gun on top mounted onto a protective shield, and the gunner's position was further enclosed on three sides by steel armor plating, against which he could lean when standing. For the gunner's seat there was a cargo strap slung between two hooks. The gunner essentially used his back to move the entire turret around. Our filthy hand-me-downs had been thoroughly used and abused by the Marines before us. Inside, they stunk of the mud of farms, diesel fuel, and canal water. The floors were caked in mud and covered in brass shell casings. To complete their battle-hardened appearance, there were shrapnel holes and dents all over them from IED blasts.

The time finally came. We were leaving the wire to go on a patrol throughout our sector for familiarization. We met up with three of the Marines; their lieutenant, a squad leader, and a Humvee driver. SSG Moon and I rode with their squad leader and the driver in one truck with me as a gunner. Echo's senior medic also rode with us. The lieutenants each commanded the other trucks, and with ours rode SGT Threatt, a 155th artillery forward observer who had been attached to us since our rotation. We took preparation seriously. I did our vehicle's radio checks and weapons functions tests with earnestness. With just as much gravity, I checked my pockets for some random articles

I'd decided to convey as good luck tokens. A piece of West Virginia coal rubbed smooth and round in the waters of the Coal River is actually the only object among them which I remember.

Our briefing was simple. The Marine's platoon leader mentioned our Rules of Engagement (ROE), emphasizing that the curfew meant that any Iraqis out after dark could be killed. We'd take three Humvees and drive almost at random around our sector, starting in the evening hours and travelling into the night. Besides driving around, we would stop at random houses and conduct 'house calls,' which were little more than questioning a random household and searching their property. Our mission was to find intelligence about the insurgents operating in the area and look for caches of illegal weapons. Anything beyond the one AK-47 with thirty rounds of ammo that each Iraqi household was allowed to have for their own defense was contraband. We were told to keep an eye out for maps, large amounts of money, bomb-making materials, or anything else unusual. The lieutenant giving the briefing seemed thoroughly bored and annoyed, ready to get it over with more than anything else.

I'll not easily forget being perched in the turret with goggles on, my full complement of gear weighing down on me, ready to go, and thinking that it was pretty exciting to be on my first patrol. I was finally doing my job after months of preparation, I felt. I had a lot to learn before that feeling became dread, but right then it was quite a rush leaving the wire the first time.

I paid close attention to the shouted remarks of SGT Ashton, the Marine squad leader who was serving as my vehicle's TC. I strained to listen to him as the driver kept the gas pedal pegged to the floor. We moved fast when we could since it made it harder to get hit by an IED.

"You don't make room for these fuckers. We got the middle of the road, yeah? They get close, you light those fuckers up, roger?" Right. Every Humvee had a sign on the back that read, "Stay back one-hundred meters or you will be shot." This was our welcome to the land of car bombs, or vehicle-borne improvised explosive devices (VBIEDs). We couldn't afford to treat any vehicle as anything less than a giant bomb on wheels. We stayed in the middle of the road to keep as much distance from the IEDs planted on the shoulders. For dealing with cars, our ROE dictated that we were to employ the principle of an escalation of force. First, we had to shout or signal, then shoot warning shots, and finally shoot to disable or kill. The general rule was that if a soldier felt threatened and used force it was a legitimate engagement. This was pretty flexible, yet it was clear enough that we had to have a good reason for opening up on Iraqis.

We drove around our sector, soon to be dubbed 'AO Battle,' and they pointed out the checkpoints (CPs) we would use to track our movement through the area. A checkpoint was a simple concept. A certain intersection, bridge, or any recognizable feature could be a numbered checkpoint. For example, the overpass just outside of Kalsu on MSR Tampa was Checkpoint 16. Everyone in our sector knew where it was, and it was useful for any number of reasons; from determining your location on a map in relation to the known point, calling in artillery or medevacs, or simply informing someone of your location. By saying, "we're crossing Checkpoint 16 heading north" everyone knew exactly where you were.

At our first house call the gunners and drivers stayed with the trucks as per SOP. I surveyed the surroundings, and the young Marine in the driver's seat and I talked. We both agreed that the flatness of the terrain was sort of unsettling.

"So hey, I wonder how many rounds it would take to cut that kid in half? That would be fuckin' awesome wouldn't it?" He was referring to a little boy standing in the yard of this house. The kid couldn't have been more than seven, although over there they were all a little scrawny for their age anyway. This was one also as raggedy as the rest. He didn't come close to the truck.

"Uh, no man." What else could I say? I really hoped he was joking.

"Fuck it, it's just hajji." He said that part with sincerity and a shrug. It was painfully obvious that he wasn't kidding. Even in that environment it was startling to hear. Our stop was thankfully brief, and we got back on the road. I didn't talk to him after that.

One of the Marines had left something at their base in FOB Iskandariyah. It was yet another Hesco basket, shower trailer, and circus tent base, except this time within the sprawling complex of a power station that was somewhat operational. It was a giant industrial dump. There was a railroad spur running parallel to the road leading in saddled with wrecked tanker cars leaking crude oil all over. The FOB itself was none too impressive. It actually seemed a lot grimier than Kalsu, even though most of its grounds were covered in gravel. We'd end up staying there for a few days in the near future. SGT Ashton and I had a moment to talk beside the Humvee while smoking a cigarette and waiting on the Marine to retrieve his stuff.

In a vague sort of way, he told me about some last-minute casualties some men in their unit had taken. A Humvee had been hit by and IED, and all four of its passengers had been killed. They'd gotten their revenge, but he didn't elaborate about how. He didn't need to. At first I thought he was messing with me, but I already knew about that patrol, and the hollow, disturbing look in his eyes told me he was being serious.

"You know...sometimes out there bad shit's gonna happen and the boys are gonna do bad shit. Don't worry about it. Bad shit happens in this place. We get hit, we hit them. Fuck these people, okay? You keep that in mind...fuck these people. Their lives don't matter. Yours does. They're fucking animals," he said calmly.

I didn't know what to think, but I began to believe then that we had entered into a different world, a bad one. These Marines had taken a lot of casualties, and it had an effect on them that I didn't quite understand. They seemed hardened to the brutal reality of what was going on there. He was trying to tell me that there was some evil in the place for which I needed to be prepared. He was letting me know that when we took casualties it was going to make us hate, and that's just the way it was. I wondered about the effect of that vicious cycle on the Iraqis' perception of US forces. Our impression of the Marines was that they didn't mind killing. The bullet holes that riddled many of the buildings we drove past, and the nonchalance with which they treated violence was a stark indication that we were in for some pretty bad times. It added something to the already sinister feeling of the place in general. It had some shock value, and it had an effect on all of us.

Night came. The Marines had never driven with night vision. In a Humvee you just used your personal NVGs mounted on your helmet. Our driver was about to have his first experience with them. It was pitch black that night, what we called 'zero illumination,' which meant that the night vision devices would have no moonlight to amplify and help us see. We left Kalsu and drove down a narrow, winding road which at one spot straddled a very deep and rapidly running canal. It was not quite a bridge, more of a culvert. I was standing tall in the turret trying to discern the outline of this dirt road through the inky, greenish-black view through my NVGs. I couldn't see a –

The back left of the Humvee slid fast off the edge of the bridge. Gravity did the rest and we plummeted into the canal.

"Rollover! Rollover," I somehow managed to scream it as I plunged down and covered my helmeted head.

SPLASH! Holy shit there's water coming in! Fuck, FUCK! I'm gonna drown! The thoughts raced through my mind. My gear had become a trap. I frantically tried to get my helmet un-snagged. I was getting wet. Someone clambered over me. There was shouting. I saw the speedometer's backlight glowing and got my bearings. It was right side up. Get the fuck out! Go straight up! I felt a hand grab my body armor and help me up. After a gasp of air, a tremble of panic washed over me. SGT Ashton glanced at me and reached into the gunner's hatch. We pulled out the rest of the guys. I was shaking from panic and the icy cold water of the canal. I heard shouts from above, and then saw lights. Help had arrived.

I carefully hopped off the roof of the Humvee across the deep, rushing water and onto the steep bank. There, I got a hand from SGT Threatt. A big guy, he hefted me up easily. I looked down into the Humvee, now filled with water and submerged up to its roof. The swift current of the canal was rocking the truck slightly. The way it landed we couldn't have hoped to have opened the doors. If it would have been upside down, it was obvious that we would have drowned. It was cold. God it was cold. The five of us were soaked in the chilled water. I was still quaking more from the fear than the cold, though. The Marine lieutenant was pissed off and yelling at the driver for not being more careful.

We had to retrieve the weapons and radios out of there since they were 'sensitive items,' or things we couldn't let the enemy get their hands on. They would retrieve the Humvee later. No one was hurt seriously. The senior medic had busted his elbow up trying to knock out the armored glass to escape. We were all shaken up, of course. SGT Ashton dropped his armor vest and blouse, then clambered on top of the truck and wormed down into its flooded compartment. We made a chain to bring all the stuff up to the road as he fished it out. We were close to the FOB, so we drove back to get checked out by the medics. The Marines didn't bother with any of that. They seemed used to bad things happening. All I remember of the short trip back to the FOB was shivering uncontrollably despite the cranking heater.

I spent that night in the squadron aid station on Kalsu. I'd never been more thankful for a thick, scratchy, Army wool blanket until then. Every hour, the medics checked my vitals and made sure I hadn't suffered a concussion. They didn't interrupt any sleep. There was none to be had that night. I was still pretty terrified. That was my *first* patrol, I kept thinking.

The next morning SSG Moon and I were alone in Alpha section, 1st platoon's new home, a claustrophobic tent called a 'GP small' with wooden floors, an AC, and fluorescent lighting. He looked at me from across the tent as we cleaned the rank mud out of our weapons. We were shoveling antibiotics into ourselves to ward off whatever we'd swallowed during our swim. He just shook his head. I said the words that were on both of our minds. It was February 5, 2005.

"Man, it's gonna be a long fuckin' year."

4

I couldn't have known then what I was getting myself into, not exactly at least. Things were happening at a rapid pace as the Marines started to pull out and we started taking more responsibility for operations in the AO. Echo Troop got shifted around a lot. One night had us in our tent in Kalsu, the next could have been on FOB Iskandariyah. It was pretty hectic in the beginning. I was rather thankful that it looked as if we'd be based on Kalsu for the remainder of the tour, regardless of the mud. Frankly, Iskandariyah was creepy. It may have been the constant hum of the power plant's machinery, or it could have been the dreary weather that appeared each time I stayed there. Whatever it was, I could never put my finger on the reason for such a feeling. It was just one of those places that kept you on edge. I had ample reason to be nervous there soon enough.

We hadn't started full operations yet. There was still some question of where exactly in the AO Echo would set up, and we were squatting in a circus tent in FOB Iskandariyah perhaps fifty meters from the base's perimeter. We didn't have a mission as of yet, so the entire Troop was shacked up in the tent basically killing time. An argument down on 1st Platoon's end of the tent had made things deathly still. SFC Green had just laid into a team leader over something in one of the rare occasions where he seemed to lose his temper. There was none of the banter that usually accompanied that many of us in one place after that. It was rather the hush of scolded children after having gotten in trouble.

WHUMP! I felt that one. It was close! I hit the floor first, then scrambled for my weapon and Kevlar and bolted for the bunker before the next round hit. Everyone lit a cigarette as soon as they got inside. The sandbags and concrete bunker muffled the next two impacts, which were much further away anyway. It was definitely a mortar attack. You could tell by a dull crump they made at a distance, just like our first at Kalsu. It really wasn't long before we started to figure these things out. The base's incoming alarm started sounding. A few guys began complaining about our cigarette smoke in the bunker.

"Quiet the fuck down," someone yelled.

"NCOs! Get accountability for your people," someone else added. Eventually, we settled down. My heart had been beating wildly. No one had been hit or injured besides one of 2nd Platoon's privates, who had clothes-lined himself on one of the tent ropes while running to the bunker. The closest mortar round actually impacted about thirty-five meters outside the wire, close enough to be loud but harmless. Everyone nervously laughed it off, helped along by the re-telling of the accident prone soldier's injury. I was unnerved. The first time on Kalsu wasn't bad. It was such a novel experience that it invoked more curiosity than fear. It didn't have the full effect for some reason. This one did.

Incoming. After that one, it was scary. From out of nowhere, there were explosive projectiles hurtling through the air. It was pure chance where they landed. There was really nothing you could do about it. If it was time for you to get hit with a mortar or rocket, you'd get hit. By the time we'd hit the ground or thought to get in a bunker, the rounds had already started landing. The feeling of helplessness that went with it only intensified the fear. Granted, we were never subjected to anything approaching an intense bombardment. Iraqi insurgents limited themselves to firing off a half-dozen rounds at most and disappearing. Still, it was enough to keep me on edge if I thought about it, so I tried not to. It wasn't easy. I always thought twice about putting headphones in both of my ears, and never did unless someone near me was kind of listening for incoming. Even when I went to sleep I had an ear out for falling bombs. But sleeping was easy, actually, since by the time we had the opportunity to do so we were nearly always exhausted, even that night after the mortar attack.

KaBOOM! Wide wake, I rolled off of my cot and hit the floor fast. Adrenaline shot through me; enough to blur my vision. Half of us were on the ground instantly. Among the shouts in the tent I heard that it was only outgoing. The Marines were shooting artillery, nothing more. I'd just slept through the alarm giving warning. Cursing myself for being so shaken up by outgoing, I tried to settle down.

KaBOOM! The howitzer shot again. I jumped even though I was prepared for it. What a sound! This was by far the closest I'd ever been to a large caliber artillery piece in action. It may have been a 105mm Howitzer. Regardless, the sound was intense enough to send a vibration through the air that you could feel. I told Steppe that this one had really scared me. He said I'd probably get used to it. Smitty was fairly used to it and shrugged it off, telling me the same thing Steppe did. I wondered if I'd reach that point. So far the only thing I'd done in Iraq was sit in my Bradley turret and wait to get hit by an IED, sit in a Humvee turret and wait on the same, or sit where I slept and wait on mortar rounds. We'd had to shoot plenty of warning shots already, but that was really the only proactive thing we'd done so far. The first two weeks or so in Iraq, really, had been a lot of hurried, seemingly pointless movement followed by long periods of waiting. The only difference was that this hurry up and wait cycle had its dangerous interruptions. How could anyone get used to that?

At the end of all that shuffling we found our home in FOB Kalsu, the small tents where SSG Moon and I had gouged filth out of our weapons and contemplated our prospects. For a grunt's needs, I can't say it was bad. Our tent was small, and originally housed my entire section: platoon leader, his Bradley crew, my Bradley crew, and the seven dismounts of 3rd Squad. Bravo Section and the platoon sergeant slept next door. The floors were plywood, lights on the ceiling fluorescent. There were plenty of power outlets for our electronic devices like MP3 or DVD players. Everyone had a cot in about a seven-by-seven-foot personal area. Army cots weren't bad if put together properly, and with our sleeping bags on top of them they were comfortable. The tent itself was surrounded by concrete barriers and had a concrete and sandbag bunker beside it to protect us from all but direct hits. There was a central air conditioning/heating duct that could put the tent in a deep freeze or make it a sauna, depending on the weather outside. For most of February, that weather was purely awful in its own way.

I've mentioned the FOB Kalsu mud. We'd arrived in the Fertile Crescent during its wet season. There wasn't much sunshine, and the temperatures remained cool during the day and cold at night. It was absolutely perfect mud weather. It rained, turning the whole countryside into a sticky, grey, slimy mess along with us and our vehicles. We tracked the mud into our tent so that the flooring ended up being covered in dried out dust after a few days. You could sweep it with a broom all day, but that powdery moon dust clung to everything just as stubbornly as the mud did. The dust became a problem in itself. There was no hope for the outside of our weapons to remain clean. Any seepage of lubricating oil was thickly coated, and the metal itself actually seemed to absorb the stuff; not to mention clothes, skin, helmets, and body armor fabric. I was filthy, without a doubt, within the first couple of weeks, and we had yet to experience how much we'd sweat in Iraq's legendary heat. The smells of Iraq permeated everything. I never felt truly clean the entire time I was there.

After what seemed like endless waiting, we finally took over operations in full around mid-February. My forecast of a "long fuckin' year" would have been gloomier still had I any idea of what exactly I was getting myself into. Logic would tell you that a front-line soldier would know a good bit about his environment and his enemy; I'd be able to see it, live it, and thus understand it. I couldn't have been further off the mark. As we took over operations from the Marines and began to get our feet wet in our AO, (besides literally, at least) it was clear that I didn't have a clue what was going on there. That place was a mystery to me. The Iraqi people and their culture were confusing. We weren't exactly told much about what was going on politically, either, although we did know that the Iraqis had just held their first election at the end of January. The only thing that was clear was that our own mission was complicated, and that counterinsurgency meant a lot more than simply killing the enemy.

We got sort of a basic explanation that was passed down from a briefing given by our squadron commander. The situation in our AO was compared to a chess game in which a lot of pieces were grey. It was up to us to defeat the opponents' pieces, help our own, and turn the neutral ones into allies. Of course, our own actions could also turn the people against us. Random violence would turn normal Iraqis into insurgents, so we had to be careful how we treated the population. We were to defeat the enemy and win the hearts and minds of the population. There was yet another twist. We'd have to do all this in conjunction with the brand new Iraqi Security Forces (ISF), composed of the Iraqi Police (IPs) and Iraqi Army (IA). We had to train them, too. We were going to have to wear a lot of hats. Moreover, the area in which we'd piece together this new way to fight a war was unforgiving and rather daunting.

For one, it was big. AO Battle contained no less than a quarter of a million people in a largely agricultural, evergreen region crisscrossed with canals. It was literally the ancient land of Babylon. Babil Province was named after that famous place, and the ruins were only a short drive from FOB Kalsu. The sector covered an area of about five-hundred square kilometers in all. The major cities, Iskandariyah and Haswah, lay just east of the Euphrates River and about twenty-five miles south of Baghdad. According to rumor, Haswah was supposed to be the next Fallujah. There were also the tiny villages of Al Hak, Diyara, and Eskan. The boundary between our sector and the unit to the north, the 3rd Armored Cavalry Regiment, was at CP 20. Our southern boundary line was roughly parallel with Kalsu. Iskandariyah was on our eastern limit, while a major canal about fifteen kilometers west of Tampa formed that boundary.

Iraqis, news media, and our military commanders called this swath of land the 'Triangle of Death' or the 'Sunni Triangle,' since the Sunni-dominated resistance to the US occupation had its stronghold there. It was also the place where the Iraqis started killing each other. Sunnis and Shiite Muslims shared the place, and their uneasy coexistence had become violent in 2004. In fact, the very concept of 'sectarian violence' was taking shape there.

In proper 2-11 tradition, Echo Troop got the most difficult job of the lot. There was a patrol base and IP station in the middle of Haswah, and it was ours to hold. In addition, we were responsible for maintaining our presence and providing security for the entire town and its environs, suburbs, and the routes leading in and out of it. Other elements of our squadron got the area around Iskandariyah, security on the main highway, or other jobs. Hotel and Delta Companies were detached from us entirely, and ended up serving all over Iraq. Charlie and Alpha companies were given different areas within the sector. It was clear that we were stretched thin. One of the men from squadron HQ told us that it was an area big enough for a brigade, or about three of our squadrons.

So we were going to do full spectrum operations, which, as the name implies, consists of quite a lot. From the patrol base in Haswah or from Kalsu, we'd do patrols on foot and in Humvees or Bradleys: presence patrols. The idea was that the Iraqis should think we were everywhere at once, so we had to stay visible. There would be raids: busting down doors to capture insurgents in their homes or hideouts. We would cordon off several blocks of Haswah and search each building systematically: cordon and searches. We'd do roadblocks and search every car in long lines of traffic – tactical checkpoints (TCPs). We'd haunt that place day and night, as much as the seventy-five or so guys of Echo Troop could, at least. We would also provide humanitarian aid and try to develop rapport with the locals.

The first thing Echo did upon taking over responsibility for the sector was head out to Haswah patrol base and establish ourselves there. One day on Kalsu, the platoon got gear together for a week's stay and drove our Bradleys out there, meeting up with another platoon there. It was a twenty-minute drive from Kalsu. As a Bradley gunner, I got to see the craters that lined the paved roads leading to Haswah. They were big and abundant. It took some force to rip a gaping hole in asphalt. The IEDs around here were no joke, apparently, for the craters were wide and deep. Incidentally, there wasn't much traffic control for a gunner to do in a Bradley. The Iraqis definitely stayed clear of us in those things. I would have, too; the things shook the ground when they drove past. The Humvees were a different story, and there were always a lot of warning shots fired as we drove around.

This patrol base was established by the Marines in a former government complex in the middle of Haswah, next to the town's major intersection and on the main north- south route in the region besides MSR Tampa, called ASR Jackson. The intersection was a constant traffic jam. When the Bradleys rolled up the Iraqis practically drove on top of one another to get out of our way. We'd shoot a few rounds in the air to hurry them up. Once the way was clear, we'd drive around the wall separating the compound from the road and carefully make our way through the concrete barriers approaching the gate. One of the two gate guards stationed there would come out of the Hesco basket bunker guarding the entrance and move a red and white toll gate to let us through. It was dusty, and there was an incredible stench coming from the major canal that cut through the middle of Haswah and right by our base. It was as polluted, dingy, and nasty as any other town I'd seen so far. It was uncomfortably crowded, and I was thankful that the whole compound was surrounded by a tall concrete wall topped by chain link fence. The Marines added the fence after they'd had hand grenades lobbed over the wall into the compound.

The roofs of every building in Iraq were flat, and ours was no different. On top of our building, the Marines had constructed guard post bunkers out of sandbags and plywood on the corners along with a couple more to watch what the others couldn't see. One tower only guarded a tiny stretch of alley. The whole roof had a four-foot wall surrounding its ledge. It was perfect cover, actually. Still, these buildings were in bad shape. The tan brick and faux stucco were deteriorated and crumbling. There were five or six rooms on the one level of the main building with an atrium in the middle, complete with a tree. The rooms were what one would imagine an Iraqi dungeon to look and smell like. I learned concrete can actually look gross. The tile that remained on some of the floors was filthy and crumbling. We slept on cots in these rooms, thankfully, because the rats were huge owing to our proximity to the canal. The Marines had tagged the insides of the rooms with black spray paint. There were lots of 'Semper Fi,' of course, their squad and platoon numbers, and a memorable one, 'Iraq: Best Hunting on Earth,' rounded it out.

Life revolved around the patrol base in a grueling cycle. For five days a platoon on security phase would provide guard shifts for the various positions and man the command post (CP) where we had wall maps, satellite imagery, and a bank of radios connecting us to Kalsu. The following five days that platoon would conduct patrols on vehicles around the surrounding area or by walking through the town. To maximize our numbers, platoons patrolled by sections. Alpha section's two Bradleys or three Humvees would spend all day on the roads, and then come back to Haswah. Meanwhile, Bravo section would have walked out the gate of Haswah and wandered around the town for a few hours. The patrol platoon would also help out should the base come under attack. The other five days were spent patrolling out of Kalsu, where at least we had good food, showers, and a clean place to sleep. Mortars or not, we preferred being on Kalsu. Haswah was a cesspool.

Spending ten days in that place, even without the grueling guard shifts or endless patrols, was tough living. The place stunk so bad that it left a taste in your mouth. Of course, the whole country stunk, but Haswah had some added flavor. As I mentioned, the main canal that ran through Haswah was disgusting. Then there were puddles of sewage in the gravel that made up the driveway into the inner compound. Our facilities consisted of a 'piss pit' (so labeled), essentially a few pipes sunk into the ground on top of which a water bottle was placed with its bottom cut out. A small target indeed, for the ground was soggy all around. It was aptly named. For other business we had two port-o-johns with holes cut out of the back. Instead of the plastic tank, there were the bottoms of fifty-five gallon drums in which we could burn our waste. Being an NCO did have its perks. I just had to make sure the soldiers on my guard shift performed this task and used enough diesel fuel. It smelled awful, but after a cold guard shift it was still pleasantly warm. I could brush my teeth, and I had to shave, but the grime that built up after being there for ten days was memorable. Armed only with baby wipes and water bottles, it was a losing battle against the filth. The grimy, filmy coating on our skin and gear never went away out there.

When we arrived and parked our vehicles, the platoon slated to rotate back to the FOB left quickly, and we set up our guard shifts. There were five or six towers plus the gate. As a sergeant I usually got the gate. There was a sergeant in charge of each shift, and the squad leaders supervised a couple of shifts and manned the CP. We pulled two hours in the guard bunkers then spent four hours resting – for five straight days. Two hours doesn't seem like much, but I remember my first few shifts rather well. The four hours in between definitely weren't much. You had to clean yourself up, eat, do work details, clean weapons, and eventually get some sleep during those off-hours. The shifts on guard blurred into a monotonous haze of night vision green and the pale tan and grey of the Haswah cityscape. They all went the same.

I had maybe just gotten to sleep, a kind of half sleep that you got on patrol bases at least, when one of the squad leaders came into the room to wake me up. It was close to four in the morning; the dawn shift, and by far the worst.

"SGT Ervin, wake up, your shift's in twenty minutes," SSG Moon mumbled. I opened my eyes. What a foul way to wake up. Tired, with gummy eyes, I went into the CP for a cup of coffee. Something had to get that awful taste out of my mouth. After lighting a cigarette, I walked back into my shift's room.

"C'mon guys, shift's in about fifteen minutes." The guys got up slowly. Wantz just sat up and stared at the floor. He was never a morning person, but he looked exhausted. I knew exactly what he was thinking. It was a raw, cold morning, and to hell with staring through those NVGs at nothing for the next two hours. On went the IBA loaded down with about three-hundred rounds of ammo. The night vision was already attached to my helmet from the ten-to-twelve shift, and it added to the weight pressing down on my sore neck. The weight of the gear seemed heavier in the morning, and it pulled straight down on my shoulders. I had a neck gaiter wrapped around my neck and head to keep the chill off. February mornings in Haswah were cool, probably only in the forties or fifties, but standing still in the bunkers made it downright cold.

After grabbing some food, relieving themselves, or whatever else, the shift met up in the courtyard. As the NCO on the shift I was responsible for making sure everyone had ammo, night vision batteries, and operating weapons, and I did so by conducting a Pre-Combat Inspections/ Checks (PCIs and PCCs). I trusted these guys, and so most often only did a cursory check. Everyone kept all their gear in their IBAs anyway, so most of the time you could assume they'd have everything. I still did spot-checks, though. Steppe was in my shift and helped me out with this. We usually had the gate together.

"You guys have all your shit?" I asked quietly. It was still during those mornings. The only sounds were the crackling voices of the patrols on the radio coming from the CP and the flicking of Bic lighters. There were maybe some grunts or mumbles, too. I really didn't need to wait for an answer. I handed out fresh batteries for the walkie-talkies in the guard posts (called ICOMs), assigned everyone a position, and everybody trudged out to relieve the guys on guard.

Steppe and I walked out to the gate. It was dark and eerily

quiet. SGT Camarillo, a funny, averagely built Mexican guy from Las Vegas and another soldier were in the guard shack at the gate.

"Alright, you guys are good. Anything new?" I asked, even though I'd have found out by now. There never usually was.

"Yo man, there's a little fuckin' mouse running' around in here somewhere. We ain't named him yet, knock yourself out. Have fun! Oh yeah, and no...there's not a damn thing going on out here. Goodnight, fuckers," said SGT Camarillo. With that, they disappeared quickly. Everyone was always glad to be relieved from guard.

The first five minutes on post we did a radio check with the CP and the other positions. Mark unloaded and loaded the machine gun, jerking the charging handle back and clicking the button to put it on safe. We quietly observed the deserted streets of Haswah. There wasn't any movement or sound, save for the occasional stray dog barking. That's just the way it was at night. After curfew, Iraqis out and about were legitimate targets, and so remained inside. As usual in those first couple of weeks, nothing stirred. Nothing happened. We just waited on the mosques to start the prayer call in the morning. The Muslim prayer call split the air every morning with its mournful cry. While it happened five times a day, just before dawn it was at its most distinct since we didn't have the advantage of any other kind of noise to drown it out. It was an unnerving chant, despite its benevolent meaning. To me, it was just another reminder that I was in a different world; one that was completely alien to me.

It wasn't bad on gate guard because I had another person with me. Steppe and I could easily pass two hours discussing our desire to blow up the mosque's loudspeaker, looking for Feivel the mouse, or just talking. Being stuck in a tower for a couple of hours at night was its own kind of miserable. There was nothing to do but look out into the inky green of the night vision with gummy eyes. At first, every shadow hid a threat. Every fifteen minutes you did a careful scan of the area. After a while, you're just bored. You stare into the green and black nothingness. Time passed slowly. The only company was the occasional remark on the ICOM. You got sleepy. You'd stand up to shake it off, maybe put some Copenhagen in your mouth since you couldn't smoke in there at night. Then there was some stamping of my feet for a while to keep the blood circulating and fight off the cold. Glancing at the luminous dials of my watch revealed that only twenty minutes of the two-hour shift had passed. So I avoided looking at it for long periods in the hope that it would pass more quickly. Maybe I could be surprised by glancing down and seeing I only had minutes left. It never happened like that, though. I just had to try my best not to think about it.

There was more liveliness during the day, of course, even while pulling guard shifts. The IPs stationed there with us were colorful characters. Most of the English they spoke was American slang, and the subjects they brought up with us were invariably sex and drinking in the US. They loved to hear our stories of carousing. We kept contact to a minimum, as we didn't trust them. They kept their faces covered while patrolling in their shot up sedans and pickup trucks. We couldn't help but see 'terrorist' when we looked at them. Our interpreters, incidentally, kept their faces covered, too. 'Thomas,' a native Iraqi interpreter who worked with Echo, explained why:

"For this job I travel far and keep my face covered. This way no one can identify me, then find my family and hurt them. No one knows I am interpreter for US." He explained that it was the same with Iraqis joining the Army and police forces. Insurgents targeted these recruits and their families as a tactic to discourage others from joining. They still did though, for the IPs were fairly thick in Haswah and neighboring Iskandariyah, regardless of their effectiveness. Their allegiances were also in question.

65

While Echo temporarily pulled security in an IP station in a small village between Haswah and Iskandariyah, for instance, a team of our Special Forces (SF) and an elite Iraqi unit actually raided the place and detained policemen thought to be infiltrators. No one ever forgot that, and we watched them almost as closely as any other Iraqis.

No one forgot our first encounters with the Iraqi Army, either. We passed by them manning checkpoints on some of the roads, but never paid much attention to them. Seeing them driving around was different. They blew past the patrol base in Haswah several times a day blasting their AK-47s into the air. It was all they could do to look tough, as they were a fairly pitiful sight that winter. They were dressed in old US desert camouflage and Kevlar helmets without cloth covers, and rode in trucks with sheets of steel welded to their sides. They were nothing more than a larger version what we called 'Bongo trucks,' which were cheap little flatbed trucks used all over the country. They flew a large Iraqi flag on each truck, and their AKs bristled over the top of the rusty steel armor. Faces covered and shooting wildly into the air, they were a sight to behold. Nevertheless, their patrolling through Haswah added a small bit of excitement to the absolute dullness of manning those guard positions.

As such, I was rather relieved each time our platoon's patrol phase in the Haswah schedule started. Besides a lot of driving, we spent a lot of time walking around Haswah. Bradley crews and dismounts alike would hit the streets throughout the five days allotted for our patrolling. Sometimes there was half of our platoon walking around. Other times there were only six or seven of us. At other times, there were other patrols walking around in other parts of the town. Everyone kept in touch with the 'man-pack' radio. On the rest of our backs was the squad gear; the detainee bag, a backpack full of blindfolds, paperwork packets, and zip-strips, or, when we didn't have our platoon medic, SPC DeGuzman with us, a Combat Lifesaver (CLS) Bag. The CLS bag complemented the one field dressing and tourniquet that everyone carried. It had splints, IV fluids and needles, more bandages, and even a coagulant called 'Quick-Clot' – a powdery substance that, when poured on bleeding wounds, caused a chemical reaction that cauterized it and burned it shut.

We preferred having DeGuzman with us. He was a soft spoken, very respectful Filipino guy. He took great care of us, and cared deeply about our health in every sense of the word. Often he'd just come into our tents or rooms to see if anyone was having any issues and to remind us to drink plenty of water.

One cold, pre-dawn February morning, Alpha section put on their gear and quietly assembled in the patrol base courtyard. 1LT Brad Kelley, our platoon leader, usually led Alpha section's patrols. He was a strictly professional officer. He wasn't someone we could joke around since he was pretty stern. A lot of guys took his professionalism for being rude or distant, but he was our platoon leader. It wasn't his job to be our friend, really, but to lead us. Smoking a huge cigar like nearly always, he laid out a simple patrol briefing:

"We're going to be patrolling the southwest quadrant of Haswah for about four hours, ending up in the main marketplace just south of the patrol base. Things have been quiet, and no one is going to be out for the first couple of hours of the patrol. We might do a couple of house calls. Squad leaders?" SSG Villacorte, a short, energetic, Filipino guy was the 3rd squad leader. He had a pretty thick accent. He was good natured in the extreme; I never saw him become angry with a soldier. He joked with us a lot, and for the most part let the team leaders run the squad, only stepping in when something needed his attention. He didn't have much to say this time. The team leaders had already made sure radio checks were done and the squad gear was doled out. Everyone's individual gear had been checked out as well, just as we did before going on guard. SSG Moon, being the senior NCO of the section, spoke up.

"You all know the drill. Maintain proper intervals. Stay alert. We're ready, sir," said SSG Moon quietly. The leaders I was around at this point were men of few words.

"Okay, let's go."

With that the dozen or so of us walked out past our parked vehicles, the sleeping IPs, and our own gate guards.

"Have fun out there," they would say, or something similarly sarcastic. The patrol filed out of the complex and into the street, heading south past the now deserted intersection. It was dark, and the only sounds were the occasional crackle of an ICOM as the squad leader told the point man (usually a team leader) which alleys to turn down. Every foot patrol at night was eerie. The streets were deserted besides stray dogs, of which there were plenty. They barked as we approached them. In fact, their barking was the only thing that marked our progress through the streets and alleys. There had to have been hundreds of them in Haswah alone. Otherwise it was a strange, Middle Eastern ghost town.

On patrol, it wasn't simply walking. I kept my head on a swivel. My eyes were looking up and down, backwards and for-wards, right and left. Sometimes I'd walk backwards just to take longer, more detailed looks behind me, especially if I was bring-ing up the rear. Everyone did this instinctively. We were watch-ing for anything, really. Creeping along, the point man up ahead held up a fist. We stopped, took a knee, and listened closely. I looked backwards and forwards; everyone in the patrol had melted into the shadows of the alleyway silently. SSG Villacorte hurried past me, bent over to stay low. I rested on one knee, weapon trained down the alley – thankfully on the single knee pad I tried to keep on for longer patrols. With one hand I tried to tighten my helmet straps since the NVGs kept pulling it down in the front. It turned out to be nothing. The point man stood up and started walking again, and the whole patrol emerged from the shadows of the alley and followed.

The streets and alleyways were very narrow, given that every Iraqi house had a five-foot wall around it with a heavy metal gate. They were littered with puddles of a kind of grey, sewage-laden sludge that wasn't quite mud. We saw puddles of odd colors, too, even purple. It stunk, of course. Walking just outside of Iraqi houses, you could smell their food as well; the smell was something like lard given their use of ghee, a cooking fat made from butter, mingled in with the aroma of fresh vegetables. Mixed with that was the smell of rancid garbage, sewage, and the ever present smell of Iraq in general. Even then, on a chilly morning, the smells were almost overbearing. It might have been the dampness that kept it smelling so ripe. Whatever the case, sometimes it was enough to make me want to gag at first. Like everything else in Iraq, it took getting used to. Yet even inured to it, though, it still wasn't pleasant.

Just before dawn the prayer call started. I knew of at least five different mosques in Haswah, and their booming cries filled the air and set the dogs off barking all around. Like an alarm clock, bongo trucks loaded with produce started appearing on their way to open up their stalls in the marketplace. Their day was getting started. The increase in traffic was signified by the noise of horns and the engines of bigger trucks lumbering down the main road. There were beginning to walk around, although they usually took another way once they saw us. Still navigating the alleyways, someone gave the word to stash our NVGs. The sun never quite penetrated the gloom on those winter mornings. It was a cool, raw dawn, beset with a humid haze. It didn't smell or look anything like a pleasant morning fog, though, more of a rank mist.

Though still early, the lieutenant wanted to get to the marketplace south of our patrol base. It was the biggest in Haswah. While the streets were lined with store front shops, bakeries, barbers, or anything else, the marketplace worked just like a farmer's market would back in the US. It was a large plaza of sorts. Being an agricultural district, the farmers of the area would bring their produce in this square to sell it locally. Many more people in the area travelled to Baghdad to sell their vegetables and animals there. They were amongst the first on the roads, and usually before curfew. Driving heavily laden trucks towards the main roads before dawn was a good way for an Iraqi to get killed by a US patrol. I never knew the reason for the curfew, just that it was an absolute.

Taking the correct streets and alleys brought us to the marketplace, just about three-hundred meters south of the patrol base on the main road. It resembled a storage area; a square of rectangular, single-story structures housed rows of stalls covered with metal sliding doors. They enclosed a parking lot, really. It was largely empty since most of the vendors had congregated closest to the road. There weren't many there. We filed past some men waiting by cars slowly and warily, making our way to the narrowest part of the market closest to the street. They might have been taxi drivers. We didn't know, since we didn't have an interpreter with us for this patrol. We just tried to look somewhat friendly while keeping a finger close to the trigger. Any time I was on a foot patrol, I instinctively kept my thumb near the safety catch, also. For that matter, any time we were walking outside of the FOB we kept our weapons locked and loaded and held close at the 'low ready', so called because we held the stocks to our shoulders and barrels pointed down, ready to raise it and aim within a split second.

I glared at them just as hard as they glared at us. They didn't look apprehensive at all, just angry. We got into the part of the marketplace that was actually pretty busy. We walked right through just like a shopper would. Getting up close to the stalls let us know that it wasn't quite like a US farmer's market. Besides stepping into ancient septic tanks like we did later, the marketplace reeked beyond anything we'd experienced yet. It was all of the filth of Iraq plus the overwhelming smell of rancid meat. The whole place and every produce item – great slabs of mutton, vegetables of all sorts, and fish that looked like carp – were all covered in swarms of flies. The old men standing behind selections of meat in the open air didn't bother to swat the flies away; the market was a cloud of them. The first few times I saw the marketplace like it was, in all its squalid glory, it was revolting. I couldn't believe Iraqis got their food there. Worse still, on the other side of town was a smaller market in which a butcher cut up sheep right behind his shop. He heaped the carcasses in a pile not ten feet away. So it was. Luckily we passed through it quickly and got onto the road.

Of course, turning onto one of the main north-to-south routes in central Iraq on foot was tricky. In a place where car bombs were a danger, walking out amidst the Iraqi cars was an anxious experience. I never thought about being blown up so much as I did about getting hit by a car, though. American patrol in the street or not, Iraqis were pretty terrible drivers by our standards; scarily so. If we had to step onto the road pointing a weapon usually did the trick to stop oncoming traffic. If not, we'd fire a couple of rounds into the pavement in front of them. Next, well, next we stopped the car according to the ROE. Traffic wasn't busy enough to require anything so dramatic on this patrol. We crossed the bridge over the canal and rounded the patrol base's perimeter. After passing the gate guard and entering the compound, our helmets came off. I carried my weapon a little easier. As we gathered in the courtyard everyone shed their body armor and made a small pile of their gear. Lighting our cigarettes and relaxing, 1LT Kelley started on an AAR. Whatever he said was rendered meaningless when he mentioned that we needed to pack up to head back to Kalsu that day in order to prepare for a big operation. It wasn't the operation that was exciting; I'd get to take a hot shower.

In an article written by our public affairs officer for the newspaper back on Fort Irwin it was called Diyara Sweep. It was a multi-faceted operation to clean up the environs of the tiny, yet notorious, village of Diyara. SF captured some insurgents, and 2-11 as a whole inundated the area to conduct a hearts and minds campaign with leaflets, flyers, and loudspeakers spouting propaganda. I called it the coldest night of my life. Whatever it was, it took all of Valentine's Day, 2005 to complete, and it taught me that the bigger operations like this were long, drawn out affairs to dread in the future.

We started getting briefings and were required to prepare vehicles, equipment, and ourselves as soon as we got to Kalsu. We had about a full day to get ready. As always in a mechanized unit, most of the work entailed maintenance on the vehicles to ensure that they would be in proper working order for the operation. For these bigger missions, CPT Harting and the first sergeant would usually do a version of a PCI for the whole Troop. Being the first squadron-sized mission, everyone treated it like a big event, although our platoon's specific role was something less than exciting. During the mission briefing for the Troop, 1st's task was explained as providing 'roving blocking positions' on the main routes surrounding Diyara. Our chain of command made quite an effort in couching things like, 'driving around in a big circle all night' in tactical terms, although the meaning was pretty clear.

We knew it was going to be cold. Alpha section got Humvees, which were a mixed blessing for this night mission.

While it was more comfortable on several levels – its seats were plushy and you could see outside – the open turret meant that regardless of the vehicle's heater, the occupants would be riding in a wind tunnel. I didn't have any illusions anyway, being the gunner, so made sure to wear every bit of cold weather gear that I could. With arctic gloves, neck gaiter, goggles, a fleece jacket over my blouse, long underwear under that, and cushy socks in Gore-Tex boots, I thought I would be okay. I couldn't dress too warmly, though, because the mission would continue into the morning, and it wouldn't be practical to call for a time-out to take many of those things off as it got warmer. For the most part, what you wore on a patrol or any other mission was for the duration. Anyway, as time came for the operation to kick off shortly after dark, Echo set up in a staging area just inside Kalsu's gate.

Last minute instructions were given, radio checks were completed, and everyone stood by their vehicles. I was perched on top of the Humvee, ready to climb down into the gunner's hatch at a moment's notice. Alone to clear my mind and reclining against the armored turret with my head turned towards the sky, I noticed it was brilliantly clear outside. With no light on Kalsu and very little in the surrounding area, I could see thousands of stars and the outline of the Milky Way perfectly. Looking in the northern sky, I could even see the International Space Station in orbit, twinkling a bit brighter and larger than the surrounding stars. It was one of the very few times I saw something so beautiful there. The sunrises and sunsets were gorgeous, but it was still Iraq. As always, it was a smell that brought me back to that reality. This time it was the exhaust of diesel engines as the unit started up engines.

"Mount up and radio in REDCON one," the call came down the line. In the pitch black, shadows hustled to waiting vehicles, all of which now had engines running. Bradley drivers were raising the hydraulic ramps as their dismounts got inside. Their sound was a slow whine that spelled, 'time to go.' Everyone got in our truck, filling every seat for this mission, unlike our skeleton-crew mounted patrols. I put my helmet on, waiting to load the machine gun until we were on the access road. We all joked around a little bit about how cold we were going to get as the different crews came on line and reported their readiness on the radio. Spirits were high. On these night missions early in the tour, we felt we had the edge on the bad guys out there. As the Troop left the gate and travelled up Tampa, other platoons split off onto their designated routes. 1st stayed on the main highway, where we would remain for most of the mission.

Since it was after curfew the roads were deserted. The only thing we had to fight off was the cold, and we lost that battle. I froze. Thirty minutes of bone-chilling wind blasting me in my face was all I could handle. We started switching gunners out. It was just too cold to leave one person up there for very long. Our truck's heater was broken, which caused all sorts of cussing. Even SSG Moon was vocal about it. Trapped, sitting still in the truck with no activity to warm our bodies, we suffered. It was the coldest night I'd ever experienced, and I was surprised it could get so bad in Iraq. It was in the thirties, but the wind made it unbearable. We didn't stop until near morning, and when we did the action got the blood pumping quickly, although it didn't do much to thaw me out.

As dawn approached things got livelier. First we encountered another unit, the cavalry scout platoon of HHT, shooting at a car and sending dismounts after it. We stopped only for a second, just long enough to hear the popping of rifle fire and smell the gunpowder in the air. We asked if they needed help. They didn't. Moving along, we came upon our designated checkpoint blocking one of the roads out of Diyara just at dawn, just

74

as SF was supposed to be finishing their raid.

They must have been done in the village, because a pair of Apaches was leveling a building beyond a treeline with rockets and 30mm cannons. It was quite a sight. The helicopters were barely visible above the trees. A salvo of rockets streaked off of their wings silently, one after another, into the ground, their detonations creating rippling flashes on the horizon. The tracers from the cannons arced towards the ground faster than the rockets. The Apaches looked like they were literally pouring a fountain of flame and sparks onto the ground. The sounds that started milliseconds after the flashes were the barely discernible, continuous whoosh of the rockets, the staccato toc-toc-toc of the cannon and, the sharp, deep bass of the explosions. I gawked, like most of us. It was awesome to see in the original sense of the word.

I still had a job to do. We had to set up a TCP and search each vehicle leaving Diyara to look for fleeing insurgents. This was one of the first among countless TCPs I'd do. Even the first time it seemed like a dangerous farce. It was always chaotic and always dicey. Each TCP had to be organized differently; adaptive to the terrain, volume of traffic, expected threat, and, of course, what kind of vehicles we had and how many soldiers we had with us. This time we'd set up at a 'T' intersection of two canal roads. We kept the Humvees on the short end of the 'T,' then sent a few soldiers about fifty meters down the long end to stop traffic. These soldiers got the occupants out, searched them and the vehicle for anything suspicious, and then sent them up to our interpreter and me, armed with a twenty-page list of bad guys.

Of course, I didn't speak or read Arabic. Our 'blacklist' of Iraqi names was written in English and spelled out phonetically. Our interpreter could barely read English, so I had to sound out the names for him. He'd look at the Iraqi's identification, something which looked like a passport written entirely in Arabic, tell me the name, and then I would have to search through the list for what looked to be the right name, judging from looking at the English spelling and just asking the interpreter.

"Jaaa...what the hell? Jalafari?" Most of the names were jaw-breakers to us English speakers.

"No, no that is tribal name. Give me family name, please," the interpreter requested. If I'd known what an Iraqi family name was I might have been able to help. Each name on the list was actually comprised of about six different names. I was lost. I started to get flustered. I tried just handing the list to the interpreter. Although he couldn't really read English, it didn't matter in that impossible situation. Meanwhile, a line of traffic had formed waiting at our checkpoint. The soldiers tasked out to search the vehicles wanted to search the vehicles further down the line so there wouldn't be a waiting car bomb. We wouldn't let them because they'd get too far away for the gunners in the trucks to cover them. The situation had devolved into a classic clusterfuck. I was getting very frustrated and the anxiety was ratcheting up. Just in time, word came down to pack it all up. SF was done with their raid, and the mission was over. Just as easily as we'd come, we left. It didn't make much sense, but I didn't care. The line of Iraqi cars and trucks waited on us to get a comfortable distance way before making their way onto the main roads and about their business.

Later that night on Kalsu, we finally got to get some sleep after what seemed like an endless twenty-four hours. We turned the heat up in our tent and crawled into our sleeping bags. There wasn't a sound after five minutes besides snoring.

WHOOOOOSH! Something shrieked through the air above our tent. *BOOM!* I hit the plywood floor. It was ear-splitting. Fuck my Kevlar and weapon, get to the bunker now, I thought as I scrambled in the dark for the tent door. That's no mortar, was my next thought. A lot of the guys had beat me out there, including 1LT Kelley in his underwear, a t-shirt, and his helmet. The sirens started wailing. Everyone who smoked lit their customary incoming cigarettes. The lieutenant joined in with his cigar. SFC Green rushed over from Bravo section's tent next door after a minute or so, excited and speaking rapidly.

"You guys okay?! That was a rocket that just hit the scout platoon's tent. Fucking close guys! Is everyone okay? NCOs?" We were fine, albeit rattled. The tent that was hit was only thirty-five meters away. Were it not for the insulation of the concrete barriers we would have felt the shockwave. The scouts' tent was shredded, but they had been out on a mission and it was empty. This is what we heard when the first sergeant stopped by our bunker a few minutes later, at least. I never ventured over there. The base's sirens sounded the 'all clear' after a quarter-of-an-hour had passed.

I stayed in the bunker for a little while and smoked a couple more cigarettes. A few of us considered sleeping out there, and one of the privates actually did. He did so somewhat jokingly, but all of us realized the reasons for his move that night. Mortars were one thing. This rocket business was pure terror. That sound was incredible! Even though I made my way back into my comfortable, warm sleeping bag, I didn't sleep much for the remainder of the night. The adrenaline was still pumping for a while. I lay awake wondering if I'd ever be able to sleep again.

5

It was after the rocket attack that things began to change. Back on Kalsu, the mortars were still falling consistently. That was nothing new, but as a unit we began noticing things – sinister things. An impromptu patrol of 2-11's command group found a mutilated Iraqi corpse just south of Haswah. The bruises and other marks on his body suggested that he'd been beaten and tortured. The fact that his heart was ripped out and that he was partially skinned suggested much more. The pictures of his body circulated around quickly. By now it had become SOP that every patrol carried a digital camera to record images of captured insurgents or anything else of intelligence value. More often than not they recorded the carnage. This incident let us know that the Iraqis were killing each other with brutality, yet another move in the chess game. We never watched the news, but we did talk to Iraqis. In that way we sort of pieced together a vague idea of what was going on. It didn't look good.

Our house calls were little more than random searches and conversations with Iraqis. We did hundreds of them, and they usually played out the same. It was a midday foot patrol through Haswah this time. The lieutenant picked a house among a row of others. We banged on the metal gate until someone came to open it. We were just visiting, and on routine patrols we didn't use force unless we met it first. An older Iraqi man, the patriarch of the household, appeared shortly after.

"Salaam halaikum," he said as he made the slightest bow and touched his right hand to his heart. It meant "peace be with you," and was a standard, formal greeting. This older man had on a full length shirt, called a thawb (we called them man dresses), and Arab headdress. A lot of the younger men wore Western clothing, and the little boys exclusively did. They all wore sandals. His left hand was behind his back. It may have been started as a rumor, but after seeing their bathroom (a hole in the ground with a faucet and tin can handy), it was easy to believe that the Iraqis actually wiped themselves with their left hand. In any event, they considered it disrespectful to wave or gesture with your left hand, spit, or display the bottom of your foot. And it was especially offensive to eyeball their daughters. To us these things were bizarre, and mindful of them as we may have been, on every foot patrol I and others spit our tobacco juice, did not let our right hands off of our weapons to gesture, and couldn't help but exchange glances with Iraqi women. A lot of them were beautiful, and they giggled at us. Many times daughters and wives would be beaten after we left a house because of this. We did not intend to insult them at every turn, but the clash of civilizations that occurred when amongst them was unavoidable.

As 1LT Kelley spoke with the Iraqi man through the interpreter, I led a few soldiers through the house on a semi-tactical search. I kept my eyes where they needed to be looking, but our posture was fairly relaxed. I'd rifle through drawers and closets without being destructive and look under beds and through their cabinets. The first priority was to locate the household AK and all of the males. Other than that, we looked for obviously suspicious things like bomb making materials, maps, large amounts of cash, or weapons. We found a lot of extra AK-47s, especially during the cordon and search we did early on, but hardly ever anything else.

Each house usually had a living room in the front furnished with long, low couches and elaborate looking rugs. Their floors were tile for the most part, and in Haswah many homes were two stories with the bedrooms on the second floor. While a team searched the interior, another searched the outside perimeter. Both teams radioed the lieutenant when they'd secured the area and completed their searches.

Having secured the single Kalashnikov rifle and posted guards outside, SSG Moon, 1LT Kelley, our interpreter, and the Iraqi man sat in the main room. I stood in the corridor, helmet off, and listened to the conversation. The cigarette smoke was thick as the old man, like most Iraqi men, was puffing away. Since he offered me one, I lit up, too. One of his two wives brought out chai tea, served piping hot and loaded with sugar. In general, the Iraqis showed us hospitality when we were in their homes and were fairly nice. Sometimes they weren't, but this family wasn't bad. Although there were usually never any ground-breaking intelligence finds during these house calls, we could at least get a sense of the people's mindset and how they were dealing with the madness. That was just as important.

"What do you think about the Coalition forces," was the first question usually asked. The interpreter waited to hear the man's answer before he relayed it to us in heavily accented English. A lot of them barely spoke English, and ours that day was notably bad.

"He say he very glad Marines gone and Army is here. He say, though, that Iraq is still very bad place. Many don't care except that you are Americans." I was surprised they knew the difference between us. The interpreters never conveyed the speaker's emotions, but you could sense frustration nonetheless. After it was relayed to us, it was apparent why.

"You Americans do not understand. If we help you, the bad people will kill me and my family. If we do not help you, you will leave us alone. We want peace. We want this to be over." He put it in stark, understandable terms. The insurgents were terrorists, and they were employing that tactic against us as well as Iraqis who supported our goals. The lieutenant asked another question in the usual blunt terms we used during those types of conversations:

"So what do you think would help?" The old man then started in on a long, animated harangue. There was still frustration in his voice. Our interpreter started translating for us, pausing every so often to ask the man a question. It may have been a clarification. Who knew?

"He say that US need to leave," was all the 'terp said. The Iraqi man muttered something after that which I understood, having had a small bit of exposure to the language at Irwin during our COB missions, and more since patrolling.

"In sha'Allah," which meant, "God willing," was what he said as he rubbed his prayer beads. It was about the same as an American saying, "We'll see." There wasn't much for anyone to say after that. The lieutenant thanked him for his time and hospitality. We donned our helmets and prepared to leave. I left the weapon and its single magazine propped against the wall as we left. They knew not to touch it until we were gone.

The interpreter, if he was a good one, would usually tell the lieutenant a little more about the interview once we got on the street. This one didn't; in fact, we barely trusted him to have translated that conversation accurately. Sometimes we wondered what exactly our 'terps were saying to the people we were interacting with, and whether it was what we intended or not. Arabic was a mystery to us, though, just like most everything else in Iraq, so we just had to go with it.

The people's indifference to our presence shone through at the most dangerous of times. We had begun to find a lot of IEDs on the roadside. Luckily, none had detonated on one of our patrols yet, but they were popping up frequently nonetheless. Bravo section found one on a patrol north of Haswah, and I gleaned what happened from the AAR which SFC Green gave afterwards. They all looked tense and were sweating, as the temperatures even in late February were getting into the high seventies during the day. The gear added several degrees to it.

They had spotted some wires coming out of a crater and halted to form a perimeter around it. According to procedure, they stopped the Iraqi traffic travelling both ways on ASR Jackson a safe distance from the suspected bomb, pulled security, and waited on one of Kalsu's Explosive Ordnance Disposal (EOD) teams. While Bravo waited, their main priority was keeping traffic at bay, which was difficult. Iraqi traffic control was frustrating. Although the soldiers had made it clear through hand signals and warning shots that the path was closed, there were still antsy drivers who kept creeping forwards. They had to shoot a lot more warning shots, nearly killing a driver of one vehicle. Stopping traffic at a suspected IED site protected soldiers from car bombs and the Iraqi motorists from the IED's blast. Even after EOD had arrived and dispatched its robot on treads to investigate the bomb (which turned out to be a dud, apparently), they had trouble keeping the cars back. The soldiers were understandably frustrated and tense as a result. A little later I saw just how dangerous finding a possible IED could be.

One day, an Iraqi man had wandered up to the patrol base and informed the IPs that there was a bomb in the alley just across the street from the patrol base. I was on Quick Reaction Force (QRF) duty with my section and went out to investigate. Sure enough, there were four or five RPG rounds in a bag lying there in an alley, though we dared not simply pick them up. We had to treat everything as if it was booby-trapped; people, cars, piles of trash, animal or human corpses on the road – everything. So we had the patrol base call EOD while we formed a perimeter around it. We watched closely, because any time something was in plain sight like that we had to assume that the bad guys

83

wanted us to find it. I kept a short distance from it, and hunkered down behind a stout wall, peering down the alleyway. There were a million things running through my head, among them to keep my head on a swivel and watch out. EOD arrived quickly and decided to blow it in place with some C4.

The kids in Iraq seemed to love American soldiers, especially the little boys. They asked us for money and cigarettes instead of candy, and offered their services in tracking down 'Ali Baba,' who they knew to run rampant in Haswah. We even paid them a dollar for every piece of ordnance they led us to or told us about. The little girls were shy. The one that popped out from around a blind corner into my section of the alley couldn't have been more than four or five years old.

"Holy shit, hey! HEY! Get, shoo! Imshi, imshi!" – Arabic for 'get away' – I yelled in a forceful tone. Still, she started wandering closer towards me, smiling obliviously, and closer to the blast that was going to go off any minute.

"Fire in the hole! Fire in the hole!" The girl disappeared behind the corner from which she'd come. All I heard after that was a 'pop,' then ringing in my ears. Debris and dust flew up into the air behind me; a few rocks and clods of dirt fell on me. When my hearing came back to normal after a few seconds, I could hear all the guys on the other ends of the alleys shouting and laughing. Everyone loved explosions, and it was gratifying to have found something of the enemy's and destroyed it. My heart was beating rapidly. I was really scared for the little girl.

We gathered up, and EOD left. I didn't mention the Iraqi girl to anyone. I'd assumed that being that young she had to have lived close by. She seemed to have gotten the message when the EOD guys shouted the warning. She had lived through the invasion and its aftermath, after all. She probably knew danger when she saw or heard it. I hoped all this at least. Haswah was proving itself to be a tough little hellhole for us to make headway in, and our commanders were attempting to change the balance of the initiative to show the residents of Haswah, and particularly its insurgents, that we meant business. It would take more than patrolling to do so.

Raids were the most carefully planned and highly anticipated operations we did. They relied on the element of surprise, above all, quickly massing men on an objective to overwhelm it and capture or kill its occupants. In other words, it was the essence of our jobs as infantrymen. Clearing rooms and buildings, among other elements of Military Operations in Urban Terrain (MOUT), was exactly the type of task we'd trained for on Irwin. Naturally, then, as soon as we got word that all of Echo Troop was going to raid about a dozen houses simultaneously we got excited. As usual with these missions, information came down the line in trickles. The whole troop would be dismounted. The rest of the squadron was supporting the raid with a cordon around the town while we hit our targets. The Iraqi Army was taking some of our detainees. Our targets were hardcore insurgents, so we could expect resistance. These things and the rest rumors and tidbits from our chain of command suggested that we were in for a big deal.

The morning before the raid the wheels were set in motion. The way operations orders were passed down the chain of command and perfected each step of the way was an interesting system. The preparation for our first Haswah raid set the precedent for Echo's later raids. CPT Harting gathered the platoon leaders and platoon sergeants together and went over the target area on a large, detailed, satellite image of Haswah. Target houses were outlined in marker, and smaller symbols drawn to pinpoint locations where he wanted security teams posted to cover the approaches to prevent any intrusions or escapes during the raid. Having gone on a small reconnaissance patrol earlier, he described some of the characteristics of the target houses. One was the biggest on the block, for instance, and most had walls around them. He explained the exact role of all of the units supporting the raid and marked their planned locations on the satellite photo. Mainly they would man the patrol base and seal off the roads around our target area with roadblocks. He covered the more mundane details of radio frequencies to use and the call signs for other units. He then told them what time to have PCIs and PCCs done, and what time he wanted his Troop ready to go.

Then it was up to SFC Green and 1LT Kelley to hammer out the details. They got in a huddle with the section and squad leaders. How many houses do we have to hit? Three. How many men do we have, and with what weapons? Were there enough detainee packets? Did we have enough man-pack radios, or did we need to make up an extra one? They discussed these things and more. As usual, we had to go with what we had, and they devised a way for us to hit the three houses and cover the two blocking positions, as well as set up a detainee collection point with a guard. We'd break up into three four-man fire teams for the houses and two fire teams for the blocking positions, where extra men could guard the prisoners. It was ad hoc, and somewhat elaborate, but we had worked well together across the dismount/mounted lines so far, so they had faith that we could pull it off without a hitch.

The platoon then gathered together, and 1LT Kelley outlined the scheme of the squadron sealing off the area and the synchronization of the attack. Then he got into the details of our three target houses and the two blocking positions we had to man. SFC Green broke down the organization we'd use. I'd lead a fire team consisting of Steppe, Wantz, and Logsdon that would hit one house. One of the dismounts' team leaders would lead a team comprised of Bravo section's Bradley crews to hit another, and so on. They needed most of the dismounts' SAWs and gre-nade launchers at the blocking positions. The squad leaders were tasked with overseeing the blocking positions and provid-ing command and control. SFC Green then told the squad lead-ers to get with their guys and go over the details. Also, get those PCIs done, and don't forget the extra gear; breaching equip-ment, detainee gear, and plenty of chemlites to mark cleared rooms.

SSG Moon was in charge of my fire team and a blocking po-sition since the two would be less than ten meters apart. He'd have three men with him there, including one of the man-pack radios, and would maintain communication with the rest of our platoon as well as the rest of Echo. He told me he'd take care of getting the guys on his position ready, and that I needed to plan out how I'd take down this house. At this point I was still offi-cially a gunner, but I was a grunt foremost. I'd acted as dismount fire team leader plenty of times already in the month or more that we'd been hitting the streets of Haswah. Besides, I had Steppe with me and knew the men on my team well. I was con-fident, although fairly anxious. Part of our briefing was that we could fully expect to be shot at inside our target houses. This was serious business. We sat in the room we were in for the day and discussed the mission with everyone in the team.

"Hey man, I got SGT Fucker's shotgun! He let me borrow it since he's sittin' in the alleyway. Fuck yes! Let me go in first!" He'd had a smile on his face since we'd first heard about the raid. The rest of team, including me, was inspired by his enthusiasm.

"It's fine by me. I'm going to take the mini sledge hammer from the breaching kit, so that should cover our breaching equipment. You go first. Logsdon after that, then Wantz, then I'll bring up the rear. We'll stack on the wall by the gate and wait for the word on the radio to go. We'll bust in through the gate, stack up again on the front door, then go inside. Number one man goes right. Number two man goes left. After that we'll go with how the room is set up. I'm coming in last, so when we all get into the main room I'll figure it out from there." No one had any real questions. It was simple enough, and we'd rehearsed similar scenarios countless times.

I checked the team's equipment thoroughly this time. A nervous feeling was building in the pit of my stomach as I did, and it grew alongside the mounting uncertainties in my head. I wondered what would happen inside that house. How many guys were in there? Did they have guns? Knives? Was the place booby-trapped? Could we get inside easily? Would they fight or give up? What if one of us got hit? It was the very type of situation which I'd been anxious about after getting promoted, actually. I was going to be in charge in there. I just hoped I wouldn't screw up.

"Hey, everybody grab some of these new zip-strips we got from the CP. I got some more batteries, too. Put fresh ones in your Surefires and NVGs." You'd be surprised by how much a grunt relied on batteries. NCOs in the platoon had boxes of all types of batteries. As the arms room guy for the platoon, I probably kept the most. The Surefire flashlights, which everyone had mounted onto their rifles and even SAWs, took a smaller battery that died quickly. Surefires were intensely bright, and would not only illuminate the inside of an Iraqi's house, it would also blind anyone who looked into it. We signaled cars with it, and it also came with an infrared lens cover so only our night vision could see its beam. It really just wasn't practical to try to clear a house with NVGs on unless we absolutely had to, though.

At dusk, the Troop gathered in the patrol base's courtyard. In the eerie twilight there was a steady hum of activity. Guys were helping each other adjust straps on gear. Prince was showing everyone the small, digital video camera he'd duct-taped to his helmet. He was excited with the rest of us, cracking jokes about how epic the video would be. There were soldiers from HHT wandering around, some hurried, others loitering around the spare corners. It was crowded. Even among the bustle I could catch glimpses of guys staring into nothing. I only saw it when I glanced up from doing the same. Probably like them, I was getting dialed in. I was helping myself to a can of Red Bull and making sure my own gear was in order for the hundredth time in twenty minutes of waiting. There were tons of details that I'd already covered with my team, but my mind was racing. It was a mix of excitement, nervousness, and fear, all of which had been steadily building. Then CPT Harting came out of the CP with the platoon leaders. Carbine in hand, with 9mm Beretta on his hip, his tall figure still stood out in the gathering darkness.

"Alright men." It was his characteristic greeting. "Tonight we're going to bring the fight to the bad guys, hooah?! Remember your training. It's going to be a long night, but we're here to see things through, so let's get to it. Platoon leaders, they're all yours." The lieutenant merely nodded to the platoon sergeant.

"Alright 1st platoon listen up, everybody be careful, watch each other's backs," SFC Green reminded us. I couldn't see facial expressions anymore. Night was setting in. We had fifteen minutes or so to wait around with our squad; REDCON one of course, just waiting on the word to go. I placed a small handful of Copenhagen in my cheek. Nothing was cutting through the tension, though. My heart was fluttering by the time the whole Troop started to move out to the compound's entrance.

Everyone was ready, NVGs flipped down. I flipped mine over my eye and took stock. In the green and black shadows, everyone lined up on either side of the road leading out of the patrol base. A group of officers, or so it looked to me at least, stood in the middle of the road and looked at their watches. The sounds coming from us had dwindled to nothing, besides

Prince, ahead of me a few guys, still laughing over something. The tension was incredible.

"Move out. Stay quiet." I don't know who said it. We filed past the gate guards. The only sounds were the shuffling of feet on the dusty pavement and the clinking and rattling of rifles and gear. Despite the chill, I started to sweat. When we reached the end of the gate complex the men– at a jog now – glided across the road and disappeared between the buildings on the other side. Most of 1st platoon's target houses were in an alleyway roughly two blocks down from the main road. I followed SSG Moon's blocking team in front of me.

SSG Moon hurried across the road and down a narrow alley that ran along the canal. It was just like the satellite photos: straight back two blocks, then hang a right. At a run, we got there in no time. SSG Moon stopped at the corner, and the guys with him flopped to the ground and spread out the bipods of their SAWs. We hustled past them until we got to our house. Then came the tricky part, as we had to time our entrance with everyone else's. Up to this point, we hadn't made a sound, and most of the Troop was across the road getting into position to hit their targets. Reaching ours, we stopped short of the gate and stacked up against the wall. The plan was that when I got word on the ICOM I was carrying, I'd slap the guy's helmet in front of me and he would pass it along. When Steppe felt a tap on his helmet he'd go. My legs were shaking and my heart was pounding out of control. The sweat that had started was pouring now, and I was oblivious to the cold. My whole body was primed for action.

The voice crackled over the ICOM: "Red platoon hit it!" That was our signal!

"Go man, go!" I'd forgotten to tap his helmet. Taking a step back for momentum, Steppe threw his whole weight into the metal gate. BANG! It wouldn't budge. Oh fuck, I thought, we're done for. BANG! He did it again. SSG Moon raced over.

"Help me give him a boost over, hurry the fuck up," he whispered excitedly. The other teams were busting doors and gates down. There was shouting all over. A shotgun was fired down the street. SSG Moon and Logsdon basically threw Steppe over the gate, and he unlocked it from the inside. As soon as he had it swung open, we filed in through the small yard and stacked up again on the door to the house.

"Go!" I said as soon as I'd reached the stack. Steppe didn't miss a beat. He flipped up his NVGs, switched on the Surefire he'd attached to the shotgun, and gave the door a hearty kick. It flew wide open this time. He disappeared into the dark, screaming as he went. The rest of us flowed into the house behind him. The first room was tiny. I hung a left, that room was small, too. It was cramped, so I stopped at the threshold. My guys have got it covered, I thought, don't crowd them.

"Rooms! Rooms!" I yelled. I didn't need to; they'd already started clearing the bedrooms.

"Get the fuck down! Get the fuck DOWN," Steppe was screaming from a room. Surefires were flashing everywhere and a few women in the house had started to shriek.

It's so fucking small, I thought. My mind scrambled.

"Clear!" I heard Logsdon shout from the furthest room.

"Guys, get them out to me, I'll cuff them!" We'd awoken these people, obviously. The house was so small that by standing in the main room you could basically see into every other room. There were three Iraqi men inside. Logsdon rushed out of a room and pushed one of them towards me, then disappeared back into the house. His hands were up. I grabbed his shirt collar and threw him to the ground, knee to the small of his back, just like they'd taught us. I got a zip-strip out, and, fighting my shaking hands and the sweat burning my eyes, managed to get them around his wrists. Logsdon and Wantz came out with the other two and handed them to me. I put them both face first on the ground, not gently, but not too roughly either. After I cuffed them, I called for one of the guys to help me search them. The tiny house was clear. The three women were crying and screaming uncontrollably. Steppe and Wantz had started to search the bedrooms more thoroughly. The whole raid had taken only minutes.

I was glad I had gloves on. The first Iraqi had the shit scared out of him; literally. None of the men had anything on them. I got on the ICOM.

"Red-two Actual, Red-two Golf, house is clear. Three detainees. Conducting search time now." The words came out hurried and tense.

"This is Red-two Actual, roger that, I'll send some help," crackled the radio in reply. I had all the detainees sequestered in the front room. It seemed stifling hot. Waving Logsdon over, I had him reach into the bag on my back and get out field dressings to use as blindfolds. Tying them over the eyes of all three, we got them up and corralled them outside. Steppe met me in the smaller room.

"There's not shit here that I can find, man. God that was fucking awesome!" He was animated, to say the least. He had the household Kalashnikov in one hand.

"Yeah, your boy here shit himself," I said as I jerked the Iraqi to his feet. My voice was still elevated, but the tension had started to pass. Steppe just laughed his dark laugh and muttered something about how none of them liked the sight of the shotgun. SSG Moon came in.

"Friendly," he shouted as he walked into the house so we wouldn't shoot him. "Oka guys, get your detainees out to the alley. Some of the others are already out there. You all find anything?"

"Negative, sergeant. Just the AK," I replied. It was the usual stuff. My fire team walked the detainees out to the alley, where the rest of the Troop had emerged from their own targets. We met up with SFC Green. He ordered us to get the detainees lined up on one side of the alley with their cuffed hands grasping the shirt of the detainee behind them. It was a hands-on process to accomplish this. The Iraqis, blindfolded and not understanding English, were helpless. We handled them roughly, but there was no beating. At most we shoved them where they needed to go. Their cuffs were tight. I know the ones I placed on the Iraqis were; the adrenaline was flowing hard when I did it. As we lined them up, we loosened the tightest ones.

Once organized, we headed back down the alley with our prisoners in tow. Now there was joking around. Everyone was excitedly telling each other about their individual raids. Ours was not the only one to have run into problems. Steppe told me he hadn't shot at the heavy metal gate for fear of ricochet. Good call. I hadn't even thought to use the sledge hammer. Prince had lost his helmet cam ducking through a narrow doorway. His team had ended up hitting a huge house with six or seven men in it, requiring them to call in for more guys from the blocking position closest to them to help. The shotgun blast was accidental; one of 2nd platoon's guy's was antsy. In short, everyone's precise, detailed, team-level plan hadn't panned out. They'd taught us that no plan survives contact with the enemy. A version of it had been proven this time. Still, as we got into the patrol base with the rest of the Troop, we felt great. We'd finally got to do our jobs, the adrenaline pumping thrill that many of us had envisioned for quite a while. We'd captured our quarry, and no one was hurt. It was a successful mission.

The Iraqi Army had showed up at the patrol base in the meantime, and it was to them that we handed over some of our prisoners. We'd rounded up about twenty-five of them in all. The Iraqi soldiers immediately placed sandbags over their heads

93

and stood them against the wall of the compound closest to the canal. One of their officers appeared. There was a cluster of Iraqi soldiers guarding the prisoners while a few more were loitering about. A lot of Echo was watching as well.

"Who the fuck is this dude," I heard someone ask. One of our officers was walking by and answered.

"That's Major Mohammed," he said.

We'd heard of him. He was the commander of the Iraqi Army battalion in our AO. Like something out of a Holocaust film, he went down the line of Iraqis, who, although had remained silent up to this point, could now be heard praying and muttering under their breath. Some of them were shaking. The Major lifted up their sandbags one by one. Cigar in his mouth, he looked closely into each of the detainee's faces, speaking to them quietly in Arabic. Moving along, sometimes the Major would stop and snarl at one of the detainees. He'd let loose in Arabic, leaving the bewildered Iraqi quaking. He grabbed one's hair and slung his head against the wall, cursing the man as he did so. With a sharp command, his soldiers grabbed these unlucky ones and formed another line with them. With another order, the Major had his men ferret away those prisoners he'd picked, and they departed the patrol base. I had a strange feeling they were going to be executed. We knew the Iraqis dealt with one another harshly. The rest of the prisoners were ours.

Despite all the units allocated to support Echo, we had to transport our prisoners in Bradleys to a collection point south of Haswah. It took until dawn, and by then everyone's adrenaline rush had turned into fatigue. I had the gunner's hatch of my Bradley open, as I usually did when I needed the cold to keep me awake. One of the soldiers had taken off his NVGs prematurely, and 1LT Kelley corrected him. The soldier said something back to him, and the situation escalated quickly until SSG Villacorte stepped in and calmed it down. We'd been up for more than twenty-four hours, and everyone was pretty testy. I was glad the detainees got handed over somewhat quickly so we could get out of there.

After assembling again at the patrol base, our platoon then made its way back to Kalsu on our Bradleys. Our first raid was over, and we'd be returning to our phase of patrolling from Kalsu. Just hours after raiding a house for the first time, I had a hot shower and a good breakfast at the chow hall back on the FOB. It would be a little while before Alpha section had to patrol again, so we could rest for a while. By then we were used to getting some sleep whenever we could. We'd close up our tent and shut the lights out, making it completely black except for the glow of some of the men's DVD players propped on their chest as they lay in their cots relaxing. Some would be reading by use of an LED headlamp. As usual, we all talked for a while until we dozed off. I didn't get to sleep for a while, though. The raid was still on my mind. I just kept thinking that nothing had gone according to plan; absolutely nothing. I was more than glad we hadn't run into opposition inside our house, but kept wondering what would have happened if we had.

At the end of February, I got a new job. Smitty had gotten pulled to go train the Iraqi Army, so I took his place as a dismounted team leader in 3rd squad under SSG Villacorte. It wasn't a huge change since I'd still patrol with Alpha section. Besides that, the distinctions between dismount and mounted men had become vaguer since the demands of a particular mission dictated organization more than anything else. Still, I wasn't responsible for a Bradley anymore. I'd likely never be a gunner in its turret again, and would certainly spend the better part of mounted patrols riding in the back, waiting on the ramp to drop.

I had two soldiers now. One was a short, slender, eighteen-year-old Italian kid from Brooklyn, PFC Delmonte. He was a smart guy, and he reminded me a lot of Prince. He was a capable soldier despite his being so new to the Army, and his accent was just what you'd think a thick, New York accent would be. The other was SPC McFarland. He was a tall, stocky guy from Florida who had been transferred from Squadron. He had spent a lot of time with the command group, but I knew he would do well as a dismount with us

I was never really hard on those two. They were intelligent enough to know that I was in charge, anyway. It was a matter of gaining respect. I'd just have to lead by example. We all had a feeling that things were heating up as assuredly as the weather was. As such, working relationships built on trust and respect were absolutely essential. I always preferred the guys to help and follow rather than be prodded or intimidated. It's what I'd learned made the best type of leader. Instead of saying, "clean your weapons," for instance, I'd start cleaning mine and say, "let's clean our weapons." I never believed you had to terrify or berate a soldier to get the best out of them. Showing them what had to be done, showing them you're following your own instructions, and at times explaining why something silly was necessary was all you needed to do.

The next time we left the wire for Haswah, I was crammed into the back of my old Bradley with my two soldiers. Being a passenger on a Bradley was an experience. We travelled to Haswah at night that time. Once the ramp was closed, the engine was idling, and the hatchway leading up into the turret was shut, a dismount was in his own little world. When the Bradley started moving and picked up speed, the rapid clanking of the metal tracks and the grinding of the sprocket was deafening. It sounded like being beside a wood chipper being fed steel rods. You could scream at the top of your lungs and still not be heard. The vibration in the back rattled your teeth and insides. We could only use dim blue lights in the back so it wouldn't be visible from the outside, and it made troop compartment in an eerie, dark blue. You couldn't see outside through the periscopes at night, and barely could in the daylight. It was only by the pitch of the engine and the sensation of the Bradley's turning that, having learned by now each turn we had to make to reach the patrol base, I could estimate where we were. The slow crawl and frequent, sharp turns of the Bradley let me know when we'd arrived that the patrol base.

It was like any other time spending ten days out there. By now the rotations had blurred together, although one night while I was on QRF stuck out. The CP received a call on the radio from squadron headquarters, call-sign 'Battle X-Ray.' There was a report of several VBIEDs en route to our location or FOB Iskandariyah. They didn't know which, but knew they were out there.

SFC Green burst into the room where my guard shift and another were relaxing.

"Everybody get your shit on and get outside," was exactly how I figured out we were in danger. He wasn't joking around one bit. We scrambled. Some of the guys went to man up Bradleys. I kept my team close and thought of what to do. They'd only said to get my guys out to the intersection and stop any oncoming cars. We got out there fast.

Across the street at the intersection was a larger building with a decent wall around it. I told Delmonte and McFarland to cover the east-west route while I hunkered down behind a utility box just off the road, looking south. We were right at the corner. I told them to take cover, even if they had to lay down in the prone. The Bradleys rushing out to cover each road would take care of warning shots. No need to be visible. I loaded an HE grenade into my grenade launcher, trained my weapon down the road, and waited. The nervous anticipation had my heart in my throat.

In the distance headlights appeared. A vehicle was approaching. There were no friendly units in the area. Had there been, they wouldn't have driven with lights on anyway. I flashed my Surefire frantically. The Bradley beside me let out a short burst of coax. Warning shots. The headlights continued to get bigger quickly. The vehicle was still racing towards us.

All hell broke loose. *Ratatatatatatat!* The Bradley's gunner laid on the trigger. A steady stream of tracers zipped out of the Bradley towards the vehicle. The headlights grew bigger still. Without thinking, I flipped up my NVGs and put the red dot of my sight above the driver's side headlight. I fired methodically; careful, aimed shots. A machine gun from a guard position at the patrol base joined in. It was deafening. The tracers poured thickly down the road. A hundred meters away, the vehicle, which I could see was a white van now, slowly rolled to a stop. No sound came from it. I'd emptied half a magazine, but the machine guns had put hundreds of rounds into it.

"Wooooohoooo! Shit!" The Bradley gunner was yelling. I kept staring at the vehicle.

Oh God, I thought, what the fuck have we done?

SFC Green rushed over with DeGuzman and a couple more men. I told my guys to stay put.

"C'mon SGT. Ervin," he said as he walked past. I didn't say a word. I reloaded magazines on the walk. My heart had stopped. The dread that overcame me wasn't like anything I'd ever experienced before. The van was just beyond the canal in the middle of the road. The Bradley kept up its scan of the road ahead and shined its headlights on the van for us while we approached it. I wondered if it was going to blow up, and warily eyed the casket strapped to the top of it. The windshield and grill were riddled with bullet holes. There was a growing pool of dark liquid underneath, and I could vaguely make out the silhouettes of the passengers, what was left of them at least. I approached it slowly, barely looking inside. I didn't want to at all. Still, we'd shot up this van thinking there was a bomb in it, so the least we could do was search it.

The smell that overpowered me when I got close was new. The sharp pungency of battery acid, the metallic, thick smell of blood and viscera, and the rotten egg scent of gunpowder mixed together in the small confine of the van. It was an evil smell. It reminded me of skinning squirrels back in West Virginia. DeGuzman stepped past me and gazed inside. The sight was even worse than the smell.

"They're definitely dead, sergeant," he said. I can't remember what was said after that. I opened the door and started to climb in with the idea of searching the interior, and had gotten my foot on a wet step when I stopped short, horrified. Inside were what remained of three men, two in the front and one behind the passenger. Their heads were gone. In their places were masses of gory pulp. Only the passenger had half of a face, and what was left of it was locked in a look of horror. The man in the back's brains had splattered all over the seat. Blood and brain matter oozed onto the vehicles floor and matted the seats surrounding the bodies.

I retched. I'd seen enough. I wasn't about to search through that gore if I could help it. I walked away from the van towards the guardrail of the bridge leading over the canal. Faucher walked over to me.

"You okay, man," he said quietly.

"That's the most horrible thing I've ever fucking seen, man. I'll be okay I think. You good?" My voice was shaky He nodded in reply.

I didn't think about a car bomb anymore. I thought about what we'd just done. Those men were shredded. I saw then what fast moving lead did to flesh. It was all horribly elemental and simple. We'd just killed three people...three human beings.

Some Iraqi Police and an ambulance showed up to clean up the mess. They were upset. How dare we shoot up men on their way to a funeral? There was some discussion about opening the casket to see if there were explosives inside of it, but the Iraqis were in an uproar about it, so we dropped the subject. We weren't there much longer when the CP got word that the threat was gone. It had evaporated just as mysteriously and quickly as it had appeared. I gathered up my men, and we made our way back into the patrol base. I didn't say much. SFC Green was asking if everyone was okay. It was some grisly stuff we'd just seen, and his concern was real. I tried my best to conceal the fact that I was horrified beyond belief and completely shaken up, although I didn't fool anyone. Anyone that had seen it was pretty shocked. I felt ashamed that I was struggling hard to keep my composure. CPT Harting had some reassuring words for us as we all coalesced in the courtyard.

We'd done well, he told us. He was impressed by our quick response. It was unfortunate that the van had gotten shot up, but it was war, and things like this were going to happen. We had done the right thing. We couldn't afford to let vehicles pass through our roadblocks. We had to do what we had to do. When he was done, SFC Green emphasized that our platoon had done its part by the book, and that there was nothing to feel bad about. I can't remember talking to anyone as we got settled into our rooms. We were all pretty subdued. I had a guard shift soon, and tried to relax a little beforehand. It was a wasted effort.

I wrote in my green, hardbound notebook that all NCOs kept. I kept trying to tell myself that these Iraqis weren't even people. They were animals that tried to kill us. I couldn't afford to be upset. If I was, that hesitation might kill me the next time. I'd done the right thing, and anyway, my fifteen bullets compared to the hundreds of the machine guns couldn't have been kill shots anyway. It was little solace. I knew I'd shot to kill. I also knew that those were human beings in there. The images and smells played over and over in my head. I kept imagining what it would have been like to have been in the firestorm of that van, to have been engulfed in that tide of lead we put into the windshield. It must have been horrible. It's what I dreamed about after I'd fallen into a fitful, restless sleep. It wasn't the last time I'd have that dream.

The next morning, I went to find Prince. He had a few songs on his MP3 player that I really liked, including some stuff from *The Thin Red Line* soundtrack, and I wanted to shoot the breeze with him anyway. I found him, as usual, sitting by himself watching a movie. So far in the tour, he'd sort of kept his distance and seemed pretty somber, but I made an effort to talk to him when I could. I knew he was fairly miserable being in Iraq. You could tell everyone was in a way, although we didn't talk about it much. He knew I was pretty shaken up from the night before, and when he handed me his music player he told me I should take it easy and not worry about things so much. That was easier said than done, and we both knew it. It was good to hear all the same, and in light of how our relationship had changed recently it was just good to have a conversation with him that went well. Something was troubling him, though, and I wondered exactly what it was besides the obvious. Of course, at that point, all of us had something on our minds to trouble us.

6

March blended in with February with the exception of my new job and the weather. During the day temperatures started reaching the nineties. Far from a dry heat like we were used to at Fort Irwin, the air was heavy with humidity. The smells were amplified, especially during foot patrols through the busy markets, and the canal running through Haswah got ripe. Now it took on a hot, raw sewage smell. We started sweating in our guard towers, and the backs of Bradleys became ovens after the sun had heated their metal hulls all day. We couldn't crack the hatch on top during patrols because it would prevent the turret from being able to traverse. So we sat in the back and sweated, hoping that the ramp would drop. At least outside the air was moving. Nights and mornings were still fairly cool. If anything, the range of temperatures had increased and made dressing appropriately impossible. Usually our patrols spanned the hours surrounding either dawn or dusk, so it was an uncomfortable period.

It was on one of those cooler mornings that we thought we'd found an IED on a mounted patrol. All I knew was that we'd left the patrol base and headed north on ASR Jackson, presumably just to drive up there to the bridge that marked our sector's northern boundary and turn around like usual. With my earplugs jammed tightly into my ears, I could tell by the vibration and movement that our Bradley was rolling to a stop. There was a heavy, metallic clank as the latch of the ramp popped open and slowly began to drop, our signal to get out.

I took out my ear plugs and adjusted my gear. In the few seconds it took the ramp to drop I wondered what we were getting into this time. As usual, I was riding in the lieutenant's track, and when the ramp hit the pavement we got out. I saw immediately that they had stopped a wall of traffic up the road from us. Oh shit, I thought. I looked up at 1LT Kelley for instructions.

"Go clear that building!" He pointed to an abandoned, two-story building seventy-five meters to the right of the road across a barren field. The Bradley behind us had dropped off its dismounts and turned around to stop traffic coming the other way. SSG Villacorte, after running up to meet us, just nodded to me, and I took off across the field. My guys followed, with the rest of the squad close behind. I didn't know what to expect.

We stacked on an open doorway. I was first. Turning to see the rest of the squad in behind me, I pivoted on my foot and raised my weapon into doorway. It was bare inside. I ran right, our squad having worked out that the first man to enter a building would always go right. The rest of the men filed in until we'd formed a line securing all angles of the room. It was obviously clear. There were some stairs that I took my guys up while Alpha team remained below. There was nothing upstairs, either. When I got back downstairs, SSG Villacorte told us what was up. He'd had time to use the man-pack to talk to the lieutenant on the Bradley.

"Hey, they've got a possible IED on the road. Once we're done here he wants us to go form a perimeter around the vehicles and wait on EOD." Simple enough; stop cars and keep a lookout for triggermen ready to blow the IED. We'd already cleared the only building in sight. As usual, we had a long wait for EOD. The increasing number of IEDs being found kept them busy. Usually they were just coming off of a mission when they were called for another one. When they arrived, they went straight to work. Watching them was always impressive.

Their team's leader climbed on top of the Bradley and had a brief conversation with the lieutenant. He peered through binoculars while listening. Then he hopped down, and after a few words of instruction he and his men began unpacking their remote-controlled robot. It wasn't big, maybe the size of a lawnmower. It travelled on treads and had optics and an arm which enabled it to lift up debris or plant explosive charges. The EOD guy had determined that they could disable this one by setting up an explosive charge to blow the fuse device off of the bomb itself. God and EOD both work in mysterious ways, so I'd heard before. The little robot made its way out to the crater with its explosives, controlled by a soldier standing at a laptop console with a joystick at the back of their Humvee. The robot stopped at the rim of the crater, and its arm plopped something on top. They raced it back to the Humvee.

"Fire in the hole!" All the dismounts echoed it as we got behind the Bradleys. There was disappointing a little pop, and one of the EOD soldiers ran out to the crater. He reached in and heaved out an artillery shell that was a couple of feet long. Carrying it away from his body (like that would help), he jogged back to the EOD truck and placed it into the trunk. They packed up and left as quickly as they had come. I remounted with my team and, putting my earplugs back in, went back into the vibrating void of the Bradley. I didn't care anymore to try to look out of the periscopes or try to judge where we were. It didn't help me understand what was happening during a patrol. Instead, I sang songs in my head or tried to doze off. Although it wasn't sleep it was an eye closing respite nonetheless. Every time the ramp dropped it wasn't necessarily action packed. Still, you never knew what was going to happen when it did.

Later, Alpha section had just finished an uneventful patrol in Bradleys. With the amount of IEDs we'd been finding, and the fact that most of our area around Haswah had paved roads, these were the preferred ride. We'd stopped at the patrol base to do a dawn foot patrol through Haswah. We had managed to pick up some of the unleavened bread we were so fond of from a baker who was just opening shop. We called it' hajji bread.' I'd first tried it on gate guard when a kabob vendor came by the gate. A kabob was just a little bit of ground lamb meat, lettuce, and to-mato wrapped up in flat bread. Their food was good compared to our MREs, despite the possible health hazards. He handed over a large bag of the stuff, and we gulped it down with coffee we'd grabbed from the CP. Before heading back to Kalsu, we had one more task.

The first sergeant hadn't come to pick up the patrol base's garbage, so before we departed we piled it into the back of one of our Bradleys. SSG Villacorte and Alpha team had to cram into the lieutenant's track with us. Seven of us, with all of our gear, made for a tight fit. I wedged myself between the turret wall and the hull on the left side of the vehicle closest to the driver's cubby hole. (Called the 'hellhole' since it stayed warm.) 1LT Kel-ley had mentioned something about driving up to the bridge and turning around before we went back to the FOB. My part of the patrol was over, at least, so I settled down with my earplugs in and dozed off.

I awoke to a loud, metallic 'pop.' All of a sudden the Bradley turned sharply to the left; ninety degrees actually. The other side of the Bradley tipped up sharply. There was split second of a sen-sation of flying through the air, and then the left side of the Bradley slammed onto the road. My head hit the turret wall, and everything was thrown around inside. The wooden benches had come apart, and heavy tools were scattered everywhere. Every-one on my side had landed on the soldiers on the other in a tan-gled, painful mess. There was screaming. I fumbled for the top hatch as I heard liquid pouring. I had no idea where we were, but drowning crossed my mind. Scrambling frantically, I actually stepped on SSG Villacorte on the way out of the hatch. Steppe was already out of the turret and had walked up the road to stop traffic. I staggered up to join him as he fired at oncoming cars. He was yelling something at me, but I couldn't hear anything. I couldn't see straight, either. I just kept shooting at what he was.

The rest of the dismounts started coming out and taking up positions all around me. We didn't know if we'd been hit by an IED or not, and in any event weren't letting any Iraqis close to the wrecked Bradley. Steppe was still yelling at me. He pointed at his ear then pointed to me. My left ear did hurt pretty badly. I touched it, and when I drew my hand back there was blood. I was dazed and didn't know what to do. I just kept my weapon trained towards traffic. SSG Villacorte ran up to me. Yelling so I could hear, he told me that I was bleeding out of my ear, and to get back behind the Bradley.

2nd platoon, on QRF from Haswah, arrived quickly. Their medic hopped out of the APC they'd sent to evacuate any hurt soldiers. He ran up to me first.

"Holy shit, SGT Ervin, I can't tell if this is coming from inside your ear or the outside. You need to get in the back of the '113 so we can get you out of here." The danger seemed to be over, so I walked over and sat in the back with the other team leader, SGT Nun, a really quiet Cambodian guy who had been in the invasion with 3rd Infantry Division. He'd messed up his leg. Considering the tangle of soldiers, tools, and equipment I was surprised more of us weren't hurt.

When they raised the ramp of the APC and started up the engine to leave, my heart dropped. The last place I wanted to be was in the troop compartment of another armored vehicle. As we raced towards the patrol base, SGT Nun and I exchanged wide-eyed glances. An APC's a bit lighter than a Bradley. When it's travelling fast enough, those in the back get the sensation that the rear of the vehicle is sliding back and forth. We were both waiting on another rollover.

At the patrol base, they decided I needed to get back to Kalsu to the squadron aid station. 2nd's medic urged me not to go to sleep. As they gathered a patrol together to get me out of there I made a request: I didn't want to ride in a track since I was still pretty shaken up. Everyone understood. IEDs or not, I preferred to ride in a Humvee that time. I don't remember much of anything about the ride other than feeling the effects of a hard hit to my head. There was a dull ache in my head along with a high-pitched ringing. I had a dazed, fatigued feeling.

Back at the aid station, the medics cleaned me up, and the squadron's doctor checked me over. The bleeding was from a cut on my ear and not from inside, thankfully. When my head hit the turret, the edge of my Kevlar had hit my head close to my ear. It had driven the hard plastic earplug I was wearing deep into my ear canal. The doc's diagnosis was a bruised ear drum and a mild concussion. His remedy was eight hours under observation in the aid station so I wouldn't fall asleep, and then a couple of days off from patrols to shake it off. I spent a long day in the aid station tent. I'd been up the entire night before but couldn't go to sleep for fear of going into a coma. It took everything I had to stay awake, and I spent most of the time sitting up or standing and talking to the medics.

I learned how we rolled over, sort of at least. At first we thought we'd been hit with an IED. But it appeared to the mechanics that the brittle, rusted tracks on the left side had simply snapped as we were belting down the road at some speed, about forty miles per hour. It may have been that the track tension was loose, causing excessive vibration. A track could be tightened or loosened around the sprocket and road wheels by pumping grease into a fitting for it. If it was too loose it could be thrown off while turning, and if too tight it could just pop off. Yet the track had simply snapped, so it's hard to tell what really happened. The Bradley driver behind us only saw a jet of dirt going into the air when we hit the dusty median.

I'll always wonder what exactly caused the rollover, but that was as much information as I'd ever get. My view towards riding in tracks changed forever, and our leaders emphasized the need to carry out proper Preventative Maintenance Checks and Services (PMCSs) before and after patrols. We also reinstalled all the metal troop seats. They were awkward, but at least stable.

The next day the whole platoon was back out on patrol, and I had the tent to myself. I never liked being in there alone. I found out that I just wondered what was going on with my section as they roamed around without me. Still, I took advantage of the relative safety and comfort of Kalsu. Besides the chow hall, showers, and our tents, there wasn't much to the place. I called home since I had a couple of hours to wait on the line. There were about twelve phones and the same number of computers with internet connection. I didn't like calling home usually, but I did it anyway. First of all, I dreaded the day when I was talking to my mother or Karen and a mortar hit close by. I also knew I couldn't hide the fact that sometimes I was just disturbed. My family was smart, so I knew I had to tell them a little of what was going on. There was no keeping them completely in the dark when news reports pointed to a worsening situation in Iraq. They knew about my Humvee rollover and now the Bradley. I kept quite a lot to myself, though. Still, I called so that I could at least let them hear that I was doing relatively well. I just hated the fact that a call home usually meant missing the place more than before.

Letters were preferable to me. No one had to hear any shakiness or moroseness in my voice, and I could sit in the bunker to write, I always loved receiving them, too. We'd put extra cots, folding chairs, and even rugs and pictures on its concrete walls. It had become a comfortable place to relax. I read books, listened to music, or watched movies. There wasn't much else to do at Kalsu. Our PX was a pretty sorry affair. There wasn't much in its stocks that I cared for except American-made cigarettes. The smokers learned that while you could buy cheaper Marlboros or other brand names from the Iraqis, the quality of the tobacco was lacking. Although a lot of guys began smoking generic brands from who knows where, like Miamis, every couple of weeks I bought a carton or two from the PX. For cash, once a month a soldier could go to an office on the FOB and draw 'casual pay.' It was less than a couple hundred dollars, but we didn't need much anyway. The Iraqis on Kalsu got most of our business, and just like at Kuwait, everything was cheap.

I was surprised by how many Iraqis were actually allowed on the FOB. They were everywhere. There was the normal compliment of vendors but also day laborers that came in each morning by the truckloads. Mostly they did menial work like filling sandbags and picking up garbage. A couple of Iraqis had a barber shop on the FOB complete with their barber chairs and equipment, right down to American magazines to read while waiting. The haircuts were free, but they took donations. We tipped well, actually, since they gave a good haircut. Still, it was a little strange to let an Iraqi so close to you with a straight razor.

I ended my brief rest in time to head back to Haswah for a ten-day stint with the platoon. We were only going to take Bradleys on this trip, and we were leaving at night. I was terrified, but I had to hide it. If any of the other guys knew I was scared to be in the back of a Bradley again, I couldn't imagine what they'd think. I thought if I distracted myself enough I could rough it out okay. At least the trip to Haswah was short.

Still, when it got dark that night and I climbed into the back of my old Bradley, I was fighting off nothing less than sheer panic. When the ramp closed my heart jumped through my throat. I grinded my teeth as my mind raced. I just kept thinking of wrecking and drowning in the back. My heart fluttered whenever the Bradley turned or the clanking and vibration changed its pitch the slightest. When we finally pulled into Haswah, I was glad the lights on in the back were dim or everyone would have seen how pale my face was. I looked at one of Bravo section's soldiers, SPC Erickson, who was in the back with me. He was a soft-spoken, knowledgeable guy who had been in the invasion. I always liked him, and felt we got along well – well enough even to confess my fears.

"Man, I don't know if I can ever get used to riding in those things again after the other day." I said it with as much nonchalance as I could muster despite the fact that I was trembling.

"I don't know. I think a Bradley's a pretty tough bitch to be honest SGT Ervin. At least you don't have to worry so much about getting hit. My last deployment I was in the back of one taking RPG rounds and we came out okay. You'll get used to it again." I don't know why I told him and no one else. I'd only hinted at my fears to Steppe.

Erickson had brought up a mental dilemma that I'd grapple with for the rest of my deployment. Was my fear of riding in Bradleys greater than my fear of getting blasted apart in a Humvee? It turned out that so far, that was the way it looked. I was helpless as a passenger either way, but at least in a Humvee I could see what was going on around me. I even had my own door wherever I sat.

Erickson was right, though. Our Humvees didn't stand much of a chance against the size of the IEDs we'd been finding: multiple 155mm artillery shells or bigger, sometimes 'daisy-chained,' or several rounds linked together and spread out along either side of a road. One of 2nd platoon's Bradleys had been hit with a big one recently, and its crew was unscathed, although understandably rattled. But to me, the vibration, noise, and motion in the back of the Bradley were unbearable. The thought of being maimed or killed by shrapnel wasn't. It turned out that a lot of us didn't even mind being shot at compared to being targeted by roadside bombs.

My first firefight started out like every other action I'd experienced so far; completely out of nowhere. My section was relaxing between patrols in one of the rooms in Haswah patrol base. Then the staccato of gunfire echoed through the courtyard.

We all looked at each other at once. There were shouts from our guys on the roof: curses and calling out directions. No words were needed. I grabbed my gear and weapon, heart racing. We bolted out of the door and onto the roof, joined by more than half the platoon. SSG McKnickles, a 3rd platoon squad leader, was on the southern wall by his soldier's guard tower. We all ran over and huddled beneath the short wall of the ledge.

Snap! Whiiizzzzhhh! Snap! Whiizzzzhh! It took me a second to realize I was being shot at. The bullets' whizzing was followed by the pop of an AK to our front.

"Suppressing fire," someone shouted. We started shooting back. The noise! Tracers were flying toward the buildings to the south and southwest. All I could hear was the tinkling of brass onto the ground and my own gunfire. I aimed at a roof a couple hundred meters away and squeezed off several shots.

"Cease fire! Cease fire! What the fuck are you all shooting at," SFC Green screamed above the din. I hadn't thought, felt, or perceived anything but the need to return fire. Some of us were laughing now. The adrenaline was rushing. I reloaded magazines.

Zzzzzip! Another round came whizzing by. Everyone got back up and started shooting again until SFC Green stopped us. Everything in Haswah had come to a standstill in the meantime. Traffic halted and the pedestrians and disappeared. Below us in the courtyard, they were throwing a patrol together to go after the shooters. SSG McKnickles tried to point out the most likely building to them, his intense, booming voice echoed off the walls.

"Alright everybody hold your fire. They're going out now, cover the rooftops around them. BE SURE OF YOUR TARGETS," SFC Green iterated.

Ten or so soldiers ran down the street and disappeared behind some buildings just short of where I'd been aiming. I watched the rooftops. Just across the canal from the patrol base, about twenty or so workers were taking cover behind the beginnings of the new police station. We yelled at them to come out. They were scared to death. There had been a lot of fire going over their heads. Hands up, they started to emerge from cover, and someone told a few of us to go round them up. We met them at the gate, lined them up, and searched them one by one. The patrol we'd sent out came back with one detainee, and we let the workers go, not having found anything on them. The prisoner was armed only with a pistol, but that was enough to get him detained since handguns were illegal.

After the excitement was over I had a little time to think about what happened, and I came to the conclusion that it had been kind of fun. It was halfway into March, and they'd finally stood up to fire a few rounds at us. It was preferable, at least, to waiting to be creamed by an IED or catch shrapnel from a mortar. There was something less menacing about it. It felt good to be shooting back at something at least. All of us lined up on the wall shooting was impressive. The noise and sights of the tracers and bullet impacts was thrilling. The miniature sonic booms of the AK rounds whizzing by our heads, which sounded exactly like that of some of the more modern war movies, were more interesting than terrifying. It was even preferable to riding in Bradleys for me, I thought. All around, though, it seemed like things were heating up. You could feel it in the air, literally and figuratively.

The temperatures were climbing steadily, and it started having an effect on us. Our leaders weren't slacking on the wear of our uniforms despite the heat. The rule was that we had to stay in full uniform and gear on patrols or in the guard towers. We longed to wear t-shirts under our gear. When I was out with the squad I unloosed my pants from my boots and rolled up the cuffs of my DCU blouse, but it didn't do much. I took the Kevlar neck guard out of my IBA, thinking that the extra inch of protection wasn't as necessary as having air on my neck. The body armor became an oven. The heavy Kevlar and ceramic plates trapped every bit of body heat inside. It wasn't long before the sweat, having soaked through a t-shirt and blouse, permeated the fabric of the IBA as well. The Kevlar helmet kept the heat around my head, too. I noticed there was a draft of hot air rising from the top of my IBA and descending from the top of my helmet. It was a small, hot current. Patrolling during the day became more and more oppressive. The heat and intense sun just sapped the energy from you, and it was only March.

Around this time 1st platoon was assigned a new platoon sergeant. SFC Green went to work for the intelligence branch of 2-11, and was replaced by SFC Torgerson, who we quickly started calling SFC 'T.' Hailing from the upper Midwest, he was a giant of a man, kept his head shaved, and came across to me as very professional and very stern. He was a worker, and expected the same out of us, as we would learn later. One of his first actions as platoon sergeant was to have us to stop smoking cigarettes on patrol. I knew what kind of leader he was immediately by that small action. It made sense; smoking was a distraction, and sometimes kept a hand busy that should be on a weapon. He had little time to get settled in with us before we had some serious work to do, though.

There was another big mission in the making late in March. The rumors surrounding this one, and the length of time our senior NCOs and officers were spending in briefings, led us to believe it was going to be the biggest yet. Word trickled down, like usual, in bits and pieces until the official briefings started on our level.

We were going to the Hateen Munitions Complex, an old Iraqi munitions factory and storage area. It was located just north of Haswah and east of ASR Jackson. We'd driven around its periphery before. There were huge abandoned buildings and bunkers all over the place. We'd only been on the roads leading in and out of it but could tell the place was expansive. We were going to employ the whole Task Force for this one. Not only was the place littered with ordnance, it was supposed to be an insurgent stronghold. The briefings on the mission we received reinforced the dire rumors more than dispelled them.

Echo's role was to conduct what amounted to a large-scale raid of this place. Dismounts from each platoon, with machine gun teams and Bradleys covering their flanks, would clear all of the buildings and bunkers in its designated zone. The timing of it all would be coordinated by using 'phase lines,' which were based on the same principle as the checkpoints only they were lines on a map. We were to use the phase lines to keep pace with the platoons on our flanks and keep the squadron commander informed of our locations. This was going to be more important this time around since, for the only time in the deployment, we'd have Navy fixed-wing aircraft on call for bombing missions in addition to our Apaches. They expected us to find weapons caches, squatters, and insurgents all over. The more I heard about the mission, the more it sounded like a traditional combined-arms attack like we'd practiced out in the Box.

I was put in charge of a weapons team consisting of a machine gunner and another soldier to carry ammo. The ammo bearer was PFC Becker, a red-haired, affable kid from the Midwest. He was a big music fan, and as he got to know us in the platoon he fit right in with our constant joking around. We would use the gun to cover the areas that the Bradleys couldn't cover for the assault squads. My own soldiers were in one of those under our squad leader. They used McFarland as a radio operator and Delmonte as a SAW gunner. No two missions were ever the same as far as allocating our soldiers went.

Once the mission's specifics had been doled out, and we'd gone over details with the men, everyone prepared for a Troop-level inspection. There were extra items for this mission, one of which was hand grenades. We took it as a clue that the mission was going to be intense, as we hadn't been issued frags yet. I didn't take any since I had a grenade launcher. We also had to cut several strips of white cloth tape – called 'engineer tape' since it was used to mark paths through minefields – to mark the ordnance we found for EOD to clear. SOP for finding random ordnance that was lying around (there was a hell of a lot of it all over Iraq for reasons we never knew) was recording its description and location in a standard report so EOD could prioritize them. As always, we had plenty of zip-strips and blindfolds. Along with a lot of extra ammo and water for myself, I was fairly loaded down. They'd also thought to issue each of us plenty of smoke grenades and flares. I still wasn't carrying nearly as much as Becker, with his thousand rounds of machine gun ammo in addition to his own gear, or even the gunner, whose twenty-pound weapons also had a two-hundred round starter belt loaded into it. If things popped off, though, I'd need the mobility. At least they didn't have to carry the tripod.

On the day of our command inspection, CPT Harting made a detailed review of his troops. He asked junior soldiers some details of the mission and to see certain items. His spot-checks showed him that his men were ready. After it was done, our platoon had a small huddle to go over details about when we needed to get the vehicles ready and such. Afterwards we were free to relax, and I was actually able to do so. I was assigned to the only Humvee that 1st was using, the lieutenant's. I was good on the radios, so 1LT Kelley liked having me in the backseat to monitor them. Every time I managed to hop a ride in a Humvee I felt bad about it. Although relieved beyond words – even elated – at not having to go through another Bradley ride, I kept it a secret. Going into the Hateen mission it seemed I wasn't as scared of anything else, really. At this point, though, the terror in the back of that thing wasn't diminishing even after several patrols. It never would.

In the middle of the night we started our day. We'd begun an interesting routine for this consisting of lots of energy drinks like Red Bull and caffeine pills. The pills I begged for in care packages, the Red Bull or other energy drinks were available at the chow hall. That pre-dawn morning, the cans opened up all over the tent. No one said much. There weren't any instructions to give the guys, having gone over minute details repeatedly already. The vehicle crews always left first. They had to walk down to the other end of the FOB to the motorpool, and then guide their vehicles on foot to the staging area. In the meantime, they were also supposed to check track tension, fluid levels, and a few other things as part of their PMCS. We took maintenance seriously, as a breakdown in a bad situation could be deadly.

I walked with the other dismounts out to the main road by the gate. It seemed like the whole Task Force was up and busy. As we got to the road, the familiar sounds and smells of the staging area came back. Shouts, tracks maneuvering into place, the squawking replies of radio checks, and tired conversations filled the air. I stashed my backpack with all the extra gear into my Humvee. Steppe was waiting by the gun. I did radio checks with all the higher nets. It was all routine now. Even though this mission had attached importance to it, in a lot of ways it was just another trip out of the wire, only our numbers were swelled. We were on time, but moving that many men and vehicles at once was slow regardless of the planning involved. We could only leave the gate singly, after all.

I don't remember the trip, only that I chugged a last Red Bull and felt the familiar tension, anxiety, and focused feeling of going on a raid. I went over our plan to assault the first set of buildings in my head. I had to set the machine gun team in place near the vehicles covering the flanks and go help with the first building since it was expected to be big. We got to the place just before dawn, and hurried commands on the radio announced it was time to go.

I jumped out of the Humvee, NVGs on already. There were IR strobe lights attached to each of us, their flashes nearly washing out our night vision. It made picking my guys out of a clump of them impossible, even though most times we could distinguish one another simply by stature and the way a soldier's gear was set up. Like all the other NCOs, I called out in a loud whisper.

"Weapons team over here!" They hurried over, and I had them take cover and keep an eye out to the right side of the building we were about to hit. The whole place was silent save for our own noise. Once everyone was ready after dismounting, SSG Villacorte started jogging off with the squad following him. The assault squad to our left was moving towards their building. The ground was scattered with craters and concrete rubble, tricky footing. When we stacked on the building, it was getting brighter out. I was maybe the fourth or fifth to get inside. It was nothing more than a bombed-out concrete shell. The second story was even gone. Our noises echoed off the concrete walls. We found a square hole in a corner and discussed checking it out.

"I'm not fuckin going down there," was the most typical refrain.

"I say we frag it," said Delmonte. It was the reason we had them. SSG Villacorte went outside with SPC McFarland to call for instructions. I peered inside of what looked like a six-foot hole leading to a tunnel; spooky. The call came back to leave it alone and get to the next building. SFC Torgerson would check it out.

Following the plan, I helped the squad clear the next building, which turned out the same as the first. It was starting to look like we would be clearing rubble all day. The intensity and motivation all but evaporated when I retrieved the machine gun team and had them plod along beside me.

The day was getting hot quickly. Making our way across the first dirt field that separated the scattered buildings and bunkers, I told Becker to drop off a couple of hundred rounds ammo with the lieutenant's truck. Eight-hundred rounds would be more than enough. The guys weren't complaining about carrying all of that weight. They never did, and they didn't have to. I'd done it before. It was simple logic to me; the vehicles were able to stay closer than we expected.

The mission was turning into a cycle of walking a few hundred meters, then setting up the gun in a pre-designated position or a spot that a squad leader pointed out. Mostly we just walked. As the morning wore on, we reached a bunker that didn't have a door, and we couldn't see a way to get on top of it either. CPT Harting decided to have a Bradley shoot through its walls. I volunteered to lead a few guys in and clear the place once it was breached.

SSG Moon and his new gunner drove up to the bunker in their Bradley, standing off about seventy-five meters. The whole Troop was excited to see this. If one thing characterizes infantry soldiers, it was the love of expending ammo. I took cover behind my truck. Everyone found a place to hide from the debris that was sure to be kicked up.

Bam! The first round was fired. *Bam! Bam! Bam!* A pause. There was dust all over the target now, but it cleared quickly to reveal an undamaged wall. I listened over the radio as they asked SSG Moon if a TOW would work. It was worth a try, he thought. The electronic whir of the TOW launcher raising was mixed in with Steppe laughing. He was excited, and had grabbed his digital camera to record all of this from his turret. He and Wantz were listening to the radios for the best time to start recording, giggling all the while.

"Hey, hey Steppe they're gonna shoot," Wantz said excitedly, "Fire in the hole!" I crouched down a bit lower behind the Humvee.

Whooosh! Boom! There was dirt and little rocks hitting the Humvee armor. A piece hit my helmet. When I looked up, there was a hint of a scratch on the bunker. There were Abrams tanks on the missions as well, so they called one over to fire a few of its AP rounds into the bunker. It seemed that Saddam's old military structures were about the only thing well-constructed in Iraq. A house in Haswah would have been leveled after all that shooting.

I put in earplugs and braced for the concussion of the tank rounds. When its 120mm main gun fired, I felt its shockwave even behind cover. It was like having a giant door slammed in your face. There were bigger chunks of debris raining down now. The tankers loosed a couple more rounds, and then announced they were ceasing fire on the radio. I got out from behind cover and yelled for the guys going with me. There was no need. There was a cluster of men around the new hole in the bunker, CPT Harting among them. They were impressed. It was thick concrete the tank rounds had penetrated, and it had curved the steel rebar inwards, yet there was still another wall a few feet beyond it. They called off searching the place, even though I told them I could make it inside. I wondered if they'd just looked for an excuse to shoot stuff. In the lull before our moving out again, I grabbed a few things from an MRE to stave off the sugar and caffeine crash.

It started to be a slog. The sun rose and heated up the bare dirt fields and concrete around us. As we wore down and got hotter, we got quieter. I let Becker drop off two-hundred more rounds of ammo and switched out backpacks with him a couple of times to give him a break. The terrain was open enough for the vehicles to support us. Every so often we'd come across a wall that the Bradleys would drive through. It was just about the only entertainment. 2nd platoon had found some squatters, but otherwise the place was empty. Well, it wasn't entirely empty.

A couple of kilometers into the complex we started seeing ordnance. They weren't part of neat little caches like we'd envisioned, but there were thousands of them. Some were small bombs and mortar rounds that one could pick up, others were artillery shells, rockets, and aircraft bombs bigger than me. The whole complex had been bombed at some point, and the stuff ended up scattered everywhere. I watched my step and ran out of engineer tape quickly. Eventually we got word to stop marking them, as there was just no way feasible that we could clear all that ordnance out of there.

Soon, we'd covered several kilometers to the last phase line planned for the mission. It was mid-afternoon and blazing hot, but we were slightly ahead of schedule. We started hearing awful rumors that since the whole Task Force was in place we could do an impromptu live-fire training exercise. I hoped it was a rumor; I was worn out already, and the reddened, quiet faces of my team told me they were done, too. They'd been plodding along without complaint all day. I remember the redness of

Becker's face, and how I gave him a little hell for it being as red as his hair. We'd been wired for the mission since well before dawn, but without anything to distract us from our own misery, the fatigue had set in quickly. With the gratitude of a worn out grunt, I heard over the radio that the mission was wrapping up, and we were headed back. Deflated and tired, I threw my backpack into the Humvee and climbed in. A Marine and his bomb sniffing dog rode with us. The German Sheppard rode on my lap all the way back to the FOB, where everyone went to sleep after an anticlimactic, exhausting day.

Halfway through April, Echo got assigned a new sector. Instead of centering our operations on Haswah, we were shifted to Diyara, a tiny village on the east side of MSR Tampa which had never really been patrolled. We also inherited its environs, in all about a quarter of AO Battle. It was a huge space, but only sparsely populated. Still, Diyara was bad news. Besides the SF raid there early in the tour, our first forays into the place didn't bode well. Four teachers were executed after the first 2-11 patrol had gone through and spoke with them. My first trip through the place I noticed that all of the stares were hard. If any place in our sector immediately seemed hostile, this was it. The word was that hardcore Saddam regime elements were all over the agricultural area surrounding it. The place hadn't been patrolled much, and they were sending Echo there to clear it out.

I didn't go on the first patrol in our new sector. It was Bravo section's turn. It was three weeks into April. The heat started with the sunrise now, and by mid-morning, when I awoke and went out to the bunker for a smoke, it was hot enough to sweat even while sitting still. Most of the guys were still asleep since we had the patrol later in the day. Then I heard about it. Bravo had been hit with an IED near CP 20.

Pretty soon they made it back. One of their gunners was

walking back holding a blackened IBA that had been cut off of someone. My heart dropped. Someone mentioned Prince. When they gathered the platoon together, minus Erickson and Prince, SFC Torgerson told us what happened. The 4th squad leader's Humvee ran over an IED buried in the road. When it detonated, it flipped the truck over. Prince had been ejected from the back, about where the blast went off, and the Humvee landed sideways on top of him, pinning him to the ground. He was unconscious, and Erickson, the gunner, had a dislocated arm. The squad leader, SSG Lutz, was okay. Prince was barely alive and had been medevaced to undergo surgery in a hospital in Baghdad.

We were in shock. Prince? He was an old hand in 1st. Hell, he was one of my best friends. I didn't know what to think at first. The mental health team, a female officer and an NCO who looked old for his rank, paid us a visit even before the news set in. They tried to get us talking, but we weren't having any of it. Most of us were cussing the fact that they'd cancelled our section's patrol that afternoon. SFC Torgerson came back in the tent after having stepped out for a minute.

"Men," his voice was shaky, so he didn't have to finish, but he choked the words out. "Prince didn't make it. He died in surgery."

There may have been a moment of silence before rage and cursing filled the tent. The Bravo guys were donning their gear. Tears streaming from our faces, and literally seeing red with rage, Steppe and I made our way to our own tent to do the same. The mental health team, in stunned silence, didn't try to intervene. Everything was entirely spontaneous. Seething with anger, we got ready to go avenge Prince. They eventually got us somewhat settled down. CPT Harting and the first sergeant talked to our platoon and halted our impromptu preparations. CPT Harting let us know he was as determined as we were to find those

123

responsible for the attack. He went about it more professionally, though.

That night we got the word that we were going into the area around the IED attack in force the next day. The whole Troop was going to fan out and search every house along the road from CP 20 to the sector's eastern boundary. We'd find out who was behind it either by catching them with bomb materials on their hands with a clever little explosives detection kit or by simply prying it from neighbors who knew. Either way we'd detain all the males. It was called, officially, a search and clear operation. We drew up rough plans and gathered the extra gear that we'd need. When I talked to my fire team, I didn't have to mention that this time we'd treat them rougher than normal. Prince was universally liked, and everyone was hurt by his death.

I was a mess of painful emotions. I'd just lost one of my best friends. There was regret at the distance that came between us and the deep pain of his loss in general. I would miss him. I was in a rage, the hatred I felt for the Iraqis that day was strong. A cowardly, faceless enemy had put a bomb in the road that murdered my buddy, and the next day we'd do our best to put faces on those enemies.

7

I didn't know what was going to happen during this mission. I knew that I didn't care about a Bradley ride as much this time. There was enough anger burning inside me to overshadow any fear. It might have been a wise call not to let us out of the wire the same day of the attack, but going out there the next day did little to diminish the anger the whole Troop felt. I'd experienced being primed for action before. This was different. This was being ready for violence. This was the hatred and anger that I imagined the Marines to have felt after losing their buddies. I understood it now. I really didn't know if I was going to kill anyone that day, but I felt like I could without being bothered by it. In the back of the Bradley on the way out that morning, already sweating, I exchanged glances with Delmonte and McFarland. Their eyes looked hard, menacing. We were ready.

When Echo's vehicles descended upon on the farmland just off of MSR Tampa and the dismounts got to work, our tempo was unlike anything I'd seen before. We swarmed on the first farms quickly. I led my guys at a run to our squad's first target house. Racing past a few women, I got to the door and kicked it in without a thought. There was a man just inside. I ran at him and pointed my weapon at his face. He put his hands up, then after my frantic yelling got on his knees. He wasn't armed, although I wished he had been so I could have blown him away. We cleared the rest of the house quickly, and I grabbed him by his collar and drug him outside. After shoving him to the ground face first and cuffing him with zip-strips, I called Delmonte over.

"Hey, blindfold this fucker and take him over to the Bradley. Be a shame if he tripped." I turned back to continue on with the search.

"Hell yeah, SGT Ervin, I got this," he replied. He was smiling. "C'mon fuckbag, on your feet." He hoisted him up by his collar and shoved him in the direction of the Bradley. I turned my attention back to searching the house. We were supposed to be thorough this time. I didn't care to be respectful of their property. Outside there were bags of animal feed. I stabbed at them with my knife to see if there was anything large in them. Inside, I tore out drawers and tipped over furniture. I smashed through doors. I broke anything I could. It felt good to be destructive, even though I didn't find anything. The women outside were wailing. I was pouring sweat already. I relished the thought that the Iraqis were more terrified of the Bradleys than I was.

Fuck him, I thought, let him be scared. I've been scared for months.

By the time we wrapped up searching the first farm, the heat was already slowing me down and dissipating some of the rage. There wasn't any shade between the farms, and we walked towards the next one in the glaring sun. Being only a few hundred meters apart, it was a waste of time to keep remounting the vehicles. Instead, they kept pace with us on the road as we moved out eastward. I heard a couple of shots to my left. On the radio, they said Bravo section had only shot a dog. We got to the second house, which was much smaller than the first. SFC Torgerson was with us for this one. His presence and the intense heat of that first hour already had the effect of calming me down. The small, mud hut was cleared in no time and we continued our push. There was yet another bare, dirt field to traverse to get to the next farm. We were actually walking across a salt flat, or so it seemed.

Old farm fields, no longer irrigated, had baked under the sun for generations. As evaporation took place it left trace amounts of salt in the soil. The white, powdery stuff we were trudging through was actually salted earth. What a hellhole. It added to the eeriness of the whole country. This field, though, had a large dug-up area. The smell of decomposition got our attention. The platoon sergeant had Delmonte grab a shovel and probe around the spot. We didn't find anything, nor did we look too hard. No one wanted to dig up a mass grave if that was what it had been. We called it in and kept moving. Several hours had passed by now, and despite sucking down water, my energy faded quickly.

This was the heat we'd heard about. It sapped strength, and it was only by sheer will that we kept going, loaded down and covered in Kevlar like we were. The ferocity I felt at the first house was gone, replaced by a lethargy that made it hard to think straight. There was a mounting frustration, though, at the fact that we weren't finding anything that pointed to Prince's killers after hours of searching.

Towards late afternoon we reached an isolated farm. Its occupants, all women and girls, were outside in the shade. Our interpreter told them we were going to search the place. They didn't protest. The oldest woman stood up and began talking. The 'terp translated her words:

"She say you all look very hot. She say sit in shade and she will bring cold water to drink." We looked at him incredulously, but he reassured us. She genuinely felt sorry for us. With one of her daughters, she disappeared into the house. We barely searched it. SFC Torgerson said it was okay for some of the guys to take a break. It was much needed. Some of them had stopped sweating; a sure sign of dehydration. I told my guys to plop down and take their Kevlars off while I pulled security on the perimeter with the platoon sergeant and SSG Villacorte.

"I think the commander's about ready to wrap up this mission," SFC Torgerson said to us quietly. "We've already gone about seven klicks and we're pretty close to the boundary. We'll pop a squat here for a few more minutes then move out," he said. He told SSG Villacorte and me to take a break ourselves if we could. I didn't. With reluctance, a few minutes later I was getting my team on their feet and ready to hit the next house. All of the steam of our operation had run out. Now we were just hot and frustrated. We plodded along another kilometer before CPT Harting ordered a short halt over the radio. The platoon met up with our vehicles on the road. One of Bravo section's tracks dropped the ramp so we could fill up water from the coolers we kept in the back. Its ice had already melted, and the lukewarm water did little to combat the sweltering heat. Most of the dismounts piled up on the back of the ramp and dozed while the vehicle crews kept watch. In the field below the road, my old Bradley was attempting to make a turn and threw its track off the sprocket. I went over with Steppe, who had been on a Humvee's gun all day, and helped him and Logsdon put it back on. I don't know where I got the energy. In the meantime, we'd gotten word that the mission was over.

In a Humvee this time, on the way out I saw HHT guys who had come out to CP 20 to collect our detainees. They had them corralled just off the overpass in a small ring of barbed wire. They were a sorry sight. I thought they looked like captured animals. We handed them one more and headed back to Kalsu.

Echo had cleared the whole area around the attack, but we didn't find any useful intelligence. The Iraqis universally claimed ignorance of the IED attack; even the house closest to the blast. I wasn't surprised, but plenty frustrated. Most of us were. A rumor spread around that our commander had shoved his 9mm into an Iraqi's face and demanded to know what happened. Of course, the Iraqi kept quiet. CPT Harting didn't hurt him. Actually besides shoving around and rough handling no one hurt any Iraqis, and we had only shot a dog. There weren't even any warning shots throughout the mission. It may have been the heat, or, more likely, it may have been the fact that we weren't as brutal as we thought we could be.

When we got back to Kalsu our exhaustion was extreme. Steppe asked for IV fluids to get hydrated again, and a lot of us followed suit. We knew how to administer the stuff, so it was only a matter of getting some extra IV bags, tubing, and needles from DeGuzman. I rather enjoyed mine, and before long a lot of us were lounging around with IV bags attached to our arms. We'd put them in the refrigerator before hooking them up. The cool liquid going through our veins did the trick. Everyone went to sleep as soon as they could; no one even took a shower. As soon as I'd gone through a large bag of lactated ringers, which had more to it than the normal saline, I crashed. We hadn't found anything that day, but by the time that ten-hour mission was over, everyone had worked the anger out for the most part. What was left was a hollowness that I couldn't describe or understand. I didn't try to either.

Prince's memorial service was pretty awful. There was the standard rifle placed in the ground by its bayonet with a helmet on top, at its base a pair of empty boots. Beside this, they'd put up a small end table with a few items on it like his Purple Heart and Bronze Star. The medals were arranged around a picture of him goofing off. It was fitting. Some of the speakers, in full gear because of the increased threat of mortars that week, said things that weren't fitting at all, though.

SGT Camarillo talked about Prince's sense of humor and how good it was to have known him. CPT Harting kept it general, and noted that Prince was a good soldier. But then others said things that only confused me. They remarked that he was proud of the mission in Iraq. They talked about his love of the Army and his dedication to helping free Iraqis. The tears that welled up in my eyes were of anger.

What, and who, were they talking about? Prince, like all the rest of us, didn't have a clue what we were doing in Iraq, and cared less about the Iraqi people. At this point, things were beginning to seem pointless, and we talked about it often. It stemmed largely from the fact that we seemed to make little discernible headway given the extraordinary efforts we made. At that, things were becoming more and more dangerous. I made my way back to the tent with the belief that my best friend had died for nothing, at least nothing I understood, and the way things looked, more would follow him.

The last week in April, Echo moved in to Diyara. The small village was about six kilometers east of CP 18 at the terminus of ASR Cleveland. The portion of road leading from Tampa to the village proper was mostly straight, although a slight bend prevented observation down its entire length. There wasn't much to see. Ramshackle Iraqi farms, palm and date trees, and empty fields lined the road on either side. Diyara was little more than a marketplace, a couple of schools, and some houses in the middle of a vast farmland. The single road leading in was, for all intent and purposes, the only practical way to reach the place. Like Haswah, Echo would conduct its operations and maintain a permanent presence there by establishing a patrol base in the town. Unlike Haswah, though, we had to construct the base from scratch. There were no Iraqi police or army units in the vicinity. Echo would be the first of any coalition forces to occupy the place.

When CPT Harting went out with 2nd and 3rd platoons to establish our foothold, it was among the last missions he'd perform with Echo. His time in command was drawing to a close, and he was slated to be replaced by CPT Frank, actually a longtime friend of his. None of us were excited at the prospect. We had, after all, been under Harting for a couple of years and had come to respect and admire the man who took us from OPFOR to combat soldiers, so we didn't want to learn how a new commander operated in a combat zone. Like the tasking of Hotel Company out of our sector at the beginning of the tour, which reduced our strength in the huge sector we had, it made little sense to me at the time.

We consoled ourselves with the fact that CPT Frank was a respected officer. Those who knew him best were looking forward to serving under him and were confident in his abilities. I couldn't say the same good feelings were present when thinking of our new patrol base. It was hard living, so we'd heard, even compared to Haswah standards. Another downside was that there were more guard positions there than in Haswah. The bright spot was that our rotations would be shortened to only a few days on security at the place.

When 1st platoon's time came to relieve 3rd out there, we loaded our vehicles full of MREs, cases of water bottles, and ammunition to add to the growing stockpile. When we showed up, 3rd platoon was more than happy to be relieved. As of yet, it was a patrol base only in name. They'd set up in a big building that dominated the entrance to the village just off the main road. It was only a single story, but its roof was high enough to allow for observation of most of the village and out onto Cleveland. A smaller, two-story building just across the main street enabled a view of most of the rest of the town. They'd closed off the main road with concertina wire – the only fortification we had thus far. Two Bradleys sat just outside the main building. The first over-watched the road coming in, the second the opposite side. Machine gun positions on the roof covered the rest. Concrete barriers or Hesco baskets had yet to arrive, so for a while our firepower was the only defense. For that matter, we didn't' even control the entire main building yet. We were sequestered in a smaller wing of the main building since we were allowing the family that lived there some time to vacate. With a CP set up and a growing amount of supplies it was a tight fit at first.

On top of that, it was hot, reaching well over a hundred degrees during the day. My first guard shift was in the Bradley watching the main road. Sitting in the gunner's position, eyes pressed to the ISU watching for fast approaching cars, I roasted. Along with the rest of the gunners who pulled shifts in the Bradleys, I did so in a t-shirt. Miserable though I was, the danger of a car bomb taking out our base was real and kept me watching with attention. We had the TOW launcher raised and all of the safeties off on the Bradley's weapons systems. They'd send out a driver now and then to start or stop the engine so the gunners could keep the ISU on and move the turret without killing the batteries. I noticed then that our view down the main route was obstructed by the slightest bend in the road. Although straight on a map, the clear line of sight down the road ended just before a bridge a few klicks away. This curvature created the same effect when vehicles perched atop the overpass at CP 18 peered down the road. ASR Cleveland had a significant amount of dead space as a result – a blind spot on our main artery to and from the patrol base.

Between shifts we tried to rest like usual. The heat did away with my appetite, so eating was out of the question. Being crammed into a room with cots literally touching each other in the broiling heat was pretty miserable. Although the guys in the CP tried to keep it down, it was a noisy, crowded place during the day. CPT Harting was making frequent trips with his replacement to check on the place. He was concerned about security and spent a lot of time with the officers and senior NCOs planning how to best to permanently fortify the place. It was in Diyara that I first met CPT Frank. We had a short conversation about our Bradley in the front being important as our first line of defense. He seemed more easy-going than CPT Harting, but professional all the same. Overall, I had a good first impression of him. After their trip, they left with the headquarters platoon escort they came with, and the guys of 1st platoon not on guard settled down in their sweaty cots. I dozed off quickly despite the heat.

WHAM! There was a tremendous, thundering explosion. The whole building shook, and I jolted awake. I was instantly terrified. Dying there was the first thought that crossed my mind as I scrambled to put on my gear with everyone else. The next was that someone had to have just gotten killed; the explosion was massive. Through the open door I saw the CO's Humvee race back into the perimeter. His gunner was screaming, helmet unstrapped, his face a mask of pure shock. Mine was probably the same.

"CPT Harting's fuckin' gone! They're both fuckin' gone!" he screamed. My only instinct was to get to the roof to help secure the perimeter. I took Delmonte with me while SSG Villacorte kept McFarland with him. I was joined on the roof by SGT Faucher. A huge, black plume of smoke was rising from a spot maybe three-hundred meters down Cleveland. We didn't have time to gawk. We were the only ones up there and started barking orders to the guys at the machine guns.

"Don't let anything fuckin' move," SGT Faucher screamed.

"Nothin' gets close to the base! Fuckin' shoot warning shots!" The words had barely gotten out of my mouth when SGT Faucher ran over to a wall and fired at a car coming towards the main road just outside of the base. He kept firing until it sped away in reverse. On the other side, a woman was calmly walking down the street towards us. Thinking only of maintaining our perimeter, I shot a few rounds into the dirt road in front of her. She disappeared. The machine gunners had their weapons to their shoulders and were ready to fire, we'd just shot first. Everyone was amped up, adrenaline pumping wildly. Voices were in shouts and hurried.

Down below, SFC Torgerson had gathered up a few guys to go out to the site. He told Steppe to grab body bags. I watched them mount up and race out there with McFarland, and I was glad that I wasn't going with them. I stayed on the roof with SGT Faucher. Our shooting had convinced the Iraqis to stay invisible for a while. In the lull, we went to each of the positions and checked on the soldiers. I was as shocked as they were. Two COs in one day? Six days after Prince got killed?

Only a few minutes had passed, and by then there were a few of us on the roof. The squad leaders were telling us we'd done a good job getting up here and coordinating security. They told us the cavalry was on the way. Squadron was sending out Alpha Troop in its Abrams tanks to lock down the place, and they were pulling us out. While SFC Torgerson and the men with him secured the area around the blast and picked up the remains of our officers, we got the full story of what happened.

As the headquarters platoon convoy of three Humvees left the patrol base, they approached a car which, for one reason or another, looked suspicious to CPT Harting. The patrol stopped the car about a hundred meters away, and our commanders walked out to search it. As the driver opened the trunk, the bomb went off. It must have been a big one. No one talked about the fact that there just wasn't much left of them but small pieces until later. At the time, Steppe was more concerned about the house they had to clear when they first got there. He said that after busting into the door with SGT Threatt it took all he had not to start shooting at the Iraqis inside. I knew the feeling. He was glad that he didn't. As usual, no one found a triggerman. We never found out exactly how the bomb detonated. The one thing we knew was that the VBIED was obviously intended for the patrol base, and had they not stopped it several more of us would have been killed. Their deaths had kept us safe. It was little consolation for the loss but a bright spot nonetheless. That was sacrifice.

The convoy that came to our relief, headed by tanks, arrived with our XO and first sergeant to gather us up and leave. The tankers and some HHT guys took over the machine gun positions, and we departed in our own, smaller column. The convoy we passed stretched out almost to the bridge and bristled with APCs, Humvees, and more tanks. They were coming in with everything. The guys waiting in their vehicles watched our convoy drive by. The looks on their faces bordered between respect and pity. I had the terrible feeling, looking back at them, that we'd been somehow defeated. Echo had just lost its outgoing and incoming commander. As of right then our XO, a first lieutenant, was acting CO. So soon after losing Kevin, though, it seemed like a nightmare. Whatever it was, it was horrible.

When we got back to Kalsu and into our tents, we learned that the all of Echo was staying at the FOB for an entire week. The reason behind it was a lengthy change-of-command inventory of the Troop's entire complement of equipment and weapons, plus time off of operations for much needed vehicle maintenance. Regardless of the official reasons, we all had the feeling that we'd been put on vacation because we'd had a hell of a week. They certainly did keep us busy with the inventory layouts and the associated paperwork.

We also had the memorial service to do. Like at Prince's, everyone had to be in full gear again because of the threat of mortars. We sweated through a higher echelon of speakers this time, some of whom had flown from Mosul and Baghdad to attend. I don't remember what any of them said. That evening, hours after the memorial service, the insurgents lobbed three mortar rounds into the FOB. For most of days out of the seven that Echo had its break on Kalsu, actually, there were mortar attacks. There was little rest to be had.

There was plenty of busy work that week, but I had a lot of time to brood. The constant mortaring didn't help, either. I thought back through the tour. I'd been on more than a hundred missions throughout our sector without being hit. I'd cruised the IED-laced roads of our sector for countless hours. I had personally searched what seemed like an equally countless number of cars. My section's patrolling had spotted several IEDs before detonation. There were close calls with Iraqi traffic – VBIEDs or not – every time we left the wire. I had been shot at with bullets, mortars, and rockets. Then there were the rollovers. An IED had killed my best friend and a car bomb my leaders. Five soldiers in the squadron were KIA so far. (Two HHT soldiers were killed in March in an accident.) A lot more patrols had been hit by IEDs on their route clearances. The opportunities to get killed or hurt were abundant, and they had hit close.

All of this caused some changes in the way I perceived things. I had been plenty scared before all of this when I thought about the danger. At first, it had been a fear of the unknown. There wasn't any mystery to it anymore. Now I knew the grim reality of the threats around us, and what happened when they materialized. I had an epiphany of my own mortality, really. Kevin was as close as they come, and he was not immune to dying here. That meant that my chances were the same. Before then, it had been a remote possibility lingering in the back of my mind. Now it was almost a certainty, a matter of time. In a way, that numbed a lot of the fear and enabled me to focus on doing my job each day.

We never talked about the fear too much. We were always cautious, we agreed that certain roads were scary and that it was getting dangerous out there. Steppe talked a lot about the "pucker factor" on certain roads like Cleveland. But we inserted humor into any discussions we had. We tried to make it unreal and make light of it. We started calling IEDs 'road monsters' and likened our enemies to phantoms. But it was still there. Sometimes you could tell when someone was scared, most of the time, though, we just paid attention to what we were doing and did our jobs. Everyone was bothered by the danger, we just never really discussed it on a deeper level. We did talk about our changing views of the Iraqis, though.

The mysterious nature of our enemies created a necessary sense of caution and callousness after that. None of the men I was closest with had ever seen a bad guy yet with certainty. Their bombs, mortars, rockets, and bullets were, as of yet, fired from what might as well have been ghosts. They were everywhere and nowhere. Iraq was a creepy, sinister place to begin with and now seemed like it was haunted by an evil that wanted to kill us. To put a face on the people trying to hurt us was impossible, but any of them could be insurgents. Therefore, giving every Iraqi the benefit of the doubt that he or she was not an enemy was dangerous. Since anyone could be the enemy that's exactly how we treated them. I never felt fully at ease with any of them, and I doubt anyone else was – even with the ISF. In a place where, in your own mind at least, everyone is out to kill you, detachment became absolutely essential. In a way, you could say that I finally understood what was going on.

Our squadron found a CO for us, CPT Ramirez. He had been the officer in charge of the Task Force's training team that was created in February to help the Iraqi Army, and had been Smitty's commander there. I don't recall my first impressions of him other than the fact that his respect for our Troop was evident. He had a hard job ahead of him in gaining our confidence and respect, though. After CPT Harting anyone would have, so we figured he would ease into his style of command gradually. It was clear that we weren't going to ease back into operations, though. Our new sector was a nightmare compared to Haswah, so I fully expected that we'd be stepping up the frequency of our missions and doing new things. Furthermore, we figured the madness to ensue as soon as we got back there.

There wasn't any craziness our first day back at Diyara. We got used to our new surroundings. It was more comfortable there since the Iraqi family had finally vacated. The place was bigger than I'd imagined. It turned out to be about the size of the Haswah complex. It had an open courtyard surrounded by several rooms, and the area where the whole platoon had slept at first was used as storage for food and water. It was big enough to have a lounge of sorts beside the CP. Engineers had constructed the standard anti-VBIED defense consisting of a maze of concrete barriers sealing off both sides of main road. The rest of the perimeter was a mixture of concrete barriers, emptied buildings, and a dirt wall in the back of the building. For a while, after every two-hour guard shift was another two hours of filling sandbags in the back yard and hauling them to the roof. Along with plywood, we made some respectable bunkers with overhead cover, but for a while it was only a few sandbags, a folding chair, and the wall on the ledge. Losing the sleep to work on the positions in the blistering heat was a necessary evil.

The mortar team that set up in the backyard was another necessary evil. In order to provide closer fire support for us, a 120mm mortar section from HHT was lent to us for a while. Squadron figured we'd need it with as dangerous as Diyara had become. They set up their weapon and the track that carried its ammunition just outside the southeast corner of the building. There were too many guard positions for the team leaders and gunners to run shifts, so I watched from a guard position as they set it up its base-plate, tube, and aiming device. Mortars, a branch of the infantry, were foreign to me except on the receiving end. It was a highly specialized combat MOS, and like others it fascinated me. I just didn't know how much it could piss me off.

It was a rare thing to actually sleep between shifts at Diyara during the day with sandbags to fill and fortifications to build. The ceiling fans in the rooms didn't do much to cut down on the sweltering heat, either. Still, being exhausted meant sleeping through a lot of heat, noise and, commotion – not explosions, though.

I woke up to the building being rocked by an explosion. Once again we scrambled to get our gear on and got ready for whatever was coming. Who knew what to expect? SFC Torgerson came into our room.

"Hey it's outgoing. The mortars are just registering." The cussing started immediately. Why would they do that without telling us first, I wondered. The whole patrol base was in a bit of an uproar. No one liked waking up to explosions, even if it was just our own mortars going off. I asked SFC Torgerson if, next time, they could come give us a warning. It was the first time I noticed that all of us were on an edge.

There was plenty to keep us on our toes in Diyara besides the mortars. Every so often, sometimes daily, we'd hear a far off rumble and wonder if a patrol had just bought it, and from the roof the black plumes of smoke from the explosions were a common sight. The sounds of warning shots coming from patrols in the vicinity became more commonplace, too. I remember sitting in a position one day and thinking it was one of the first times it sounded like a war was going on out there.

We were eating in our room in Diyara a couple of days after getting used to the mortars being there. SSG Chavez came in. He was a Mexican guy from Texas who was loud in a boisterous sort of way, quick to crack a smile. When he came in with a frown, somber and subdued, I knew something was wrong. He delivered us the news he'd heard at the CP. Smitty was riding in a shoddily armored IA bongo truck through CP 18 and had been killed. He'd taken shrapnel from the IED in his thigh and had bled to death from his femoral artery. They'd done what they could for him, but it was a mortal wound.

"I'm sorry, I know a few of you were pretty close to him," was all he said before he left. We sat there for a minute in shock. I didn't feel anything. I wasn't overcome with grief and anger like with Kevin's death, or shock and defeat like our COs. This time I was numb when I first heard. I hadn't seen much of him recently, the last time being a month or so before, when we sat in our bunker and had a smoke. Maybe that helped.

I wrote a letter home that day. After all the bad news of the previous weeks, I had to tell them something about how I was coping. "You guys must think we are superhuman being able to deal with all of this. No, we aren't...We're a bunch of young men and kids making the best of an adverse and potentially dangerous environment. We're not full of courage; we just swallow that wad of stomach in our throats and do our thing. No big deal." I went on to remark that I wouldn't have anything to complain about in the states, knowing that I'd "been through worse."

When I actually had the time I got really down about his death. He was a really close friend, and I'd missed him while he was on another FOB. I just forced myself not to dwell on it, and did my best to block it all out. We attended his memorial service, something which had become routine, unfortunately, and I don't remember any details about it. There was no break or special operation in response. The only real change was that on patrols we were told to focus on CP 18. That particular place, and ASR Cleveland along with it, was a big deal, although one that I wisely did not mention in any letters home.

The six-kilometer stretch of Cleveland between Diyara and CP 18 and the checkpoint itself became Echo's new battleground. Although required to patrol the extensive farmlands around Diyara, the checkpoint and main road was our lifeline to the FOB. We began calling it the 'gauntlet.' With all the extra attention this relatively small area needed, our resources appeared to be thin. Even as a junior NCO I could readily see that we didn't have enough grunts to properly secure the area. We tried to make up for it with technology for the most part. Perched on top of the overpass on CP 18, a Bradley's ISU could range far down Cleveland. The northwest guard position at the patrol base could see a kilometer or so. We pooled all the optic equipment together that we could, and put a scope on the machine guns ranging the road. We also used a Javelin anti-tank missile's optics for its magnification and thermal imaging capabilities. Yet the blind spot remained. There were other ways to keep eyes on it, though.

Setting up a three-man observation post (OP) in the middle of the night was the best assignment available in my opinion. Like raids, this kind of mission was exactly what we'd trained for – this was literally hunting for bad guys. The idea was that three soldiers hiding in the darkness stood a good chance of catching an insurgent in the act of emplacing an IED. The mission was less intended to engage the enemy, instead to report any contact through the chain of command. Calling in a QRF patrol, Apache helicopters, or even mortar or artillery fire with a radio was all possible to do while remaining hidden. Shooting at them with only three guys was fairly risky. Nevertheless, we went out on these OPs prepared to do just that. Their planning and preparation were unlike anything else we did, which was maybe one reason I enjoyed them so much. Steppe lived for them.

For one, OPs were made up completely of volunteers, including the sergeant leading it. On 1st platoon's guard rotations in Diyara there was never any shortage of them. Steppe was usually first to volunteer, followed by me. The platoon sergeant or lieutenant running the CP would talk over the plan with the sergeant. They always let us pick where we'd set up and would approve the location if we could explain to them why it was easy to secure, offered good lines of sight on areas we needed to watch, and was easily accessible in case of an emergency. It was all, really, on us to figure out, even down to where we'd call in a medevac if the need arose. We were similarly entrusted with preparing the soldiers and the specific equipment we needed.

Optics, communications, and weapons were key elements. First on the list for me was the handheld thermal scope that each section usually carried on patrol. It had good magnification, and the thermals didn't depend on moonlight. The shades of green in our NVGs just didn't cut it sometimes. I also carried illumination flares and red star clusters for my grenade launcher in addition to an IR strobe light. The illumination rounds lit up the surrounding area like daylight. A red star cluster flare was a universal signal for 'the shit has hit the fan and we need help,' and being close enough for the patrol base to see it was a comfort. The IR strobe I carried so we didn't get shot up by our own Apaches or patrols. As for the weapons, a SAW gunner, my grenade launcher, and rifleman would provide the necessary firepower. The first couple of OPs I led, sacrificing my four hours off of guard, were pretty much getting to learn the area. We ended up moving around a lot, because without posting on top of a building the flat terrain prevented our seeing very far. We'd have plenty of time to find the best spots.

Back on Kalsu, I kept busy with all of my extra responsibilities like the arms room and never-ending issues with our communications equipment in the vehicles. I'd taken on the communications role inadvertently. I was one of the only ones who knew how to use the small device which programmed the coded frequencies into our radios each week, called an ANCD. Instead of using a single channel which could be monitored by our enemies with a captured radio, most US forces operated on 'frequency hop.' Each radio was synchronized to switch frequencies on an exact schedule. On a specific day every week at 0300, the radios would need to be changed over to a new timetable. It was a pain, to say the least, and had to be done even during patrols. The arms room tasks were easier, even if not always pleasant.

Smitty's M4 carbine made it back to our Troop. Our supply sergeant had gotten in back from HHT shortly after he died, minus its destroyed scope. It was in rough shape, and had only been wiped down of whatever covered it, but it still worked. I found about it first since I was in the arms room frequently. I couldn't imagine anyone else getting it, so I worked it out with the armorer so I could. Putting it out of my mind that it could be blood I was picking out if its crevices, I cleaned it up, attached my grenade launcher and sights to it, and then zeroed it. At first it was strange holding the weapon of a guy who had been killed so recently, but he was my friend. It somehow comforted me, and I vowed to make good use of it in the coming months as we tried to clean out Diyara. I figured I'd have many opportunities.

8

I was back on patrol before I knew it. I adjusted my grip on Smitty's M4, muzzle down between my legs. I tried not to think about what would happen to the HE grenades strapped to my chest if we were hit. Just another patrol. I was already drenched in sweat although we'd only just begun our mounted patrol in Humvees. The heat was growing more intense by the day. I was in my usual spot behind 1LT Kelley with the radio handset pressed against my ear. The squadron-level channel wasn't bad to monitor. I just radioed in checkpoints as we reached them and listened to the other patrols do the same. I liked it because I always knew what was going on in the sector. The whine of the engine was loud, and the breeze coming through the gunner's hatch was hot. I was already bored, although I wasn't looking forward to our first house call or hasty checkpoint, either. Our countless TCPs had all gone like the first, chaotic and dangerous. I was really hoping that the lieutenant didn't feel like doing much at all on this patrol. Sometimes we kept them uneventful on purpose, but other times we couldn't. After all, we didn't call the shots all the time.

We'd just turned off the highway and were headed towards Haswah when I heard a thud off in the distance. Fear came over me mingled with excitement. This wasn't going to be an uneventful patrol at all.

"SGT Ervin..." the lieutenant began.

"Yessir, wait one." I knew to listen to the radio for what was going on. Within a few seconds a panicked voice broke the silence of the channel.

"Battle X-ray this is Killer Blue two, our middle vehicle has just been hit," crackled the voice.

It was a Charlie Company patrol. A flurry of shocked, hurried conversation filled the airwaves. They were just across the road from Hateen Munitions Complex, maybe a mile from us. They weren't sure about casualties but thought they were all dead. The vehicle was burning and ammunition was cooking off so they couldn't get close enough to confirm. After I'd relayed all of this to the lieutenant, he had me inform squadron headquarters that we were en route to help. Wantz had already started going faster as the lieutenant radioed the other two Humvees of the patrol to tell them what was happening. Off to my right, I could see the black plume of smoke rising in the distance. It occurred to me that they hadn't called for a medevac, and that wasn't a good sign.

It only took us a few minutes to get there. They were just a short distance north of Haswah on ASR Jackson. The fireball and the smoke on the railroad tracks a few hundred meters to the right of the road was all I could see as we raced into the adjacent field. A sickening dread came over me at the sight. Charlie Company's other two Humvees were on either side of the burning wreck with soldiers clustered about them. As we approached to within a few hundred meters the lieutenant had the patrol stop. We could hear the ammunition cooking off in the vehicle; bullets, rocket launchers, grenades. It sounded like fireworks. I thought I heard something else – something terrible – but wasn't sure. The Humvee was not distinguishable as such. It was an inferno. The front half of the vehicle was simply gone, and the rest was burning. Petrified, I got out of the truck when we came to a stop. The Charlie soldiers were yelling at us to keep back from the wreckage. My first instinct was to grab the fire extinguisher, but it dawned on me that it would be useless. I stood and watched for a moment. We heard there were four men in that Humvee.

The lieutenant was busy on the radio, and as always we were establishing a perimeter and keeping an eye out for any possible threats. Within a few minutes, the QRF patrol from squadron was there. 1LT Kelley sent my squad leader's Humvee chasing after an Iraqi van that was driving off to the west several hundred meters away. Then they sent SSG Moon's to clear some buildings in the distance. I went with them. It turned out to be the same buildings we'd cleared when we'd found an IED on Jackson months earlier. Just as then, there weren't any people in them or any sign of anything suspicious. Nevertheless, we took our time. No one really wanted to go back to the scene of the attack. After about twenty minutes of searching the building and its surroundings, though, we mounted up and made our way back.

By then several vehicles had showed up. There was probably a dozen there now, including a wrecker they'd brought along. There were several soldiers working around what was left of the truck, having put out the fire when we were gone. As I got out of the truck and walked towards the wreckage, someone called my name. It was 1LT Capps manning a Humvee turret, who had been 1st platoon's commander for a year back at Fort Irwin. On any other occasion it would have been good to see him. I had been his driver on his first ride in the Box and had helped the platoon come up with his nickname, Clark Kent.

"Hey SGT Ervin." His face was expressionless, his words subdued.

"Hello, sir," I replied.

That was the extent of the conversation, but we gazed at one another with a knowing look. This was a bad day. There was a sickening, solemn feeling in the air, and the work before us now was grim and terrible. I turned away from him and walked a little closer to the wreck.

There were four body bags laid out, and a medic standing by them handing out latex gloves to soldiers. The driver and TC had been blown to pieces and scattered all over. We had to cover a large search area. The two soldiers who were in the back of the Humvee were burned beyond recognition, but their bodies were mostly intact. Their black, charred remains filled two of the body bags. Everyone was picking up pieces of the others – with instructions to just fill the bags evenly if we couldn't tell what was what. I took a single glove from the medic and started walking towards the patch of dirt to which he'd pointed.

I guiltily hoped that I wouldn't find anything. What I was looking for was disgusting, but they were our own. It didn't feel right to be revolted at the horrible sights of their remains. More than anything else, I just didn't want to be there.

The body parts glinted in the sunlight, so they stood out among the dirt. It was just small pieces; small pieces that gave meaning to the phrase 'blown away.' I found a piece of a boot. Its desert tan color would have left it hidden if not for the sole of a man's foot melted to it. I found a back pocket for the same reason. The rest was just pieces of flesh. I didn't have anything to put the stuff in, so I just walked back to the body bags each time my gloved hand was full of gore. I don't know how I managed not to throw up. I just tried not to think about the fact that those little pieces could be me one day, if not on this very patrol. I couldn't dwell on any of it though, so I just shut it all down.

After a while, we stopped finding pieces and the search was called off. The Humvee wreckage had been loaded onto a flatbed truck, and anyone who hadn't been policing up the remains was standing around ready to leave. And that was that. There wasn't a lot of talking, everything was just loaded up and everyone made their way back to their respective vehicles. As we mounted up and did our radio checks between the vehicles of the patrol, I did my best to get back into a working mindset. We had several hours left to drive around even after that horrific break, and it didn't do any good to dwell on what I'd just seen and done. We went through the motions for the rest of the patrol. No one spoke. Everyone was just waiting on our time to be up so we could drive back to Kalsu. The remaining hours went slowly, but they went, and before long we were pulling into the FOB's perimeter.

After we'd downloaded the weapons and other gear from the trucks, we trudged through the hot dust back to our tent. Upon dropping my things off at my cot, I went outside to the bunker to smoke cigarettes. I didn't want to be inside the tent any more than I wanted to still be on that patrol. I listened to some Pink Floyd to distract me. Before long one of Bravo section's soldiers came over and asked about the patrol. It was SPC Villalobos, a soldier from Costa Rica who had served with Steppe in Fort Hood. He was a big guy but had lost a lot of weight since our arrival. He'd brought his guitar with him on the deployment, and often his music filled the air outside the bunkers. He was a pretty serious, reserved guy at the best of times, so I only told him enough of what had happened so that he had a general idea of what I saw. By now we'd all been through it one way or another, anyway.

"That's a bad fucking day, SGT Ervin," he said. We didn't make eye contact, but instead each of us stared into space with a grim, hollow look.

"You got that right, man. That was horrible. Horrible." I stopped there. There was nothing more to say. He'd been on the patrol when Prince was killed. I considered myself lucky that as terrible as that whole ordeal had been, at least I didn't know those men personally. I did my best that night to put the sights and sounds of the day out of my mind, but it wasn't easy. It was a grotesque display of our enemy's firepower and their ability to use it effectively that I'd just seen. More than that, though, as this had merely reinforced what I already knew about how bad an IED could be, was something even more terrible There wasn't anyone I could really ask, and I hardly wanted to bring it up. I thought I'd heard the soldiers inside that Humvee screaming when we approached it. I decided for my own sanity's sake that the sounds I heard were merely the roaring of the flames. It didn't matter too much, though, because the fact that it was a haunting, evil sound didn't change at all.

Around this time, it was decided that we needed to crack down on the main roads in the sector. This meant manning the overpasses. There were four overpasses in AO Battle; CP 16 was closest to the FOB, and a few more running north all the way to CP 20 on our sector's boundary. A military police (MP) company from Fort Bragg had responsibility for Tampa south of CP 16. HHT took over 16, and then Echo got responsibility for CP 18. I didn't see it as a good sign that almost halfway into our tour we had to shift our focus to the main road. One would think, it being a main supply route, that its security would have been a top priority upon our arrival in the sector. It seemed that it had gotten worse since then. I'll admit that it was embarrassing to have convoys hit IEDs on a stretch of road that was our responsibility to secure.

So between patrols and stints at Diyara, then, our new task would be to sit on the overpass at CP 18 and watch MSR Tampa and ASR Cleveland. Shifts at CP 18 and the mounted patrols were twelve hours now as well, increased from their usual six or eight. The first time I was on CP 18 felt like an eternity. We rolled out of Kalsu with two Bradleys to man the place. CP 18, like all the other checkpoints on Tampa, would be familiar to anyone who's been on the US interstate system. Setting the Bradleys on each end of the overpass bridge, we used their optics to peer down

Cleveland and Tampa, even if we couldn't see all the way down the former. A dismount's job was easier on the checkpoint. I looked down the road on occasion with binoculars, but our main purpose was to protect the Bradleys while they watched. There was no traffic allowed on the overpass, and we weren't stopping any cars passing by to search them. The closest vehicles came to us were the ones using the entrance and exit ramps to get onto the highway from Cleveland. Unless something happened it was just going to be a long, hot day under the Iraqi sun.

The heat had intensified into something none of us had ever experienced unless they'd been there before. It had been hot, getting into the nineties during the day even in late March, and creeping up into the hundreds for most of April. But if we were sweating in March and April, by now in late May we were melting. I started sweating in places I didn't know possible; through my boots, through my pants, and even into the cloth cover of my helmet. I could wring out sweat from my chin strap after a patrol. Once our uniform blouses dried out, the salt and grime left over made them stiff enough to stand up on their own. More than that, though, it played hell on our minds. It was hard to think straight sweltering under all that gear. It was a lot easier to get frustrated, and even easier to stop caring so much about what happened on a patrol. The Bradley rides were hellish. Sweating in the back of them, all I could think about was the ramp dropping so I could breathe a little easier. At least outside the air was moving. A handful of Humvees had air conditioners, but they were rare. For the most part we had to live with the heat.

So CP 18 duty was especially miserable, since we roasted on the asphalt without any kind of shade to keep off the sun besides our helmets. All day we looked down the road. I wondered what would happen if any one of the several oil convoys passing below were to be hit with an IED. We figured that the fireball would probably engulf the overpass. We had a lot of time to think up there. It wasn't always uneventful, though.

At night we called in illumination rounds from the mortars, now back at Kalsu. 1LT Kelley let me adjust the fire once or twice by radio, a task for which all of us had trained but was a rarity to perform on a real mission. Any time the need for fire missions was expected our forward observers or an officer would call the shots. Our mortars were accurate, and the instant daylight that lit up the target area when the parachute flare opened was impressive. We were setting pre-designated targets for the mortars – target reference points (TRPs). Telling the mortars to fire, say, two-hundred meters west of TRP 1, would let them know exactly where to aim their weapons. We didn't have to go through the task of determining the exact coordinates in a hurry, something useful for medevacs also.

Despite the heat, we were on edge on CP 18. We knew it was an evil place. So there was immediate tension when we saw two Iraqi vehicles stop on the exit ramp closest to Diyara one evening, one a Bongo truck and the other a van. The driver of the truck, dressed in a white thawb and holding a cell phone, had gotten out and was talking with the three men in the van. Soon they were all standing by their vehicles. They kept their eyes on us and continued talking. By their gestures we could tell they were talking about us. In a place where the enemy was difficult to distinguish, this certainly looked suspicious. Cell phones we knew to be a rarity except among insurgents. I listened on the ICOM as 1LT Kelley and SSG Villacorte talked about what to do. The interpreter was saying they were up to no good. All of a sudden we had the eerie feeling that there was an attack being planned in front of us. I don't think anyone said it, we just knew it. I was on the opposite side of the overpass from them. Steppe was in the Bradley closest to them, turret locked on to them.

I started walking over to the Bradley. I was turned away from the sight for a split second when I heard shouting. They'd sent a team to question the Iraqis, and the driver of the truck jumped in his vehicle and made a run for it. Steppe let loose some warning shots from the Bradley, but the truck kept going. About the time I got my sights on the truck Steppe started shooting it with coax, so I joined in. The stream of red tracers going into the truck was steady until it rolled to a stop and we stopped shooting. Still not knowing exactly what was going on, I had my guys stay put on the other side and ran over to talk with the 1LT Kelley and Steppe. The ICOMs had gone silent. The lieutenant looked at me from the top of the turret, his vehicle helmet on and handset pressed to an ear under it. No wonder the ICOM was silent. He shouted some orders. There were already soldiers detaining the Iraqis by the van. I was instructed to go secure the truck. I got Walters and McFarland to go with me. Walters was a recent addition to our section. He was young, and his boyish, seemingly innocent face had made me balk at my orders at first. I hated telling anyone to do what we were about to do. I had a pretty good idea of what to expect down there, and had even put on gloves. They followed me down the off-ramp without a word.

It was the same smell as the van we'd shot up in Haswah; battery acid, metal, burning plastic, and of course human guts, and it overpowered my senses as I approached the truck. Here we go again, I thought, but it didn't bother me much. Peering inside, I could see that the Iraqi man was twitching grotesquely. I opened the door, and he slumped over to the passenger side, leaking brains and blood from his head onto the floor. He had several bullet holes through him, and his body was still convulsing and making a hideous sucking sound. 1LT Kelley was yelling over the ICOM.

"SGT Ervin is he alive?" I really didn't know how to answer the question. If he was, he wouldn't be for long. I was annoyed that he was asking me when I was half inside the vehicle.

"Well, sir, his brains are leaking out on the floor so I don't think he is." It was the truth.

"I need a yes or no SGT Ervin." He was more adamant this time. I reached to feel for a pulse and his body twitched violently just as I touched his neck. I recoiled.

"Yeah sir, he's fuckin dead alright...Fucking radio," I added once my transmission was over. Everyone wanted to know what was happening as it was happening. I handed the ICOM to McFarland.

"Look, I'm going to search this truck and get it over with. It fucking stinks." I wasn't about to ask McFarland or Walters to do it, although they would have. There wasn't any more movement coming from the body. It was definitely a corpse now. I didn't want to be reaching over the body searching through the vehicle, so I grabbed the collar of his blood soaked garment and pulled him out. His limp body flopped to the ground with a thud. I dragged the corpse away from the vehicle a little ways and rifled through his pockets, finding a small notebook, his wallet, and a cell phone. I handed all this to McFarland to bag up, then flipped the body over again to search his back pocket. I didn't want to see his face anymore, either, as I'd been avoiding looking at it the whole time. Just like they'd taught us in basic training, having searched and cleared the corpse, I crossed its legs and spread its arms outward. It struck me that it looked a lot like a crucifixion.

I sorted through the few contents of the truck. There was the usual small assortment of tools (their cars were always breaking down), several papers, and a second cell phone. I handed it all to McFarland, thinking to myself that I might have just found valuable intelligence. I stayed out of the passenger side as much as possible. The pool of pink and red fluid on the floor there smelled strong and sickening. The acrid stench of battery acid and burning synthetic fabric or plastic added to it, so I made short work of all of it. I'd searched hundreds of cars, and the inside of a bongo truck wasn't big. I looked over the outside and its undercarriage after I climbed out and breathed in relatively fresh air. The flies were already starting to get to the body, though. We were ready to get out of there. I radioed in that we'd searched everything, then I took off my gloves and threw them on the corpse. I was never going to wear them again anyway. Leaving the body, we walked back to the overpass.

It was getting dark. SSG Villacorte had the three of us take a break while the other half of the squad continued to guard the detainees, having already started filling out the paperwork needed to turn them into the MPs on Kalsu. Things had calmed down. SSG Villacorte told us 3rd platoon was dispatching a QRF patrol from Diyara to take the prisoners off our hands while we continued our watch. Steppe was still ensconced in his turret, and the lieutenant was up there with him talking on the radios. As usual, all the higher echelons of our chain of command wanted to know exactly what happened. I kept looking at the corpse down below. I didn't feel bad about shooting him. We were all convinced the guy was an insurgent.

It was getting dark. All of a sudden there was an acute, deep rumble out towards Diyara. The sky lit up for an instant. IED. The dread followed immediately. We all knew the QRF had been hit. The lieutenant called out from his turret that there was wounded and they had to go help. They took off down the road in a hurry, leaving the other Bradley and all the dismounts on the checkpoint. We had little to do but wait, guard the detainees, and think about who might have gotten hurt. SSG Moon and SSG Villacorte talked for a little while, their conversation interrupted occasionally by SSG Moon listening closely to the radio. SSG Villacorte called the team leaders over.

"Hey, uh, Maida and Bondarenko are going to need a medevac chopper. They're bringing more wounded back in the Bradley, and we're taking it to Kalsu. SGT Ervin, need you to gun on the LT's track, Steppe's still down there with 3rd platoon waiting on the medevac. They're sendin' another patrol out here soon."

With a nod and a "roger" we geared up to leave. The Bradley returned in moments. The rest of the squad got in the other Bradley with the detainees, and I wiggled my way into the lieutenant's turret and put on Steppe's vehicle helmet. It didn't fit well, so I could barely hear the intercom system. There wasn't much to hear, anyway, besides the lieutenant telling the other track we were going to haul ass back to the FOB as fast as we could. I still didn't know who was back there, or how many of them there were. Just as instructed, we raced down the highway back to the FOB. Without stopping at the gate to clear weapons like usual, 1LT Kelley had me hop off the track to help the others with the detainees. He was going to remain in the Bradley and race through the base to the aid station, ignoring the rule that a vehicle had to be guided by foot.

After a few hours of doing all the paperwork on the detainees and handing them over, we got back to the tent and everyone waited nervously for news. Some went to the bunker with me to smoke cigarettes, some to Bravo's tent, and some sat on their cots alone with their thoughts. SSG Moon's crew had been back for a while already, but not Steppe and Wantz. I had just snubbed out my fifth or sixth cigarette and gotten back into the tent when I saw Wantz open the flap. I looked at him

"You okay, man? Where's Steppe," I asked.

"I'm good. I guess. I just passed him ...he's uh...he's right outside. He's kind of shaken up," he replied. He looked like he was, too. When bad things happened everyone had a grim, awful look on their face, and his voice was quiet. I went out to find Steppe. I was worried about him.

I found him sitting on the concrete barrier outside of our

tent by himself in the dark and silence. Mark's entire top half was covered in blood. He was just sitting there, stunned and mute. I put my hand on his shoulder and gave him a cigarette. He barely moved, and I lit it for him. I'd never seen Steppe shaken up like that. I didn't know what to say. I suppose we didn't have to talk at that point. He knew a lot of things without my saying, among them that he could talk to me if he needed to. With all that blood on him, though, I knew it had been bad out there. I never asked him what he'd done out there, but I learned a little of what happened.

The first real news I got was that Maida hadn't survived his wounds. He'd taken a lot of shrapnel to his legs and a piece through his neck, and was dead before the medevac got there. His BC, SSG Bondarenko, had been medevaced on the chopper, too. He'd suffered a terrible wound to his arm and ended up losing it. PFC Terry Rogers, who had been on the gun, had taken shrapnel to his face, and we'd taken him out of there in our Bradley. I can't remember who was in the back with him. Steppe had stayed at the site of the attack. The things he saw must have been horrendous considering he'd loaded those men onto the chopper. CPT Ramirez had given him a ride back to the FOB afterwards, and he'd walked to our tents alone and hid outside so no one had to see his bloody uniform.

The reason the IED had been so devastating was that it was different than most. They told us eventually that it was an EFP (explosively formed projectile) designed to penetrate armor. It had indeed gone right through the Humvee. They said it had gone off when their truck, the first in the small convoy, had set off the trip wire set up between the guard rails of the bridge. It was the first we'd ever heard of this weapon, and it showed us that the insurgents were stepping up their game.

Maida's death hit the Troop hard – very hard. There were a lot of tears at his memorial service. He was a universally liked soldier. His easy-going attitude and constant smile had been around Echo since before I'd arrived in the unit back in November of 2002. I never remember him having anything but a cheerful attitude even in Kuwait and Iraq. This was saying something, since he was already supposed to be out of the Army by the time we deployed. He hadn't flinched in going with us, though. I always respected him for that, and admired his sense of loyalty to the men in his platoon and the Troop. It was a tough pill to swallow that he wouldn't have been there if not for stop-loss, though, and combined with my grief at his passing, I got angry at the whole situation.

Now the thought of dying past the date I'd have gotten out of the Army bothered me in the extreme. A lot of men were re-enlisting and staying back on the FOB. I don't know the details surrounding those situations, and I knew that just as many were still busting their humps out on patrol after extending, but something still bothered me about it. I just had a sense, however unwarranted, that something was awry. It wasn't a proud moment when I spoke out against what I thought was an unfair practice. I had a sense of duty and honor, I felt, but I'd also seen close friends whose future plans were cut short by their terrible deaths in this hellhole. It bothered me enough to speak up one day, much to my regret.

It was during an NCO meeting one morning that I did it. I was pissed off that day; that worn out, frayed-nerve feeling of angst that made me want to crawl into a hole.

"Why don't we give all the stop-lossed guys jobs on the FOB? Really, they're supposed to be out of the Army, anyway." The glares I received were deserved. Someone told me to can it, and my squad leader told me later, outside in a special chewing out session, that it wasn't any of my business to question orders, the way the squadron was run, or anything for that matter. He was right, and I was ashamed for speaking up. It wasn't all that was bothering me. I blamed Maida's death on the fact that we had shot up that truck. I couldn't help but feel that it was in some way our fault. That it was a miserable time for me I remember well. I wondered who would be next.

As with everything else, I had to put it out of my mind to keep going. I did have a couple of things to look forward to, the most exciting by far being my chance to go home on leave. Beginning around March, our squadron rotated soldiers back to the states on a two-week mid tour leave. With the trip from Kalsu to Balad, the location of LSA Anaconda and a major airbase, on to Kuwait, and then to the states and back a soldier was gone for about three weeks. Leave slots were doled at random near the beginning of the tour, and we were allowed to trade with one another to a degree. I had ended up with a slot in July, so as June approached it was actually realistic that I would get to take it. There was also a chance to have an entirely new job altogether.

Our commanders decided to influx a lot of new advisers into the Iraqi Army in the hopes that before the end of our tour we could hand over responsibility for combat operations to them. We even heard that by October we'd be playing volleyball on the FOB, only occasionally helping them out as QRF. To accomplish this, each platoon had to give up three or four NCOs for military transition teams (MiTT), which was to be called Operational Detachment Echo. Smitty had been among the first of these. While it had its real dangers, I also saw it as a chance to do something new. I'll admit, also, that not having to be around Bradleys also entered into my thinking. It had been months since the rollover, but the edge never dissipated. Moreover, I had a sense that training the Iraqis would be a more significant contribution than anything else I'd done up to this point. It was a unique opportunity, and I let everyone know I was willing to do it. Some guys were outright against being assigned there, some indifferent, while others, like me, were enthusiastic. The specific assignments would be figured out by around the time I took leave.

There was no break after Maida was killed. Our Humvee patrols through the farmland surrounding Diyara continued the day after his memorial service. The battle of observation on Cleveland did as well. Now our OPs were exclusively conducted on that road. It was six kilometers of proven danger now. This stretch of road, more than anything else during the whole deployment, illustrated that we just didn't have enough soldiers for the job. When I took out two men on an OP near the bridge shortly after Maida was killed, I would have liked to have an entire squad with me. We had every reason to expect that we'd encounter something. Still, with two men we could at least be stealthy. It was what we could spare, anyway.

After having discussed my plan with our lieutenant in the CP at Diyara, I got my volunteers ready. I was taking Smith and McFarland. Smith was a new soldier, only a PFC, but one of the oldest men in the platoon. He was a tall black guy from Los Angeles, and was one of the most unique characters I ever met while serving. He had sort of a strange personality, and had lived an interesting life. Both of them had been on several OPs before, and even more patrols and guard shifts, so my only PCI was asking if they needed batteries for anything. We were taking a thermal scope, Smith's SAW, my grenade launcher, McFarland's rifle, and most importantly, the radio. I had the grid coordinates of the bridge written on the back of my map, and had decided that if we caught anyone that looked as if they were emplacing bombs (digging holes by the road was a sure sign of this) I would ask for permission to call in mortars. Steppe and I were vying to be the first to nail some insurgents with their own medicine. When we slipped out of the perimeter of Diyara that night it was pitch black. I wondered if I'd be able to see anything at all.

The going was rough. We were a short distance from the bridge, but we didn't dare walk on the road. Instead we had to traverse the fields adjacent to the road. Every so often we'd come up on a canal that we had to figure out how to cross, usually by locating the small foot bridge that allowed the workers in the fields to get around. Sometimes we just had to go through the mire. It wasn't easy. Our NVGs were almost useless that night. There was no moon. We floundered through mud and walked into bushes until finally, almost two-hundred meters short of the bridge, I found a spot in a ditch that afforded us good lines of sight and decent security. The bridge was at our eleven o'clock, and a farmhouse with a single light on to our one o'clock a hundred meters from our ditch. I radioed in our location.

"Diyara X-ray this is Reaper Red three Bravo," I whispered into the handset as I pressed it hard against my ear. Its volume was as low as it could go.

"Diyara X-ray, over." 1LT Kelley's voice came through clearly.

"Roger Diyara X-ray, I'm set in location in treeline two-hundred meters northeast of the bridge. I have eyes on objective."

"This is Diyara X-ray, roger that. Tower two has eyes on your IR strobe. Will standby for SITREP." Every fifteen minutes I had to call in the situation report. Comforted by the fact that the guard in the tower observing the road could see us, we settled in to wait.

As the name of an OP implies, we hid in the bushes and watched – or tried to at least. It was dark as hell, and I was glad we had the thermal scope. We'd been noisy getting into position despite our best efforts, and I wondered if we were the ones being watched. The three of us took turns clipping the radio handset to our chinstrap to listen and call in our SITREPs, and we all watched one another's backs. The patrol base could see us, but they probably wouldn't be able to see someone creeping up on us. More or less we just watched the road and listened to the noises around us. It wasn't quite silent. There was the gurgling sound of a canal and the distant drone of generators. The occasional dog bark or rooster crow mingled in occasionally. Mostly it was the bugs; sand gnats. What terrible little creatures. They were smaller than mosquitoes, flesh-toned, and their bite stung before it started itching. They buzzed in our ears and all over our faces. Any exposed skin was open game for them. The sweat added to the itch. Nights by now were still hot enough to keep us fairly drenched in the stuff.

Swatting constantly at the sand gnats and wiping sweat from my eyes, I kept my attention on the bridge until our two hours was up, and we started to leave. Nothing had happened, like usual. There wasn't a single vehicle or Iraqi moving around that night. It was almost as if they knew when our OPs and patrols were coming and going. It wouldn't have been hard, we reasoned, to have a guy with a cell phone in town call his buddies by the bridge when we headed out. Being less careful this time, the boredom, heat, and frustration having sapped some of my attentiveness, we trudged back to the patrol base. In another hour or so we'd have to go on a guard shift, just in time for the rising sun of Diyara and another day that promised to be melting hot. OPs meant one thing for certain; you wouldn't be sleeping for a good while if you went on one.

No infantryman is a stranger to sleep deprivation. The most sleep in one stretch I could get at a patrol base on security phase was about three hours, and then it would be back to a guard position for another two. So in a way, I was always operating on a sleep deficit. It wasn't just guard duty that cut into that sleep. Besides eating and trying to stay clean, during the day there was always work to be done, even after our fortifications were constructed. We had to maintain our gear, first and foremost. The dust that summer reached into every crevice of our weapons and equipment, and their cleanliness affected their reliability. We cleaned our living quarters as best we could, and kept our storerooms clean to cut down on rats and other vermin. We made improvements on the fortifications and the perimeter by setting up trip-flares in some of the hard-to-see spots, and replacing sandbags that had come apart. There was always something.

For all the interruptions though, the men on guard stayed awake. There were a lot of creative ways to do this. One of the most popular was playing trivia games on the ICOM radios or just telling jokes. Smith and McFarland were masters at sports trivia. Whoever was in charge of a guard shift would bring coffee or other things to the guards. There was a lot of use of chewing tobacco or snuff. Some soldiers stood up for most of their shift. Some sang quietly to themselves. We brought snacks and chugged water. We got to learn the comings and goings of the Iraqis intimately. Mostly we just stared at nothing and waited until the shift was over. It was a matter of doing whatever it took to stay awake. Sleeping on guard was dangerous for everyone, and it was also a dereliction of duty punishable by the Uniform Code of Military Justice (UCMJ), and rightly so. I only heard of it happening once during the whole year It was dealt with swiftly, although not as harshly as legal punishment.

My added responsibilities, particularly the radios, crept into the few hours I did manage to find away from guard or other work. Sometimes, for any number of reasons but mostly user error, the radios would lose their 'fill' and they'd wake me up to fix it. If the commo NCO wasn't there, I was the one who troubleshot the equipment and reprogrammed everything. He usually wasn't. Primarily, he was needed on the FOB to maintain the whole Troop's equipment. SFC Torgerson, my squad leader, and the lieutenant knew I could handle more technical tasks and always called upon me to do them. Staying busy wasn't a bad thing, though, so I never complained about the loss of sleep. I'd become inured to operating without it.

The first full twenty-hours without sleep were actually easy. It was the hours after that when I really noticed the effects. For one, my eyes felt like they were glued open. They were sticky, dry, and hard to focus at times. I wasn't sleepy. Some second wind always caught me on the second day and prevented that, yet I was tired; dragging both mentally and physically. In a trick of the mind that I noticed as far back as basic training, I had the feeling of being more alert and having sharper senses. The lack of clear thinking mitigated any advantage from the feeling though. Sometimes it just took my brain a few seconds to register what was going on. I could zone out tying my boots or programming a radio frequency. I may have been awake in the guard towers after thirty-six continuous hours without sleep, but it was a vacant stare into my sector. It was true for all of us that something always kept us going, fortitude, discipline, or both.

Kalsu continued to remain a veritable vacation spot compared to Diyara. The mortar and rocket attacks were ever present though, and I had a couple of close calls by June. The first close one was close indeed. I was walking from our tents to the motorpool, a completely open area, with Smith and Walters. Just outside the berm we heard a series of small thumps – too quiet for an IED. Smith said something first as we all looked at one another, puzzled.

"Hey that's a fuckin mortar shooting!" He was right.

CRUMP! Without thinking I started running towards a bunker several paces away. Smith and Walters had already hit the ground, hands over their heads. They stood up and followed me.

CRUMP! CRUMP! I heard and felt them hitting not a hundred meters away. I practically dove into the bunker, and Smith and Walters tumbled in after me. That feeling of helplessness came over me. I tensed up and waited on the next round to hit. Nothing happened. I radioed in our status, lit a cigarette, and waited on the all clear siren.

As soon as it was over, I knew I'd done exactly what I shouldn't have. I should have hit the dirt like Walters and Smith. I told them they'd made the right call afterwards; the attack was over before we'd even reached the safety of the bunker. Admitting mistakes to subordinates wasn't always a good idea, as it could undermine your own authority. However, in this case I didn't think twice about it. It was a life-or-death situation, and they had done the right thing. I didn't admit that it was fear that had clouded my judgment. Of course, the impact of mortar rounds still never bothered me as much as rockets.

I was hanging out in the bunker a few days later, laughing hard at one of SGT Camarillo's jokes when something ripped through air above us.

WHOOOOOOSH...BOOM! We both hit the ground despite being inside the bunker. It was a deafening, tremendous noise.

"Holy shit!" SGT Camarillo said it all right. That went right over our heads. The tent emptied into the bunker, and everyone lit their customary cigarettes like any other time we'd had incoming. Unlike other times, though, SFC Powell, 2nd's platoon sergeant, and our XO, the quiet, mild-mannered CPT LaRocca, came limping into the bunker bleeding. They'd both been hit, and the XO had a wound through his calf and was bleeding a lot. He was pale and shaken. I snapped at someone to grab our CLS bag from the tent. When Smith got back with it, I had him put a field dressing over the XO's calf and elevate his leg. We went about the first aid just as we had in training. Somehow I remained calm. There was a lot of blood from a small wound. SFC Powell had a smaller wound and was taking care of it on his own. It wasn't bleeding much. He kept saying the wound burned because the shrapnel was hot.

It was surreal. The rocket had hit the squadron headquarters building not fifty meters from our tents. They had been just beyond the concrete barrier protecting our tent, and hadn't had time to hit the ground, much less get into a bunker.

A couple of soldiers helped CPT LaRocca to the aid station while we inspected the concrete barriers outside our tents for shrapnel marks. The HQ building, for its part, wasn't even damaged. It was a Saddam-era military building designed, apparently, to withstand more. There was a pock mark on its concrete wall near its roof. That was it. We didn't figure our tents would have fared as well. These close calls, and especially the rocket, changed how I thought about incoming. Now there was blood involved. Like the IEDs and car bombs that had turned out fatal, now there was something very real to be frightened of with incoming. The insurgents were doing their best to drive home the point that we had to live under fire even in our bases. They did a good job of unnerving us.

Talking to SSG Chavez one day outside of Bravo section's tent, SPC Reardon bolted outside, pushed past us, and ran to the bunker. I was instantly scared. We followed out of instinct, and it was only when we all got there that he asked us if we'd heard a rocket. No, we hadn't. He'd been dozing off, he said, and thought he'd heard one. SSG Chavez made some wisecrack about him scaring us, and we all laughed it off together. Reardon was among the most intelligent, level-headed soldiers I knew, one of the men who had a lot going for him outside of the Army. He was a rational, sensible, guy, so I knew that if things were getting to him, it was evidence that all of this was taking its toll. Sometimes I wondered how much we could take.

9

June was miserably hot, but I welcomed it all the same. It meant I was closer to going home on leave and perhaps getting a new assignment training the Iraqi Army. I saw change as a good thing, regardless of the form it took. For at this point, about halfway through the tour, a dreadful monotony had set in that was almost unbearable. We alternated between sweating out at Diyara or on patrol in our Bradleys and Humvees. We searched house after house, trudged through the irrigated farm fields, and did a raid or two. All the while we hoped no one else would be killed or wounded. SFC Torgerson and I, although we had differing patrol schedules, kept a running countdown until our leave slot came up. There was a growing impatience as it got closer, but for the meantime I had to plod along, make sure my soldiers were doing their jobs, and try not to do anything too brave or reckless.

Personnel came and went frequently, and the composition of my fire team changed quite often, although McFarland was sort of a mainstay. 1st platoon received a couple more soldiers that month in addition to the few soldiers we'd gotten earlier. One was SPC Walker, who had been to Iraq already with the 82nd Airborne Division. I remember that he was sandy haired and sort of intense. He was disciplined, and would answer my questions quickly with a "sergeant" tacked onto the end of his reply. He was a knowledgeable light infantry soldier, even if he came across to some as being cocky. The other was SPC Graham, a stocky, tall soldier who had served with the 1st Cavalry Division and knew Bradleys well. He was a nice guy, also disciplined, but he seemed preoccupied with problems at home and brooded a lot. Both of them were hard workers and good soldiers. Having been stateside for a while, I hoped they'd get into the swing of things quickly.

It was on one of my first patrols with Graham that I learned that this was easier said than done. He was the gunner on a Humvee I was commanding for the patrol, and we had set up a checkpoint on a dirt road just to the east of Tampa. It was before dawn, and the Humvee was partially hidden by some tall grass. We were conducting more of an ambush than a checkpoint, since our intention was to discourage the Iraqis from getting on the roads before curfew ended. It was very quiet, but before long I could hear the sound of an engine coming down the road. It was barely light outside. Soon headlights appeared on the horizon.

"Graham, he probably can't see us, you'll have to shoot warning shots when you think it's best." He had a better view from atop the turret than I did standing behind the opened passenger side door.

"Roger, sergeant," he acknowledged while looking down the sights of the machine gun, ready. Twenty seconds went by. The vehicle was really close, now, and coming on fast. Whether he didn't see us or was coming in fast on purpose didn't matter.

"Graham, fucking shoot! Shoot!" Nothing. The vehicle was a mere hundred meters away and closing. I was the only other one facing the road. I dropped the radio handset and put my weapon to my shoulder, flipping the safety off as I did.

POP! POP! I shot well in advance of the vehicle, kicking up dust about ten feet in front of it. The vehicle, which I could tell by now was a bongo truck, came to an abrupt stop. Two men got out of the cab, hands up. They looked scared. Weapon pointed towards them, I started walking, taking McFarland with me. My

ICOM was blaring; the lieutenant asking me what was going on. As I approached, I motioned for the occupants of the vehicle to approach us. They did so timidly. While McFarland covered me, I searched them quickly so I could move on to the vehicle itself. It was just another bongo truck laden with produce. I had them get back in their vehicle after warning them about curfew with a mixture of hand signals and the little Arabic I knew. I turned my attention to Graham. He looked devastated as I approached.

"Graham. Jesus, man, you have to shoot when I tell you. Hop off the gun. McFarland will take your place. You can drive." I tried not to make it sound too harsh.

I understood what had happened. He'd frozen up. Nothing of the sort had occurred yet in the tour, and it rattled me. Later, he told me that he had indeed frozen. It was his first time having to pull the trigger since his last deployment, and he said his mind had simply stopped working. I couldn't very well punish him, nor would I have thought to do so in the circumstances. It happened. I told him that it might be better if he wasn't a gunner when we took Humvees for a while. Humvee gunners always did most of any shooting that had to be done. He agreed. I felt pretty bad for him, but I had to make sure we were safe. Of course, the opposite could be true as well.

Maybe it was the edginess engendered by the proximity of my leave date, but I started to get sort of trigger-happy when it came to warning shots. We were leaving Diyara one day in Humvees, and I was on the gun of the rear vehicle. A car had come up on us quickly, and despite my frantic hand signals, kept racing towards us. Without thinking, I shot a burst in front of him and he came to a stop. Seconds later, we got a call from the patrol base. A few of their guards had heard bullets ricocheting overhead. I knew they were mine instantly. I was mortified. I'd almost been the cause of a friendly fire incident. I got a talking-to by the platoon sergeant, had to apologize to the soldiers in the patrol base later, and then teach a class about target awareness. Warning shots were always tricky, and that snap judgment not always the best.

June passed quickly, and it was finally time to go on leave after we'd shot off some flares in Diyara for Independence Day. We didn't pack much, basically just a knapsack full of clean socks, t-shirts, and hygiene items. We turned in our weapons, night vision, and other sensitive items into the arms room and stripped our body armor of ammo pouches and all the rest. We only needed our helmets and the armor itself for the trip. It was odd to be without a weapon and ammunition. For six straight months I'd kept it within arm's reach, the rare exceptions being going to take a shower and using the bathroom. I didn't feel right without it.

As I sat in the tent before going out to catch our flight to Balad, it really hit me that I wasn't comfortable leaving my soldiers or friends behind, even for a few weeks. I knew that a lot could happen in that time span. I did not want to miss out on anything – especially anything bad. I didn't want them to suffer it without me. It felt a lot like abandoning them, and I couldn't help but wonder who would be hurt or killed when I was back home in West Virginia. I said my goodbyes with a heavy heart. When I told Steppe that I'd see him soon, I tried to ignore the fact that my seeing him again depended on whether or not he'd be killed or wounded. Feeling not a little guilty, when SFC Torgerson popped his head in our tent to tell me it was time to go, I took one last look around at the guys in the tent and told them to be safe.

The excitement really kicked in at the helipad. There were four or five of us waiting there to begin the first leg of our journey. A Blackhawk helicopter would take us to Balad, an airbase north of Baghdad, and from there we would fly on a C-130 to Kuwait to catch our MAC flights back to the United States.

There were a few soldiers from 2-11 with us; a medic from HHT who had treated me after the Humvee rollover, a platoon sergeant from Hotel Company, and my platoon sergeant. There were a couple more enlisted soldiers, but SFC Torgerson and I were the only ones from Echo. I was surprised at how relaxed we all became upon arriving at the helipad. We were already leaving the war behind mentally. It was exciting to be taking my first helicopter ride as well. We were fairly jovial when the chopper arrived and we hustled out to the helipad.

The Blackhawk touched down. The crew member motioned for us to come in and have a seat. It was incredibly loud, a high-pitched whine accentuated with the deep *thwump-thwump-thwump* of the rotor blades. I just followed the actions of the guys around me. The troop seats in the back of the helicopter were pretty small, and had a five-point seatbelt, much like one that a racecar driver would wear. SFC Torgerson looked over to ensure I had figured it out. Once strapped in, we gave our thumbs up to the two crew members now manning the machine guns, and they passed it along to the pilots. The rotors sped up and we lifted off. The doors were open, so it was really only the seatbelt that held us in our seats. The helicopter corkscrewed up to cruising altitude and took off. I looked below me at FOB Kalsu. It looked small, and as we gained altitude, and then a little distance, it seemed like dusty little island.

It was somewhat like sightseeing on the flight to Balad. The flat terrain of Iraq only allowed you to see to the next treeline or slight rise from the ground, but flying above it all I could see the lay of the land. It was crisscrossed with straight canals and roads. I thought it looked more like Vietnam than Iraq. The highway cut through the tapestry of the farmlands like a ribbon. Before long the greenery vanished, as we were making a wide arc to avoid flying over Baghdad airspace. There was still a danger of being shot down, after all, even if this was our vacation. The desert that stretched out below me was entirely featureless. There were few roads and even fewer dwellings, and out in the desert there were interesting irrigation systems. The fields of green, standing out amidst all the brown dust, were circular. There were long watering machines that swung around them like the hand of a clock. I was impressed since I was used to the ancient canal system of central Iraq. This seemed more modern, and modern in Iraq stood out.

The flight was short. Before long we could see the giant base in the distance. Balad, or LSA Anaconda, was one of the largest bases in Iraq at the time. Not only was it a major airfield, but most of the supplies flown or trucked into Iraq passed through the place. It was built on an old Iraqi airfield, and much of it was still in use, including the concrete hangars. As we approached the huge tarmac we could see the fighter jets in bunkers, C-130s, and other cargo aircraft. The scale of the place was impressive. Even from above it seemed to stretch out past the horizon. Seeing the grandeur of the place was a reminder that I was a very small part of a very large machine. All of this, the airfield, the giant supply yards, the vast motorpools, were there to support our operations across the whole country. There were a few times when I caught a glimpse of the massive undertaking that was the Iraq War, and this was one of them.

The base was so big that we had to take a bus to the depot for soldiers travelling in and out of the country on an individual basis. It was called 'Catfish Air.' We reported in, and they informed us that it would be a couple of days before we could catch a plane to Camp Doha, Kuwait, the travel depot for the entire theatre of operations. In the meantime, they set us up in some transitory barracks which were little more than plywood buildings with bunk beds and air conditioners. Still, it was an improvement over our dusty tents in Kalsu, and luxurious compared to the patrols bases. There was a lot to do in Balad. As I studied the color-coded bus schedule and the directory of things to do there, it actually dawned on me that there was more to this place than at Fort Irwin. We were excited, and caught the first bus we could to get to the center of the base where all the goodies were.

I was amazed. Clustered around the PX (bigger than Irwin's) was a veritable strip mall. There was a Pizza Hut, Burger King, ice cream stand, several trailers with phones, a giant, immaculate dining facility, individual trailers in which soldiers lived, and an old hanger turned into a massive recreation center. Inside of it were computers, gaming consoles, big screen televisions, pool tables, foosball and ping-pong tables, a stage for putting on USO shows, and couches and chairs – real, comfortable, plushy couches and chairs, the American stuff. My first order of business, since I had a soft spot for them, was to get a cheeseburger. The medic with us picked pizza, but the thought of eating a cheeseburger, milkshake, and fries from a real restaurant (even fast food) seemed heavenly after six months in Kalsu.

It was still blistering hot out, though. We had to eat outside in a shaded area by the row of restaurants. I didn't gorge myself, but I enjoyed enough to upset my stomach. I just wasn't used to the richness of the food. After eating, we made our way over to the recreation building, and sitting on a couch in an air conditioned room calmed my stomach. From there we split up. I went to make a few phone calls before going back to our billets on the other side of the base to relax. Venturing around the place alone, I started noticing that Balad had more than restaurants, an Olympic sized swimming pool, and real couches. There were a lot of American women there, too. Most were soldiers, others were Air Force. Balad was the type of place that had plenty of support personnel, so there were naturally more women. There were only a handful on Kalsu, and I rarely saw them around. Balad was different. They were everywhere.

I believe that's just when I realized how far away I'd been from everything I knew. I'd been looking forward to seeing Karen, sure, but there was something about the presence of American women, and really attractive ones at that, which made me extremely homesick. There's no doubt that being in a woman's company was on my mind a lot, but the longer I spent in Iraq it was more and more an abstract. All of us talked about it plenty, but in reality we were just never around American women. (For a myriad of reasons, Iraqi women were not an option.) Seeing them reminded me of the part of human existence I'd been missing for so long. It wasn't sexual so much as it was the recognition that women embodied the antithesis of what we were doing out there beyond the wire every day as grunts. It was a poignant reminder that there was indeed more to life than the patrols, heat, and fear.

Being around all these reminders reinforced the excitement of going home. Not only were there going to be luxuries there, it was West Virginia in the summertime. I couldn't wait to have a cold beer on a porch while listening to birds and bugs. The journey wasn't over yet, though. After a couple of days our turn to leave came up. It was mid-afternoon when we left, and stifling hot. After catching a bus to the Catfish Air terminal, and then another to the runway, we filed aboard a C-130 with its engines warmed up and running. The loadmaster in the back didn't give any instructions. It was easy to figure out. The seats were arranged so that the rows faced each other. Passengers were squeezed so close together that our legs were interlocked the whole way down the row. It was cramped, and as we sat there on the runway waiting for takeoff clearance, the back of the C-130 turned out to be an oven just the same as a Bradley was.

Everyone was drenched in sweat, but it didn't matter. The

next foot we stepped off of this plane was not going to be in Iraq. When the wheels left the runway I was gladdened, even if I knew I had to go back eventually. The pilots did a combat ascent, meaning they ascended in a tight corkscrew pattern above the airfield to gain altitude quickly so as to avoid ground fire. In spite of my churning stomach and discomfort, I smiled at the thought of leaving Iraq.

Kuwait turned out to be hotter and drier than Iraq. When I stepped off of the plane onto the runway, I thought I was feeling the aircraft's engine exhaust, but it was just the wind. It felt something like putting your head in a dryer. The sun was intense as well. The whole place seemed to broil in the light. We were bussed to Camp Doha, where we would get some logistics of the journey out of the way. We accomplished everything the first night. The bus took us to the different stations; turning in our helmet and body armor for storage, receiving a travel briefing, getting our plane tickets, and completing all the necessary paperwork. After sleeping in a giant warehouse with bunk beds, the next day we received our official travel orders. Each of us had a couple of days to kill in Kuwait before we caught our flights, so we made the best of the amenities there. Like Balad, Doha had it all, but since it was the final stop before getting out of the Middle East, the time seemed to crawl by slowly.

After two days, it was finally time to climb aboard a plane bound for the United States. There was no climactic feeling stepping onto that plane, no finality of an actual exodus from the Middle East. It was a welcomed, though temporary respite. The moment the plane took off it seemed like the clock was ticking. I tried to put it out of my mind. I was determined to make the best of the couple of weeks home that I had. My mind was free to anticipate a million things to do when I got home now. After a stopover in Germany, during which I nearly froze to death in seventy-degree weather, it was on to Atlanta and then to

Charleston, West Virginia.

Taking in the first lungful of West Virginia's summer air when I stepped off the plane was a beautiful moment. The air was so clean! It was an overcast, humid day, the type of weather West Virginians would call muggy. But it carried such wonderful smells with it; green trees, fresh rain, and even wet dirt. It had just rained a warm, summer rain. It brought my mind right back to home. I'd had a similar sensation on the several occasions in which I flew back home from California, but this time the contrast was much more vivid. I'd taken a lot of things for granted until then. Iraq had a way of putting things into perspective.

Iraq also had a way of following me home. I certainly hadn't anticipated it, but once we got on the highway in Karen's car, my nerves started playing havoc. At first it was the speed at which we were travelling. For more than half a year I'd never gone faster than fifty miles-per-hour or so in a Humvee, and slower in Bradley. All of a sudden we were going seventy. My body wasn't used to the sensation of travelling that fast, and I was frightened. I got a grip on whatever I could and gritted my teeth. We seemed to be engulfed in traffic, and the closeness of the vehicles around us was astounding. I felt like yelling at the gunner to get them away. My eyes scanned the guardrails and the shoulders of the highway for any debris or disturbed ground that could yield an IED. I had no idea any of this would happen to me. The extent to which I was on edge scared me. It dissipated as I got used to it, although certain jumpiness stayed with me.

My first night back I drank a lot. It was beautiful outside. Karen took me to a bar that had a patio, and a lot of my friends from my high school years came to visit like they normally did when I came home on leave. They were glad to see me. I'd had the opportunity to speak to a few of them on the telephone and write letters to more. They had a vague idea of what I'd been up against, but their imaginations probably filled in the rest. At one point, leaving the bar, a friend asked if I wanted him to break one of my legs in his car door. I looked at him and laughed. He didn't. He was actually being serious. I had to explain to him that staying back from this one would be worse than going back and finishing it. I don't think they knew the connection that I'd formed with the men I'd been with for several years, how our shared fear had the effect of bringing us closer together. It was something that transcended friendship, bordered on brother-hood, and that I was only just beginning to understand. It was the reason I had an odd desire to get back and get the rest of the tour over with. I could rest when we were all home.

Friends and family did their very best to make me feel wel-come and allow me to relax. They gave me a wide berth and didn't make demands on my time. I only had a few things in mind that I wanted to do while I was home. One was spending time with Karen. Being with her was such a radical departure from what had become normal in my six months in Iraq. The hard life I'd been leading melted away when I was with her. She helped me simply enjoy the moments in which I found myself. She didn't treat me like a hero or anything, but she did an amaz-ing job of helping me have fun. While I was away she'd gotten us tickets to see Tom Petty in Indianapolis. Despite the tornado that touched down nearby during the concert, and a subsequent cancelling of the rest of his set, we had an absolute blast. We shared many quiet moments, too, not having to talk a lot. I think we were just thankful to be around one another, even if I wasn't entirely the same person I was before I'd left.

I knew that I had changed while I was away, even though I didn't know how exactly, to what extent, or if anyone else no-ticed it. I felt different. They did notice that I'd lost a significant amount of weight, and probably because of that anyone I visited offered me good food and plenty of it. I figured I'd lost about ten or fifteen pounds, which was a lot considering I only weighed about 170 when I deployed. Everyone, and especially my mother, thought that I looked unhealthily gaunt. It wasn't surprising. I told them all that I probably drank more than two liters of water a day over there, but lost at least that much in sweat. The constant stress was more than likely the cause. It was a lot easier to hide the mental changes as long as I didn't talk about the bad things. I tried not to divulge anything. It wasn't hard. I didn't want to think about it.

It was also a bit difficult to realize that for all the strangeness of my life the past six months, everything at home had gone on uninterrupted. People lived their lives regardless of the war. A friend of mine travelled the country with a band on tour, and Karen had completed her first half of summer classes. They had been accumulating experiences just as I had, although theirs were radically different. I had the feeling of missing out on a lot, and while on leave it felt like I was missing out on two parts of my life, one at war and one here at home. It seemed like purgatory.

The two weeks passed much too quickly, and before I knew it I was preparing to leave. I was sad to leave home behind. I dreaded returning. There was an air of excitement to that first trip across the ocean that characterizes any new type of experience. This time I knew what to expect. The goodness of all that I was leaving behind was more poignant as well. I'd had a good time – some of the best I'd ever had – and I knew I was returning to what promised to be more of the worst times of my life. That contrast was startling. The morning I put on my uniform and packed my bag was terrible. Everyone looked at me with thinly veiled pity and heartache. They felt sorry for me, feared for my safety, and hated to see me go. I understood something on that last morning home that I hadn't really considered before: they had missed me, too.

Karen made the good-byes easier. She was stoic, which was

good, because if she hadn't been I would have cried, too. I certainly did not want to leave her and everything I knew. But I was also missing my comrades. In the back of my mind during my time at home had been a nagging feeling of dread regarding them. I didn't know what was happening over there, if anyone had been hurt or killed, or if we had gotten a new sector, or anything else. Some things I knew. One was that I was going back to the heat and nastiness that was Iraq. The other was that it was a dangerous place, and after living in the safety of home for two weeks it brought a pang of fear when I contemplated going back on patrol. These things clouded over my mind as I turned my back to the terminal, my girlfriend, and home, and stepped aboard a plane to go back to war.

As I made my way through the complicated series of flights, stopovers, and waiting periods, the homesickness sunk in deeply. I hadn't experienced it when I left the first time. But now, in Balad again and back in the heat, it was crushing. I listened to the CDs I'd bought back home and thought endlessly of being with Karen. The music had a way of making me think of home. That much had remained the same before and after the break. I listened to a lot of calm music: Pink Floyd, the Grateful Dead, Dave Matthews Band, Simon and Garfunkel, and Beethoven. Music was one of the best ways to escape whatever reality you were trying to in that place. At present, I was making the best of a day's wait in Balad with the Grateful Dead, but it only served to remind me of what I was missing. I struggled to get my head back in the game, and the return journey turned out to be fairly miserable.

I received good news as the other soldiers in the squadron whom I'd gone on leave with reunited in Balad. No one had gotten hurt while we were gone. SFC Torgerson said he'd been in touch with one of the NCOs, and that nothing really amiss happened, although there had been some changes.

The assignments for the IA training detachment had finally come out, and I hadn't been selected. I didn't mind too much. Steppe hadn't even volunteered for the assignment, so at least I would have him with me in the section. I didn't much look forward to operating with our reduced numbers, though. The ranks of sergeant and staff sergeant had been pretty well cleaned out, with each platoon offering up at least four soldiers for the Operational Detachment Echo. Among 1st's were SGT Camarillo, SGT Faucher, and SSG Nun, who had recently been promoted. Already overstretched, it meant that we'd each be pulling a little more weight.

We didn't skip a beat when we arrived back on Kalsu. We touched down just at dark. 1st platoon was on patrol phase, but the next evening we would be going to Diyara for security at the patrol base. We rustled up our armorer, got our weapons and other gear out of storage, and spent that evening catching up with the guys and preparing our gear to get back to work. It was good to see everyone, and they had some stories to tell.

The dreaded bridge on ASR Cleveland had been replaced by a wider one, and during its construction a squad had had to stay out there and provided security. My squad had been attacked by mortars when it was out there. No one was hurt, but it was close enough to rattle everyone and let them know that the insurgents could shoot those things with a fair amount of accuracy. Regardless, the bridge had been widened, which was supposed to increase our safety. There were other changes.

That late July, Diyara patrol base was undergoing a transformation. The plan was for us to hand the place over to the Iraqi Army eventually, but it needed some work to make it a proper base, even for them. The squadron hired an Iraqi construction company to do a few things. One was installing air conditioners in the rooms where we slept, much to our relief. Another was refurbishing the guard positions, which they did so with brick and plaster. I'm not sure if it was safer that way, but then I was never too sure about the sandbags, either. The contractors slept in the smaller building of the complex, on top of which an additional two guard positions were placed. That meant more men on a guard shift at any given time, but it afforded us another angle of view down Cleveland and guarded the flanks of the complex better. Before, we'd simply put trip-flares in the abandoned buildings just outside the perimeter. The work had barely started when I left and was in full swing when I got back.

My tent on Kalsu was a little sparser than before. They'd given all the squad leaders in the Troop one tent, the platoon leaders and platoon sergeants another, leaving us a lot of room. My jobs changed slightly. I took over as Alpha team leader since Nun had left, and I was now the senior team leader in the squad. I had a new squad leader, too. He'd been in charge of 4th squad in Bravo section previously, and I'd always liked him. He was a soft spoken, laid back guy from North Carolina, SSG Lutz. He thought I was capable, knew I was pretty intelligent, and so in a tongue-in-cheek kind of way let me know he didn't want to change anything around. He appreciated my knowledge about the radios and all the weapons systems. He was pretty hands-off in that he let me do my job and would only randomly check to see that I and my soldiers were doing what we were supposed to. We got along on a personal level, too. We'd both been raised in the country, relatively, so we had a lot in common. I still had McFarland on my fire team, although I can't remember who else composed Alpha team, 3rd squad at that point.

The night we went back out to Diyara went like it usually did. Hectic. Some of us had to get vehicles ready, some had to pick up boxes of MREs and other food from the chow hall. On top of that, we had to secure a trailer full of fuel for the generator to a Humvee. No matter how many times we'd done that same thing, it was always chaotic. Something usually went wrong. A trailer hitch would be busted, one of the vehicles we'd planned on taking would be broken down, or an interpreter slated to go with us couldn't be found. It was always something. We always figured out who was riding where the day prior, so at least stashing our personal gear on a vehicle was simplified. Having completed all that, for a few minutes everything got calm as we gathered by the gate, ready to go, and waited on the lieutenant and platoon sergeant to give us a short briefing. For this first time back out I was in the lieutenant's Humvee. I felt safe with Steppe on the gun. It was also nice not having to hop in a Bradley yet.

It finally felt like I was back when I smelled the interior of the Humvee, that rich, musky, rotten odor of the mud and dust mingled with the smell of diesel fuel and gunpowder. When we left the wire with our lights out and got onto the highway, the whine of the Humvee's diesel engine and the hot wind from the gunner's hatch was all too familiar. The sinking feeling in my gut was not. After having been away from it for a while, it was all a bit much.

As many times as I'd shut out the possibility of being hit with an IED, this wasn't one of them. Something had changed when I was home on leave, and everything was more intense now. The fear was there, and hard to keep down. All I could do was strain my mind to pay attention to the radio chatter on the squadron frequency. I was gritting my teeth and cinched up like a knot all over, but I was still monitoring that radio. Pressing the handset against my ear and focusing all my energy on it, I managed to get through the short trip without freaking out. It would take a while before I got used to everything again.

Arriving at Diyara patrol base to relieve the security platoon was just as chaotic as preparing to leave Kalsu. Guards had to be relieved, vehicles unloaded and loaded quickly to carry men and their equipment back to Kalsu. The trailer had to come off, all of the food and fuel unloaded quickly, and we had to keep track of any extra equipment that we'd brought like optics, radios, detainee bags, and the like. All of it was done in the pitch black dark and in a hurry. Nothing could be left behind, because my Humvee was being manned by a 3rd platoon crew that was being relieved as we arrived. When 1st platoon's guards had taken over and everything was off-loaded, 3rd platoon departed. All of it took maybe half-an-hour. Steppe and I walked out in front of the main building for a smoke just as 3rd platoon's vehicles made it out onto Cleveland.

Then the sky lit up. It's difficult to describe the sound that followed. A detonation like that was something you felt throughout your entire being more than you simply heard. If you're close enough, like I was then, you can feel the earth tremble slightly beneath your feet. That deep, sharp, thunderclap was low-pitched enough to feel in your chest. Then my brain added to it. The sudden realization that the terribly intense sound was, in fact, an enemy trying to hurt your buddies manifested itself as an instant shot of adrenaline and a wrenched knot somewhere between the pit of your stomach and your bowels. It was a bodily experience, one which always amazed me in a terrifying sort of way.

"Holy fucking shit, man," I said.

"Welcome back to hell, buddy, welcome back to hell," said Steppe. He followed it up with that dark laugh of his and slapped me on the back. We went back into the main building and waited outside the CP to hear what had happened over the radios. One of 3rd platoon's vehicles had been hit, but the blast wasn't too bad. The driver of the Humvee got some shrapnel in his foot. The vehicle wasn't disabled, and they could evacuate him to Kalsu themselves.

It had been only minutes since I'd passed the exact same spot on the road. Either the insurgents had failed to hit us as we passed or had set it up in anticipation of a platoon leaving shortly after we'd arrived. Either way, they'd scored a hit. They also managed to shake me up pretty bad. Later that night, as I sat in a guard tower sweating, all I could think about was how many more times I had to travel ASR Cleveland until I got back home.

10

I awoke earlier than usual for my guard shift. Shortly after dawn was the most pleasant temperatures of the day in late summer. I tried to rise earlier to drink some coffee and eat a little before the shift. If I did so, I was less groggy and in a slightly better mood when the two-hour stint began. After a cup of coffee and a few cigarettes, I donned my gear to talk with the men manning the positions on the roof. Putting on the filthy, heavy helmet and body armor was always the worst in the morning. Perhaps it was the lack of sleep that made me more acutely aware of the filth. I had been in Diyara only two days, but the constant sweating had made my uniform stiff with salt. The grime on my helmet's chin strap and the outer edges of the body armor smelled and was almost slimy to the touch. Everything smelled like old sweat, including me. I felt gross, even after shaving with bottled water and brushing my teeth.

In spite of the foulness and the filth that surrounded the patrol base on all sides, as I walked onto the roof there was a cool and oddly refreshing breeze. I walked up to one of the positions and asked the guard what had transpired during his shift. "Nothing," was the answer I expected and received. All of the soldiers I visited in their positions were glad to see me, though, because that meant their relief had been awakened and they would be able to catch a few hours of sleep very soon. The graveyard shift, from about four to six in the morning, always dragged on the longest. The fatigue was etched into their faces from what was then their sixth or seventh shift. Although we'd reduced the number of days we spent doing security Diyara to three or four, the duty of being on QRF, OPs, or work details during the off-hours meant that everyone was always exhausted. There was a reason I always asked for caffeine pills in my care packages.

I walked over to the guard position on the northeast corner of the roof. It offered an almost unobstructed view down a significant stretch of Cleveland.

"Anything happen on your shift?" I asked Larson, a 4th squad soldier who had been looking down the road with binoculars when I approached him. I didn't know him well. He was a recent addition to the platoon and I rarely worked with him. He generally kept to himself anyway.

"Well, sergeant, we had an SF convoy come through right before I took over, they told us to keep an eye out for them. That's it, you know how it goes," he replied.

Just as he finished talking we could hear their vehicles heading towards us from just north of the village. Humvees and Toyota trucks loaded down with Iraqi Special Forces appeared and hung a right, taking them down route Cleveland and away from us. They disappeared through the early morning haze, and Larson set his binoculars down. I told him he didn't have much longer to go. No doubt he knew it already and had been thinking about it since he relieved the previous guard.

The sudden flash was like lightning in the early morning twilight. The sound followed a split second later: *KrrThwump!* T his IED sounded big, bigger than the one I'd heard two nights ago. I could see the tail end of the convoy just short of the bend in the road and a growing plume of smoke just off to the left of them. Larson was already calling down to the CP on the ICOM, and the convoy had already started shooting. There were at least three machine guns going off, and also the hollow, metallic thud of an automatic grenade launcher. Mingled in the staccato of gunfire were the grenades' dull detonations. My heart dropped as I thought of the destruction some Iraqis' house was going through.

I didn't say anything. I just looked. Larson handed me the ICOM. More soldiers were getting on the roof now to see what had happened.

"SGT Ervin how far down the road?" It was 1LT Kelley. He sounded groggy and bored. IEDs were becoming routine.

"About eight-hundred meters, sir. I can't tell if any of their vehicles got hit, but nothing's on fire."

"Roger."

"There's a lot of shooting down there, sir."

"Roger, we're monitoring their radio traffic now, no casualties. They're not waiting on EOD." His voice was so calm. It seemed out of place with what I was seeing. The shooting stopped, and the convoy disappeared from sight, leaving only a small plume of dust and smoke from the detonation. Although I couldn't tell, they probably left some civilian casualties in their wake. It didn't matter. The decision to send a patrol down there wasn't up to me, and I had a guard shift to run. Larson's team leader had come over, so I went back downstairs to gather up the guys on my shift so we could take over from the weary guards. The noise and commotion had a lot of guys awake wondering what was going on. I had a brief conversation with Steppe before we headed up to the roof.

"Man, SF wasn't fucking around. You should have seen it," I said.

"Oh I know dude, I heard it down here. Fucking awesome, huh?" Steppe loved a display of firepower. We all did.

"Yeah, crazy, they opened up as soon as they got hit. I'm just glad we don't have to go down there and play in the mess." I said that part with relief, and I meant it. I didn't have to go see the aftermath. Instead, all I had to look forward to were a couple of hours in the relative calm of a guard tower. I wouldn't be fighting off sleep, this time. Underneath the fascination I displayed to everyone around me, my fear was continuing to grow. I'd seen two IED detonations on Cleveland in nearly as many days. It was unreal. That little stretch was getting nastier by the day, and I had several months to go in the tour. In a day or so, I'd be back out there, driving up and down those roads in a Humvee. I became more than homesick. I started to feel trapped in a nightmare.

"Well SSG Moon, I guess it looks like I'm going to be your gunner for this patrol. Don't worry, I still remember how," I joked with him as we met up near the gate. I was in the Humvee turret for this patrol. I wasn't too pleased about it but tried to keep a light heart. The radio checks were done. Logsdon, still SSG Moon's driver, had given the vehicle a brief inspection. We were ready to go. It was still early in the morning, but the sun was beating down on us already. It was going to be a hot one. I regretted the full breakfast I'd eaten earlier.

"Yeah, well, don't be shooting everything we see," said SSG Moon. He was never the most jovial, and I could tell he was pretty tense at the moment. After being around everyone for so long, the little things like that were easier and easier to see. I was tense, too. We made it back from Diyara without any problems after our security phase, but this was going to be my first actual patrol since being back. I shuddered at the thought of having to pass all those craters on the road for the next ten hours or so – and Cleveland especially. After the lieutenant arrived and asked SSG Moon if everything was ready to go we got a short briefing. By now, the lieutenant left it to the NCOs most of the time. Everything had become routine and normal.

"Alright listen up," SSG Moon began. "First we're going out to the patrol base to clear Cleveland. We'll do our foot patrol about halfway through the patrol. \ Keep drinking water, pay attention, and remember to follow rules of engagement. Radio checks done?" The gunners of the three Humvees all nodded their heads. "You got anything to add, sir," he asked the lieutenant.

"Cleveland's been hot, so we'll probably spend most of our time there and on the approaches to it. We may do a few house calls, and the foot patrol we do will be at least an hour. We'll have to use the interpreter at the patrol base. We'll probably do a hasty TCP at some point. SSG Moon, if you don't have anything else, we'll go ahead and mount up." He put his helmet on.

"Alright men, let's go. Do radio checks when you mount up," said SSG Moon. With that, he donned his helmet. I climbed into the Humvee turret, opened the feed tray of the machine gun, and laid the belt of ammo on it. After slamming the feed tray back down and pulling back on the charging handle, the weapon was ready to fire after disengaging the safety. I moved the turret all around with my back to ensure there were no new snags since we'd loaded up. We were the lead vehicle on the way out to the patrol base, so I could expect that any shooting at vehicles that wandered too close to the convoy would be done by me. There was always a bit of anxiety that accompanied those warning shots, for me at least. I always wondered whether I was doing things properly: if I was shooting according to ROE, if I was putting the rounds where they needed to be, if I had shot soon enough to avoid being blown up, and above all, if it was the right decision or not. I took a deep breath and hunkered down. Hopefully this patrol I just wouldn't have to shoot.

When we left Kalsu's gate and made it onto the highway it started. My heart began pounding, and I broke out in a cold sweat. I gritted my teeth and squeezed the stock of the machine gun with white knuckles. I told myself not to think about what could happen, focus on what was happening. It was hard. My mind raced. How many IED detonations had I seen since I'd returned from leave? How many times had I travelled these roads without getting hit, and how many more times could I do so before it happened? I'd rolled the dice too many times not to expect it now. The odds were turning against me. It was simple mathematical probability. I couldn't put it out of my mind. This patrol just seemed like the one where I'd get hit.

I noticed everything that could hide a bomb: the slightest indentation on the side of the road, a piece of garbage, a segment of a tire. The guard rails and the spots of disturbed earth on the shoulder were menacing. With each potential danger I let out a half-choked gasp. No vehicles were coming close to us, so I didn't have to stand up and expose myself. I touched my hand to the front of my helmet and extended it to the edge of the turret, making an invisible line so I made sure that my head was below it. No sense in riding in an armored vehicle if your head is hanging out of it. I thought all of these things at once. Then my stomach started churning. Then I got worried about my condition. Being scared wasn't so bad, but I thought I was going to lose it. Everything was just so intense. I dared not say anything for fear that something in my voice would give away the fact that I was flipping out – that wouldn't do for a sergeant. Things were snowballing fast, though.

When we pulled off of Tampa and descended ASR Cleveland towards the patrol base, my heart jumped into my throat. This was the road where it would happen, if any of them. It was paved, but hadn't been resurfaced in a long time. It was bumpy and uneven, and every time the Humvee lurched or hit a bump my heart rate increased. It was like bracing for an impact that never came. SSG Moon broke the relative silence halfway down the road:

"Hey when we get to the patrol base, turn around. We're

gonna make another pass on Cleveland, thought they saw something back there," he yelled above the engine. Logsdon nodded and continued driving calmly. It was business as usual. Route clearance meant that we made sure the road was clear of bombs. If we drove through it without getting hit, it was clear. If we drove through it and got blasted, it was also clear since we'd detonated what was there. But the despair that I felt at those words and the increasing sense of doom was all new. I was losing it. Even through the vibration of the vehicle I could tell I was trembling.

"You've gotta be fucking kidding me," I said under my breath. Fear had taken over my thought process entirely. We reached the intersection by the patrol base and turned around. Twice more we drove its length, each time going slower than before. I had the time to notice every small and potentially deadly detail of the road. The craters were everywhere from all the IEDs, and there was more trash and debris on Cleveland than on Tampa. It was the perfect road for bombs, we knew it as well as the insurgents did. Somehow I managed to hold it together on the first trip back out, but as we came closer to the patrol base on our third trip, I started to crack up.

"Hey, SSG Moon, is that it? I really don't feel like fucking dying on this road because the LT wants to go up and down it all day." Even as I said it I knew I'd crossed a line. Never, ever give soldiers below you reason to think you're scared, because if you are, they certainly will be, too.

"SGT Ervin what the fuck? Just pay attention," he said. Finally, we made it into the wire of the patrol base. All of the dust stirred up made it harder to breathe and I could smell the rankness of the canal nearby. My stomach was already churning and it made me nauseous. When the vehicle stopped and everyone got out, I climbed out of the turret and started puking beside the Humvee.

"Oh there he goes! Ha! Too many Red Bulls or what?" said Steppe, laughing. I wasn't really aware of it. My head was buzzing in a bad way. 1LT Kelley walked over.

"Hey, you alright?" He asked it in a serious tone. I sensed he knew what was happening.

"Sir my stomach is fucked. I don't know what's going on," I managed to choke out. I was glad I was puking, actually, because it gave me an excuse to be debilitated. "I feel pretty woozy." By this time SSG Lutz had walked over, too.

"Well goddamn, you gonna make it?" He was smiling, too, as he asked me in his Southern drawl. Being in the infantry, things like vomiting had their humorous side to most.

"Yeah I don't know sergeant, something's not right," I said. Then I turned away and dry-heaved a few times.

"Hey, SGT Ervin, get some water and go take a break. We'll make a short circuit and come back to get you, okay?" said 1LT Kelly. He was giving me a way out for a minute.

Avoiding the 3rd platoon soldiers milling around, I had their platoon leader point me to a room where no one was sleeping so I could chill out for a minute. When I got into the room and took all my gear off it hit me hard.

What exactly it was that hit me I could only describe as an avalanche of horror and hopelessness. I felt like I was trapped in my own death. There was no way out, and I had to play the dice game over and over. It didn't matter if it happened today, tomorrow, or in the coming months, but it was going to happen, and it was going to be painful, brutal, and ugly. As much as I tried, I couldn't muster up another thought. It was just all so fucked up, I thought. There was nothing good about this place except for surviving a patrol, and when that happened it just meant that you'd be right back out there the next day. The tears began to well up, but then reason took over. I lit a cigarette.

Somehow I began to calm down. I looked down at my gear

and breathed deeply, drying my eyes. There was no getting out of it. It finally made sense again. The only way to make it through the rest of the tour without going crazy was to realize the fact that I was already as good as dead, and it was only a matter of time before it happened. I didn't need to be afraid. Fuck it, I told myself, there's nothing I'm going to be able to do, really, to avoid being hit by an IED. With that out of the way, I could focus on everything else besides myself.

That was it. I'd finally figured it out. It wasn't pleasant by any means, but it was enough rationalization to get me on my feet putting on my helmet and body armor. If I treated my death or maiming like a known fact, I'd be fine. Just do what I have to do and don't dwell on it. I couldn't function if I was petrified, and actually my chances of missing something important would increase if I was scared out of my wits. It may have been a morbid, disturbing thought process, but it was working. It dawned on me that I'd already undergone this mental process before going on leave, and I could do it again.

When the patrol returned and I took over the turret in SSG Moon's Humvee, I did so with a renewed calm and focus. Looking at my gear in that room made me realize that I was a professional, and that part of my job was to overcome this fear and focus on the task at hand. For now, it was ensuring that no vehicles ventured too close to our Humvees, pulling security when we halted by standing up and scanning the horizon, listening to the radio when the TC was out of the truck, and making sure I was doing these things in tandem with the other gunners. I knew how to do this. I had already done it countless times. I didn't have any other choice, so I'd better keep it up. It was a hell of a mental pep talk I'd just gone through. The best part of it was that I was pretty sure no one was aware of exactly what had happened to me back there. I didn't, either, but I was pretty sure I'd just had a nervous breakdown. I was also glad that I'd snapped out of it. We had a lot to do before we came home for good.

The next several patrols were no problem. It took a little while, but I got back into the groove of being out there beyond the wire all the time amidst the danger, real or perceived. The mental conditioning I'd undergone during the six months before taking my leave had gone deeper than I thought. I'd had a lot of time to process things gradually. Returning from leave was different, because I had to deal with everything bad that I knew all at once. There were no mysteries about the place anymore, and I had to get used to this reality quickly, in one gulp, and I had to do it alone. I could not afford to let anyone know how scared I'd become after that trip home. It was pride, but it was also a feeling of not wanting to let my superiors, my soldiers, and my peers down. They had to suffer the same things I did for the same amount of time. They didn't crack up, and some of them were on their second tour, so I had no right to crack up, either. I had soldiers to lead and some complicated missions to perform. The transition period from leave was over, and it was time to finish my war, come what may.

What came my way shortly after that were a couple of things. The first was some changes for our off-time. It was decided by someone (definitely not anyone who went patrolling regularly) that not only did we need to start conducting training classes on our down time, but we also had to do PT. If that wasn't enough, we'd also have a PT test in the near future. The classes I could understand a bit. It would do us well to brush up on things we didn't do too often, and even on some of the things we did all the time. Practice and proficiency were good for us.

It was up to the NCOs in the squads and sections to devise what classes we'd teach. I had grown pretty annoyed with the fact that I was the only one who knew how to switch out the encryption codes in the radio, so I decided on that class easily.

The other NCOs picked a range of things; weapons assembly and disassembly, battle drills, medevac procedures, proper radio etiquette, first aid, and someone brought up the fact that everyone needed to sight their weapons in again at the range on Kalsu.

PT was another story. A lot of the men went to the small gym on Kalsu and lifted weights as a way to blow off steam after a patrol. I never did. To me, going on patrols was physically exhausting. If that didn't do it, then working on the Bradleys or Humvees after the patrol did the trick, and either way the heat took most of the energy out of us. Were it not for that, I saw the logic in keeping us healthy. But there were some people that didn't have duties so physically demanding. A PT test, though?

We could hardly believe it. Normally we had to have weapons, ammunition, and a field dressing with us at all times. Not so when we were doing PT. Either way, we had to do it, and did. SSG Lutz was a runner, when we had a chance we'd run around the perimeter of Kalsu or go to the gym. They set our PT test for some time in October. I wondered if I'd pass it, but didn't put too much thought into it. I didn't care much, either. My time in the Army was rapidly coming to a close.

I managed to settle back into a routine that included the training, anyway. It was only a couple of hours of our days "off" that were taken up by the added training. The rest of the time was more or less ours, and we spent them how we chose. Nothing much had changed, but we did enjoy slightly better living arrangements. Throughout the tour we had purchased or acquired things to make our few square feet of home more bearable. We added a refrigerator, television, and even a few rugs to the tent. I had added a thin foam mattress to my cot. With a thick sleeping bag on top it was very comfortable, actually. I put a plastic chest of drawers on top of my foot locker, and so was able to have somewhat of a dresser. It was worlds better than living out of a duffel bag. On the side of the drawers facing my bed I taped up pictures from home: Karen, some of my friends, views of my mother's front yard in the wintertime, and anything else that I found comforting.

During down time I also read – a lot. I'd always been an avid reader, and I was thankful that there were tons of free books to be had on FOB Kalsu. The chaplain kept a pretty well-stocked library, my family sent me books, I'd brought a few with me, and all of us traded them around as we read them. I read a little bit of everything. My brother had sent Superman comics which were good for unwinding. A 2nd platoon squad leader, SSG Seth Lombardy, lent me a copy of *Atlas Shrugged* by Ayn Rand. It took me a while to read, but it was engrossing to say the least. SSG Lombardy was as intellectual as they came, and applied it to the technical aspects of a grunt's job. I always admired him for that, and we became friends despite our not working together. I devoured books on military history, especially on the American Revolution and the Civil War. I read some novels, and re-read some of the classics like *1984*. I wasn't incredibly picky. I'd found that reading was a great way to switch gears mentally, and an even better way to calm my mind down enough to sleep. There were other ways to pass the time, too.

We joked around constantly, played pranks, and ribbed one another. We devised a water balloon sling-shot to hurl things at the chow hall, but never used it. We filmed ridiculous videos of us dancing around and goofing off. Lightsaber battles were staged, and Smith came up with an elaborate board game for us to play. We traded music and split up the contents of the plentiful care packages between us. A lot of times we just had conversations; what was going on in the sector, when we thought we were redeploying, how things were going with families. We spent a lot of time together, so naturally we all got pretty close and familiar with one another.

When our section was off duty we watched the pirated DVDs

that were abundant in Iraq. Everyone back home was surprised to learn that we saw films that were in the theaters back in the states. As such, we didn't have to wait until our return to see *Star Wars: Episode III* or any of the other blockbusters that came out that year. Although of terrible quality, they were new movies nonetheless. Most of the soldiers also had personal DVD players. I'd walk into the tent sometimes and find all the lights out and the soldiers lying on their cots with the players on their chest, earphones in place, completely in their own worlds. During the daytime, if we were off, we kept the lights out in the tent so people could sleep if they wanted. Everyone kept quiet during days when we had to get some sleep. Living in such close proximity to one another, we did all we could to keep from driving each other crazy.

That didn't always work, though. If there was one thing I hated about living in a tent it was that there was no such thing as privacy. It kept me from sleeping a lot, actually. We slept close enough to one another that snoring was an issue. Sometimes most of the tent would want to watch a movie or play cards. The majority ruled I wouldn't dare to pull rank on guys for doing what they wanted. As long as men were getting enough rest to perform missions and we didn't have any pressing matters to attend to, it wasn't my place to regulate how they spent their time. If a soldier wanted to play video games all day and had completed all of his work, who was I to tell him not to? There was one thing I learned being an NCO over there, and I took it to heart: there were times that I needed to assert myself and make people do things. There were also times when I needed to leave people alone. Our down time was a good time to leave guys alone. Everyone had their own ways of unwinding, and it was absolutely necessary that they be allowed to do so. We lived in an extremely stressful environment, so there was no reason to add to that stress if I could avoid it.

I understood this, perhaps, because I spent so much time outside the wire. There were a lot of people on Kalsu who didn't understand that aspect of the deployment. It's widely known that there are more support personnel in a combat zone than there are combat arms soldiers. It takes a lot of work to keep operations going, and much of it had to be done on the FOB. I understood this. When it became problematic was when these individuals forgot exactly what it was we did outside the wire. There were those who treated FOB Kalsu like a garrison base back in the United States. We dealt with it all the time. Sometimes coming off of a patrol, wretchedly filthy and sweaty, we'd head straight to the chow hall to eat. (Since they'd curtailed its hours, you simply had to go when it was open. If you didn't have time to clean up beforehand, so be it. We had to eat.) More than a few times I was told to leave and come back with a clean uniform and a shave. We got told to blouse our boots properly, get our hats washed, straighten up our helmet, or whatever else someone decided to point out. Our little pet peeves went the other way. I couldn't stand seeing uniforms that looked like they were pressed, but even worse was how the shoulder holsters for the side arms waved the muzzle around behind its wearer.

Naturally, there was some tension between the soldiers who left the wire daily and the soldiers who never left, or at least spent the majority of their time in the relative safety of the FOB. It was subtle for the most part, but present all the same. We took to calling them 'Fobbits,' a play on the words 'Hobbit' and FOB. It wasn't as if we resented our duty out there. It was more that we felt that when we were back on the FOB we should be given a little leeway. Sometimes, going to the chow hall dirty was necessary. The reason we were so dirty is that we hadn't been around a shower in a week. There were soldiers who took things like showering and eating in a dining facility for granted. I always understood that uniform wear and cleanliness were important, I just felt that the tough, exacting duties we had changed our priorities. Often I heard complaining about the people who didn't leave the FOB hogging what little access to telephones and internet we had. It was true; the grunts didn't have nearly as much time to spend waiting on a phone than others. The resentment stemmed mainly from the fact that the people who seemed to run the FOB did not share the degree of exposure to danger or the stress that accompanied it. There was always plenty of danger and stress for us.

In a way I felt that we were overworked. QRF duty was a good example of the things that led to this thinking. Within our relentless schedule, sometimes we had a day or two for vehicle maintenance or other housekeeping items. During this down time, we'd end up with twelve or so hours of QRF duty for the FOB. During those hours we had to have vehicles and ourselves ready to go into action within minutes. It was even a rule to sleep with boots on. Being on QRF meant that if we were attacked by mortars we'd be dispatched to the area from which the rounds were fired. (The base had radar which detected this.) It could also mean responding to a patrol that had been hit just outside the perimeter, or anything else that was considered an emergency.

The duty itself wasn't the problem. The bad part was that there were hundreds of soldiers who never had to do much out there that could have done it just as well. In other words, the same soldiers left the wire day after day. I understood this was our lot, but at the time it was hard not to be resentful. We were worn out most of the time and coveted our respites back on Kalsu.

The grueling cycle of patrols, raids, and stints at the patrol base continued unabated. The rural area surrounding Diyara turned out to be much larger than Haswah's environs. The canal roads that disappeared into the hazy horizon were endless, it seemed, and we spent most of our time driving around them and visiting the farm houses out there. We'd drive slowly to ensure not slipping off the edges of the road, and most of the time used Humvees. There was always a question of whether those roads would support the weight of a Bradley, and the Humvees were more maneuverable in that terrain, anyway. I didn't mind this at all. Despite the length of time that had passed since both of my rollovers I still fought off panic while riding in the back of a Bradley. I obsessively ensured that chemlites were taped onto all the hatch handles in case we rolled into a canal in the dark. I welcomed a patrol in Humvees anytime, and especially after 1st platoon had its third rollover of the tour.

It was during another hectic changeover in Diyara one night that it happened. Our platoon had travelled out there in two Bradleys and two Humvees. The first three vehicles made it into the patrol base's perimeter before we realized that the rear vehicle, commanded by SSG Bryan, who had taken over my job as SSG Moon's gunner, had fallen into the canal just outside the base.

It wasn't exactly shocking. There were a few reasons why it seemed inevitable. One was that it was pitch black that night, so even with night vision the driver and BC could hardly see the road. Green and black shapes were the best we could hope for on nights like that, and depth perception was nil. Additionally, the Bradley's turret had been facing the backwards to cover the convoy's rear. As such, the BC's hatch actually obscured the commander's field of vision. No one was at fault, really, it was just bad luck. The Bradley's front had gone over the edge of the canal. Once it started, the weight of the engine pulled the vehicle down into the ditch, probably fifteen feet in depth. Once the front of the Bradley hit the bottom, its back end tumbled over, leaving the vehicle upside down in the ditch. It took a while to notice that it had happened in all the hectic business of the changeover.

Steppe was one of the first soldiers out there first trying to help the occupants out, and he described a pretty bad scene to me later. SSG Bryan and SPC Villalobos, the gunner, were trapped in the turret. Upside down, their hatches were just above the surface of the water. The driver and Larson, the single passenger, managed to crawl out of the rear troop door hatch with great difficulty, but it took digging through some mud and a little swimming on the part of the SSG Bryan and SPC Villalobos to get out. When I talked to Villalobos later, he said he was sure they would drown in the muddy, rank water, and it had freaked him out. And especially rank it was. Once they were fished out, they came back into the patrol base. They were covered in canal water and oil that had spilled out of the Bradley. Steppe was as well, since he'd volunteered to climb around in the thing gathering up what weapons and equipment he could. They reeked. Imagine bathing in sewage on a hot day – it smelled the same.

The guys who rolled over were also extremely shaken up. I could relate. Not only did they just face their deaths, but drowning in the shitty canal water of Iraq, in the dark, was a terrible way to go. They probably realized what I'd known for a while, that after the prospect of such a death being blown up by insurgents' bombs was preferable. I didn't need to discuss it with them. I could see it in their faces and had been through it before. I felt sorry for them, because a rollover was something that could make even the most mundane things frightening beyond belief. If we did a lot of anything in Iraq, and especially around Diyara, it was drive around canal roads. I was pretty sure that now they'd carry that nagging feeling of claustrophobia and fear of drowning with them forever. I hoped not, but after what Villalobos had said, I doubted it. Shaken up and covered in filth, the platoon

201

we relieved took them back to Kalsu to get cleaned up.

I was glad to be in charge of the first guard shift. I made sure all the machine guns in the positions were switched out and that my men had stashed their gear in our assigned room. I didn't have to deal with the hectic things like unloading fuel and food. As everyone got settled into the towers, and the departing platoon left the base, things settled down. I was left to my own guard position and my own thoughts. The wrecker had come out and was lifting the Bradley out of the water down below with some difficulty. The thirty-three tons of armored vehicle had fallen in partly because the road had crumbled at the edge of the canal. It was my worst fear – it had been after my first patrol and would continue to be until I left Iraq. I did a radio check on the ICOM, undid my chin strap to keep its foulness off my face, and peered through the green murkiness of my NVGs and the sweat that accumulated around my eyes. The next two hours I'd think about drowning in a Bradley. Although I'd managed to stop dwelling on the fear of death by enemy action, the mundane was still terrifying.

The cycles continued, and we stayed busy enough that time passed quickly. Before long it was August, and we actually reached the point in our tour that we could say it was two-thirds over. August was quite a month, though. Edging that close to our redeployment made going home a reality for most of us. It was no longer some far off, unattainable goal that we shouldn't even think about. As such, no one took any chances. Although we had become familiar with the range of operations we had to conduct, and could plan a raid in our sleep, we got careful. The gunners in the Humvees were more apt to take warning shots. Drivers navigated the canal roads gingerly, and if they didn't the gunners and TCs reminded them to do so. In short, everyone saw that they'd made it this far and had a real chance of surviving the tour, and everyone had become inured to taking shots at Iraqis.

Sometimes, though, I took chances I shouldn't have. During a maintenance day, SSG Diaz poked his head into our tent. He was short, stocky, animated guy who had been with Echo for a long time. He was originally the HQ platoon sergeant, but had been tasked with being in charge of EOD's escort.

"Hey, who wants to go blow a bunch of shit up? EOD is doing a controlled detonation at Hateen," he asked while looking at Steppe. He knew who to ask.

"Fuck yeah. Count me in, when are we going SSG Diaz?" Steppe couldn't contain his smile.

"Hey man, as soon as you get enough guys together to man a truck we're going to roll." I wasn't doing anything else, so I volunteered. Graham did, too. The three of us got our gear together and made our way to the motorpool to ready the truck. Echo's HQ platoon had filled a five-ton armored truck with ordnance: Hellfire missiles, mortar rounds, artillery shells, defused IEDs, and dud rounds of all sorts. The EOD vehicle and SSG Diaz, riding in another Humvee, met us at the gate with the munitions-laden truck. It was an ad hoc mission, so there was no kind of briefing besides an admonishment to keep a safe distance from the five-ton. It had enough munitions on it to create quite a large explosion if it got hit. The EOD truck was packed full of C4 as well. Steppe and I glanced at one another and jokingly agreed that our mothers were better off not knowing we'd volunteered for this.

When we arrived at a dirt field in Hateen's expansive complex, we off-loaded the ordnance and placed it in a large pile, probably twenty-five feet by twenty-five feet, and at least four feet high. The EOD guys tossed us long, rectangular blocks of C4 and instructed us to place them on the ordnance, making sure that all of the blocks touched one another. The grunts han-dled the stuff more gingerly than they did. We weren't used to it, and even though we knew it wouldn't blow up without a fuse, it was still unsettling to have it tossed our way so casually. I was surprised that there was no exact science to its placement. After emptying two crates of C4, they told us to move at least five-hundred meters away to keep clear of the blast radius. They knew we'd want to be as close as was safe. Steppe and I agreed that an estimated four-hundred meters was plenty of distance, drove our Humvee out there, and waited.

"Fire in the hole," came over the frequency. Graham and Steppe both had their digital cameras out. When it went off, it was deafening even at that distance. The Hellfires and mortar rounds shot off in every direction, and the mushroom cloud be-gan to take shape almost immediately. I noticed the ground be-tween us and the blast ripple as the shockwave approached. When it hit, it felt like a powerful, hot gust of wind – it was over in an instant but its strength was impressive. It was forceful enough to hurt a little, actually. As the mushroom cloud grew, debris began to rain down on us. There were hot little pieces of metal and rock landing on the Humvee and on top of our hel-mets. It was over in a few seconds, and the whooping and yelling could be heard from the men in the other vehicles in the dis-tance.

It was one of the most remarkable things I'd seen over there. It was a huge explosion, like something out of an action movie, and we could enjoy it since it wasn't directed at us We happily got in our truck and drove back to the FOB, glad that we'd vol-unteered for something like this, and gladder still that we didn't get hit on the way out there. As we cruised back to Kalsu we were all smiles. We'd finally gotten to see something blow up that wasn't ending someone's life. It was all about the little things.

11

As summer waned and September rolled around, the situation in AO Battle continued to change. Some of it was progress, some of it a regression. Operational Detachment Echo's Iraqi Army soldiers deployed to Diyara patrol base as a step towards the transition of operational responsibility to them. Although they didn't take a leading role in operations or providing security at the patrol base yet, they did conduct their own patrols, and often we took them as dismounts for QRF missions from Diyara. We had doubts that they'd be self-sustaining by October, but any progress was progress. The security situation wasn't improving in the meantime, though. The IEDs were still abundant.

The Iraqis in AO Battle were killing each other a lot more as time went on as well, and in late August and early September we could see that their fight was intensifying. We had chances to observe this first-hand, and the Iraqis began to speak about it more often. With their help, we had ascertained that Iraqis who actively helped us accomplish our mission were targeted by insurgents, but other than that we really didn't understand what was going on across the country or in our corner of the Sunni Triangle. (We didn't follow any sort of news.) What we could see with our own eyes was disturbing enough, though.

Steppe and I were on QRF duty one day in Diyara. Around mid-morning, SFC Torgerson came into our room and instructed us to get two Bradleys ready to venture out onto Cleveland. An Iraqi contractor had been gunned down on the road.

No patrols were expected to come by anytime soon, so we had to retrieve the body. It was just a couple of kilometers away near the bridge, and just out of the sight and range of the weapons from the patrol base. Whether or not the insurgents were waiting there to ambush whoever came along to get the body was an open question, but it was one that we didn't think much about. We were tired, the day was already hot, and my only thoughts were getting it over with as quickly as possible. Steppe and I were both thinking the same thing as we mounted the Bradley's commanders' hatches and did our radio checks: who cared about an Iraqi corpse? We didn't want to risk our necks just to bring him back to the patrol base.

It only took a couple of minutes to get out there. When we approached the truck the Iraqi had been driving, we stopped a few meters short of it and had our gunners scan the horizon for anyone watching the area. They didn't see anything out of the ordinary. Not having any soldiers to send out to the truck, Steppe and I decided that we would dismount and take care of it, leaving the gunners in charge of the vehicles. I hopped down off my Bradley with my carbine in hand. When Steppe and I approached the cab of the truck, it was pretty easy to see what had happened. There were several bullet holes in the windshield of the truck, and the driver was in his seat, mouth open, also riddled with bullet holes. He'd been dead long enough that the blood had stopped flowing and was congealed in the floor of the truck. Not ten meters in front of the truck was a scattered pile of shell casings from an AK-47. Steppe and I looked at one another.

"I mean fucking brazen, right? It looks like these dudes just hopped out in front of the truck and shot him. Ballsy," I said, shaking my head. Steppe nodded.

"Wish they had those sorts of balls with us. Well, let's get this asshole in a body bag and get the fuck out of here." I nodded in agreement. It was stifling hot, and the corpse was already stinking. We had one of the Bradleys pull in front of the truck to cover us while we extricated the corpse. We weren't exactly taking our time doing so. We didn't have to search the truck or anything, just get the body out. Steppe had his Bradley driver drop the ramp so he could retrieve a body bag while I climbed up into the cab of the truck. The smell was awful. There were flies buzzing around inside, swarming on the corpse's open eyes and mouth. When they started buzzing around me and landing on my face I shuddered. It was disgusting. Beyond that there was no emotional reaction besides being annoyed. Impatiently, I considered how to get him out of the truck. I pulled the knife off of my body armor and sliced the seatbelt off of him. Then, stepping out of the cab, I pulled on his arm until he flopped out of the truck.

"Oh, Jesus man. Dead weight, huh?" Steppe asked with a laugh.

"Man, I'm not putting this guy in the back of a Bradley. We'll never get the smell out. What do you think? Put him on the back deck?" I asked. I was referring to the small area behind the turret and above the troop compartment.

"Yeah, if we can get him up there." Steppe yelled into the Bradley for the Wantz to come out and help us. He wasn't very motivated. I didn't blame him. Neither were we.

Not exactly gingerly, Steppe and I maneuvered the corpse into a body bag and zipped it up. We considered how to get the bag on top of my Bradley. Steppe mentioned that we'd either have to man-handle it up there or heave it. We decided on heaving it. We picked up either end of the body bag and began swinging it back and forth to gain momentum.

"Okay, 1...2...3," I counted down. We let go of the handles. The body bag hit the top half of the ramp, then hit the ground with a thud. We laughed. Steppe told Wantz to get in the middle and help it up there. We decided to hold on to it this time. With another count, another heave, and Wantz's push from the middle, we finally managed to get the body bag on top of the Bradley. When we mounted back up I got on the radio to inform the patrol base that we were headed back. I asked what they wanted us to do with the truck. Get it out of the middle of the road was the reply. Steppe yelled at me from his turret. Simple, we could just nudge it off the road with the Bradley. After the five minutes it took to plow the Bradley into the truck and scoot it off the road, we drove back to the patrol base.

When we arrived there were a few IA soldiers standing around their half of the building watching us return with grim faces. I didn't pay any mind to them. When the Bradley was parked my gunner and I climbed out of the turret and stood above the body. We didn't discuss how we'd get the body down. We just nodded and kicked it off. It landed heavily in the dust. The Iraqi soldiers started talking amongst themselves in Arabic. It looked like they were pissed off that we were handling the body so roughly. It wasn't like the dead Iraqi was an insurgent, but to me it was just another corpse. I hadn't killed him, nor had I created the situation in which he was killed. I simply didn't care. His life mattered little to me. I walked back into the base to report to our platoon sergeant that we were back and everyone was accounted for. I told him the body was outside.

With that, I grabbed a bottle of water and some soap and tried to clean the smell of rotting corpse off of my hands. It was a stubborn, evil smell, to say the least. With only another thirty minutes or so before I had to go back on guard, I briefly considered eating and decided against it. Instead I walked out to the front courtyard and smoked a couple of cigarettes. The body bag laid there in the dust.

Shortly after that, I was on a night patrol cruising up and

down Tampa. Patrolling in Humvees this time, I was in my usual spot behind the lieutenant, listening to the sparse radio traffic that night. The breeze coming from the gunner's hatch, despite smelling like Iraq always smelled, was refreshingly cool. I watched the side of the road as we drove, looking for anything distinguishable in the green and black luminescence of my night vision. Hooking the radio handset to my chin strap, I pulled on the back straps of my helmet to tighten it. Not only did they work loose on their own, but the weight of the night vision attached to the front pulled the helmet down over my eyes if I didn't keep it tightened. I overheard some commotion on the radio. There had been a convoy passing through earlier that had seen what they thought was a firefight near CP 20 on Tampa. I listened as they confirmed there were no friendly units in the area. After relaying this to 1LT Kelley, he had me tell them we were on our way to the location. HQ ordered us to keep our distance.

We pulled up to the overpass of CP 20. We could see green tracers zipping back and forth a few kilometers off to the east. The staccato of gunfire was audible, and there were dull thumps of what we figured were mortars or RPGs. It was a full-scale firefight. We all gazed at the flashes of light on the horizon. I wondered then what exactly it was that we were doing out there. If we weren't there to prevent the Iraqis from killing each other, then what purpose did we really serve? As I thought more about it, the reasoning behind letting that particular firefight continue became clearer. There really was no way to determine which side we should help. We could have added a lot of firepower to the fray, but it would have been pointless. We would more than likely be shot at by both sides on our approach, so we watched as spectators.

The following day we took CPT Ramirez out to the area of the firefight. It was easy to find. We made our way down the canal road west of CP 20 a couple of kilometers and simply asked Iraqis where the fight had been. They pointed out the house which had come under attack, and we pulled up to it.

It was abandoned. The mud and brick structure was riddled with bullet holes. One of the walls was partially burned. Another wall was collapsed, and looked as if it had taken a direct hit from a mortar or RPG. When I walked onto the roof, my boots kicked around piles and piles of brass shell casings. There had indeed been one hell of a fight. It was eerily quiet and deserted; there were no bodies, no signs of life at all. We could not determine the position of the attackers had been after searching the surrounding area. We took photographs with digital cameras, wrote down the coordinates of the place, and left.

The firefight we'd witnessed, the mutilated corpses that appeared near Haswah during the beginning of our tour, the mass grave we thought we'd found the day after Prince had been killed, and the murdered Iraqi contractor confirmed what we had been hearing from the Iraqis throughout the tour. There was a significant amount of violence directed at Iraqis that sided with us or that were neutral, and the levels of violence had increased the longer we were there. In February and March there had been car bombs which targeted civilians in Haswah. One of them detonated just outside the perimeter of the patrol base and killed several Iraqi bystanders. An IED had destroyed a billboard with a propaganda placard just outside of town as well. It was clear that the violence wasn't always directed at us. We were told as much, and I noticed small things on my own that pointed to some of the reasons for it.

On a foot patrol in Diyara one day I remember walking past a group of kids. We were far enough into the tour that we didn't pay any attention to them anymore. (If they were conspicuously absent, though, it usually meant trouble.) Most of the young ones had an innocent fascination with being around soldiers, but the older ones seemed to resent our presence. Once, passing a secondary school in Haswah, our patrol was pelted with rocks. We couldn't very well shoot at them, or even shoot into the air, for fear of pissing off the whole town. We just ran away. But on this foot patrol in Diyara, I realized that these kids hated each other, too. One of the little boys around us ran up to another kid, smaller than himself, and started kicking him. He spat on him and slapped him around. I looked over at the interpreter and asked what in the hell the smaller kid had done wrong. Well, nothing, it turned out. The older boy was a Shia, the younger one a Sunni.

It was right then that I realized that our mission as US soldiers was much, much more complex than I ever could have realized. We were dealing with two segments of Iraqis that had a deep-rooted hatred for one another. It was puzzling, because to us an Iraqi was an Iraqi. While we understood the distinction between Sunni and Shia, and even that Saddam had been a Sunni, we couldn't understand how such a division could give them cause to kill one another. It was a bit of a mystery, and a disturbing one at that. But we still did our best to win all of them over to our side.

There was a campaign for the hearts and minds that was a part of our mission, too, and since we had started from scratch in Diyara it was recognizable. For one, we were expected to treat Iraqis with a modicum of respect. It was clear that our superiors didn't want us to terrorize the people of Iraq. Instead, it was our job to show them that we were a better choice of allegiance than insurgents. On nearly every patrol we had to load boxes of propaganda flyers, Iraqi flags, or candy, for example, as part of psychological operations (PSYOPs). We kicked soccer balls to the kids from the roof of Diyara patrol base. We had specific missions for the distribution of 'humanitarian aid bags' filled with soap and food items. I can't say we were enthusiastic about it;

most of the time we just lobbed the stuff in their general direction. After one of 3rd platoon's humanitarian missions was hit by an IED outside a small village, it just seemed dumb to most of us, and although we understood the purpose, we hated doing it all the same.

We also undertook projects that would help the Iraqis live better. Shortly after our arrival in Diyara, we installed generator and water pump within our compound for the town to use. To maintain it, our officers had found a technically capable Iraqi man that lived in town. We eventually learned to trust him, and we realized that providing electricity and water to the town demonstrated our interest in helping them probably more than anything else. Behind the scenes our officers negotiated and built relationships with tribal and religious leaders in the area. But the prerequisite for any of this work to be effective was security, and as grunts it was our primary focus to root out the enemies. Sometimes we were more successful than others.

In late September, we did a raid on a farmhouse a few kilometers away from the patrol base. It was memorable. One reason is that it hadn't cooled down that night at all. It was one of the hottest I remember; sticky, drenched in sweat, and difficulty-thinking-straight-hot. We called it 'stupid hot,' because it was almost beyond comprehension. We prepared for the raid in the inner courtyard of the patrol base, the exhaust from the window-sized air conditioners surrounding it added to the heat. We had satellite photos, grid coordinates, and a general idea that the targets were major players in the insurgency. From the photos, we could tell that the house was just off of a canal road, and it was nearly a straight shot from the patrol base. It was a platoon-sized operation, and even though the target was on a canal road, we used two Bradleys and an M113. I had to ride in the M113 with my fire team. Since that particular vehicle hadn't been used on missions much, I spent most of the day ensuring that it was stocked with proper equipment and supplies, the radios were in working order, and that it was in good working condition. I probably should have been sleeping.

The plan was simple. We would drive right up to the house, and then my squad would dismount and run to the door. The other squad, split up between the Bradleys, would dismount and take up blocking positions around the house to cover escape routes and ensure that no one came to help the insurgents. It was a small farm. Everything looked straightforward enough from the satellite pictures, and we'd done enough raids by this point that no one was abnormally amped up for this one. We did our normal round of planning, the same as we'd done in Haswah, but on a smaller scale. SSG Lutz told me to make sure the guys had their equipment in order, and, as usual, to be careful.

I was less worried about being careful on the raid itself than I was being careful on the drive to the target, which was saying a lot since I was going to be the first one in the house. The canal roads just outside of Diyara were notoriously narrow. Although an M113 was narrower and lighter than a Bradley, its driver's night sight was of a lesser quality, and the soldier who was chosen to drive it made me nervous as well. Luckily, an M113 has a large hatch above the troop compartment which we were going to keep open. It was less a safety measure than a way to stay as cool as possible, but it served both purposes.

The tension of anticipation grew once we piled into the back of the track. We were wedged in tightly. The heat was unbearable. All of us had sweat running up our cloth helmet covers, our faces were wet, and it was a night when you could sweat through your boots. Someone broke out a digital camera and photographed us on the ride. We looked tired, hot, and dirty when I saw the pictures later. Our jumping off signal was going to be the ramp dropping. Not knowing how long the trip to the target would be, I settled in uneasily. I kept wondering if it was possible to bail out of the M113 if I felt it beginning to tip over.

We rolled to a stop. I flipped down my night vision as the ramp lowered. From the photos I knew the target house was off to the right of the road, and we'd halted just short of it. As the first man out of the vehicle, I took off at a jog towards the house, taking care not to outpace Graham and McFarland behind me. When I stepped down off of the canal road I sunk into some mud up to my knees. Still trying to be quiet, our whole squad struggled through the slop. It was deep and thick, the kind of sticky mud that stunk and tried to suck your boots off. There was nothing quick about that little jaunt. If I wasn't so keyed up I may have laughed, but right then it was a dangerous hindrance. We needed to get inside quickly, because it was unlikely that the occupants of the house hadn't heard the armored vehicles pulling up and dropping ramp. My team and SSG Lutz made it to the door split seconds after I did.

"Ready?" I asked in a whisper behind me. We had stacked on the door – all of us in a line waiting to go in after I kicked down the door. SSG Lutz gave me the signal to kick it down. I lifted one leg up to do so and fell flat on my back, my muddy boots slipping on the smooth tile of the porch.

Uh oh, I thought, this is not going well. McFarland stepped right over me and kicked in the door. The fire team flooded into the house without a word, turning the flashlights on their rifles on as they did so. It only took a second. I scrambled to my feet and followed them inside. SSG Lutz was already in there directing men around the house. Within half a minute we had cleared its entirety and began moving up to the roof to see if anyone was sleeping up there. There was no furniture of any kind, actually no signs at all that the house had been occupied. With that the tension disappeared. It was just an abandoned house. Drenched in sweat, we all met up in the front room and had a good laugh.

"Goddamn, you went straight down," SSG Lutz said as he laughed.

"Yeah I did. No traction on that porch," I said. I was chuckling about it now, although minutes earlier the rush of adrenaline had me ready to shoot someone, and terrified that I was on my back when the door was breached. I was glad the house was empty; it made for a short night. We radioed the men in the vehicles that we'd either hit the wrong house or the occupants were long gone. The lieutenant dismounted and met us inside. He agreed with us that there was no sign of anyone living in there for some time, but we had the right house. The element of surprise and stealth irrelevant now, we had a cigarette, took some pictures, and laughed about the guys who had been forced to slog through the mud all the way to their blocking positions.

1LT Kelley decided to have us question the people in the house across the road from our target. Thoroughly drenched in sweat, I hated the idea of going back inside anything. Their house was very small, though, and didn't take long to secure. At the rear of the house was a kitchen. When I opened the door to it there must have been dozens of huge rats that squeaked and scurried away. I was disgusted at the sight, and could hardly believe the squalor of this house. The farmhouses were nothing like the dwellings in the towns. I could have been looking at a hut from the Middle Ages if not for the bare light bulbs hanging from the ceiling. While I'd been searching the back rooms with my team (although I stopped short of a thorough search of that kitchen), the lieutenant and our interpreter questioned the old man. He was a sorry sight himself, terribly skinny and wearing their traditional garb. He chain-smoked cigarettes as they talked with him.

No, he told us, no one had lived in that house for many months. They were surprised that we'd raided it. He said he was sorry he couldn't be more helpful. We mounted up and left them, concluding our mission.

We were happy when we got back to the patrol base. Although soaked entirely through with sweat, my squad managed to smile for a picture. We may not have captured any bad guys, but no one had been hurt. There were no IEDs on the way, no rollovers, and there was even a good laugh about the mud-slog we'd had to do. The higher echelons of command may not have called it a successful raid, but we did. There was nothing we could do to change the accuracy of the intelligence we were provided to accomplish our mission. I often wondered where it originated, since for the most part it wasn't close to accurate. Many of us suspected that our raids rarely resulted in the capture of real insurgents, not that we had any way of knowing.

That's not to say that these enemies remained elusive all of the time. 2nd platoon had been in a firefight one night on the outskirts of Diyara and had killed a couple of insurgents. 3rd platoon had been ambushed with RPGs and small arms fire west of CP 20, and we continued to interdict IEDs on a regular basis – either by setting them off or, more rarely, finding them before they hit a patrol. There was enough to keep us on our toes and alert when we were on operations. More often it seemed like a wild goose chase and endless driving and walking around. It's been said many times that warfare is long periods of boredom interrupted by moments of sheer terror. That's exactly what was happening. Sometimes, of course, the moments of terror came from unlikely places.

Since ASR Cleveland was Echo's lifeline to the Diyara we continued to focus our attention there. We'd stepped up the amount of OPs we did, and had recently begun doing squad-sized ambushes. A lot of times we'd do the ambushes in conjunction with our patrols, and one night shortly after our raid the lieutenant had decided that an ambush near the bridge on

Cleveland would be in order. We went over the fairly simple plan one evening before heading out on patrol. We would take two Bradleys so that all of us dismounts could be together, not having to man a Humvee. Right around the bridge we were to dismount and head north on a dirt road, setting in an ambush with the hopes of catching insurgents making their way out to Cleveland under the cover of darkness. The difference between an ambush and an OP to me was that we'd be able to shoot. Seven of us brought to bear a lot more firepower than three.

There was no special preparation for an ambush. We took the usual squad equipment; handheld thermal sight, backpack with detainee materials, man-pack radio, GPS, and the like. We had two SAWs, two grenade launchers, and several rifles. In fact, everything went as a normal patrol would, except this time when we got out of the Bradleys by the bridge, our rides kept on going until getting in the patrol base. They'd stand by there and be ready if we needed help, but for now we were on our own. We felt safe with each other even as the sound of the Bradleys faded down the road.

We took cover and waited until they were gone before stepping out onto the dirt road. It was eerily quiet, lacking even the animal noises or the gurgling of the canal typical of this area. Silently, we made our way down the canal road until coming upon an intersection that made a right angle. SSG Lutz pointed to us individually then pointed to spots on the sides of both roads, placing us in positions. When we were set, we formed an 'L.' It was a textbook infantry ambush. We could observe all around us, were behind the cover of the elevated canal road, and could concentrate our fire on the area we thought was the most likely avenue of approach of the enemy.

SSG Lutz took his place in the middle of the angle we'd formed beside the radio operator, with me on the other side of him. He had me call in to the patrol base that we'd set up our position and would call in SITREPs every quarter-hour. We settled in to wait, hoping we'd bag some insurgents making their way to plant bombs on the road.

We'd been there an hour or more. The moon was bright enough that I could see well with my night vision, and we could hear very well in the silence. No one spoke, and all kept as still as possible. Just like on OPs, it felt a lot like deer hunting that I'd done as a kid – it was just hotter, and we were hunting human beings. From a distance I heard the beating of rotor blades. This was not unusual. Apaches patrolled our sector in pairs pretty much constantly. SSG Lutz told me to get my IR strobe light out and turn it on, and to pass the word along the line. Within seconds, all of us were blinking in the night vision. No one wanted to be shot up by our own helicopters. SSG Lutz then asked me to get on the radio and make sure squadron had our location and knew what we were doing. The Apaches rarely monitored our frequencies unless they sent us chasing after a certain vehicle or something, and we could never raise them on theirs. Our man pack radio wasn't strong enough to reach the FOB, so we had to relay everything through Diyara. They assured me that they'd inform the FOB, and in turn the Apaches. I started getting nervous.

We didn't know how long this would take, but the Apaches had already crested the treeline a few hundred meters away. Our IR strobes were designed to be seen from the air, and each of us had IR reflective tape on our sleeves and the tops of our helmets. This was still no guarantee they could identify us as friendly forces. The tension grew. It was probably good that the other men in the squad couldn't hear me talking on the radio or to SSG Lutz, as I was getting antsy.

"Diyara X-ray this is Reaper Red three Alpha, over," I said in a loud whisper.

"Red three Alpha this is Diyara X-ray, go ahead, over," 1LT

Kelley's deep voice came crackling over the net.

"Diyara X-ray, these birds are on top of us and I'm again requesting confirmation that they know our coordinates, over."

"Red three Alpha, wait one." I could have screamed. I was scared now. I'd seen what those choppers could do to a target. They passed overhead and made a wide turn behind us. Then they started flying back, lower this time. By now we were waving our IR strobes in the air, hoping that the pilots would waggle their wings in recognition. They didn't. When they got directly above us they just started circling our position.

"Holy fuck, we're going to get lit up," I said under my breath. I figured they were just then radioing the FOB to figure out who it was they were circling.

"Red three Alpha this is Diyara X-ray, Warmonger has your location marked and is moving off station." 'Warmonger' was the Apaches' call sign. The relief was instant.

"Diyara, Red three Alpha, tango mike," I replied, using radio jargon to tell the lieutenant thanks. I could have hugged him for the relief I felt. I told SSG Lutz we were safe, and he had us pass it along down the line. Most of the men put their IR strobes in the dirt in front of them, still being cautious. The Apaches made a couple more circles around us then flew away. I wondered exactly what kind of support they offered us if we couldn't usually communicate with them directly. We stayed for another hour or so, but SSG Lutz figured that the Apaches had deterred anyone from using that route against us for the night. We marched back to the patrol base and had a good bitch session about the communications with the pilots.

Friendly fire was a real concern. Snipers out on Tampa had been shot at by passing convoys on occasion because convoys never monitored the frequencies in areas they traversed. We were careful around sector boundaries for the same reason. We were in a precision business where the slightest details mattered, and we got constant reminders.

At the end of the summer an element of Echo Troop was out in the boonies helping the artillerymen of the 155th on Kalsu register their guns. Registration of an artillery piece basically meant ensuring that the guns hit the coordinates at which the gunners were aiming. It required a team on the ground near the target to call in small corrections. By calculating the projectile's actual trajectory compared to the information put into the targeting system, the artilleryman could adjust for conditions. It's somewhat like a highly technical version of Kentucky windage with a 155mm artillery shell. It was important to select a large, uninhabited area for this procedure owing to the fact that the guns may be off by a few hundred meters. We learned that they could be off much further than that.

Through the grapevine, we heard that the 155th gunners missed their target by several thousand meters. It was far enough away that the observers could only see a plume of smoke in the distance. Fearing hitting our own troops or innocent civilians, the rest of the registration mission was cancelled, and CPT Ramirez led a patrol to the point of impact to assess the damage. The howitzer round had gone through the roof on an Iraqi family's home. It killed several of the family members and completely destroyed the house.

It was a costly mistake. For the rest of the tour Echo took care of the family who had been hit. We compensated them monetarily, trucked supplies to their home, and did everything in our power to save face with them. If winning the hearts and minds of normal Iraqis was difficult before, for this family it would be impossible. Mistakes happened, but we did our best to be professionals in spite of the sometimes impossible situation.

The men of Echo Troop believed themselves to be among the best in the squadron. This idea was reinforced by the fact that for as long as I could remember, Echo had been given the toughest jobs to be had in the squadron. It was why we'd been sent to Haswah in the beginning, and why we were dispatched to Diyara later. We knew we were the main effort. It may have been a compliment to our skills as soldiers, but being the go-getters for a squadron in the Sunni Triangle had cost us dearly. We were glad when Hotel Company was finally re-assigned to AO Battle in July. They'd taken casualties outside of Haswah shortly after arriving, but the feeling of having another 2-11 in-fantry company to share some of the burden was welcomed. We knew they were good, and would make an impact in our sector. We needed it.

In the simplest of terms we were getting tired. By that Sep-tember, complacency became a problem, somewhat inured as we were to the dangers we faced. It was a combination of the effects of growing used to our jobs over there and realizing that our alertness, useful though it was, didn't prevent us being at-tacked. We'd even grown used to mortar attacks on Kalsu – so much so, in fact, that we went to our bunkers almost begrudg-ingly. It almost seemed that we were getting lazy, and may have appeared so on the surface. Sometimes a soldier would hold his rifle lower, sometimes we'd get out of the sweltering Bradley a little slower. Constant tension and fear could only be sustained for so long before a person feels the effects of being strung out. We were getting there.

12

Before I knew it, the blur that was the summer was over and October rolled around. The daytime temperatures still soared, but it wasn't as bad, and the days were shorter. Our remaining time in Iraq was considerably shorter as well. We still didn't know exactly when we would depart, but most of the rumors floating around suggested we'd be going home in January or February. As I'd learned coming into Iraq, deployment was an amazingly complex and time consuming process for an armored cavalry squadron. It was a process which had taken months before even boarding a plane, but it had not started on Kalsu as of yet. The Iraqi Army had not taken over responsibility for the sector yet, either, so it was business as usual for the time being, and I tried not to think too much about going home. There was plenty to keep us busy. Besides the twelve-hour patrols from Kalsu, stints at Diyara, and shifts at the overpass on CP 18, we spent a lot of time working on vehicles.

Pulling maintenance on Bradleys at Irwin may have been hard work, but doing it in Iraqi weather was brutal. It was a constant process. The tempo of our operations started out high and did not diminish as the tour went on, so the wear and tear on the armored vehicles was extreme. In the US, a Bradley would be driven a hundred miles or so in a month. Its actual operation time was quite short, limited as it was to training missions. At that, the terrain the vehicles navigated was the Mojave Desert. The wear on the treads and rubber track pads traversing dirt was mild compared to the baking hot asphalt and concrete of the major roads in our sector of Iraq. It took no time at all for the pads to disintegrate, leaving the metal track shoes to eat up the road and become brittle themselves. (It's probably why we flipped a Bradley early in the tour.) Simply put, we were driving our vehicles to death.

Most of the days that we didn't have missions were devoted to maintaining these vehicles. Dismounts and crews alike pitched in to help. As a former crewmember, I was adamant that the soldiers who rode in the vehicles contributed to their maintenance. Many times in Fort Irwin I'd spent hours at the motorpool while the dismounts did training classes or shammed out. After having been a dismount team leader for a while, I realized that we depended on our vehicles' operability just as much as the crews did, and any maintenance problem which occurred out on a mission would affect us equally. On certain days the entire platoon would go to the motorpool and work all day in the searing sun and heat. We changed the tracks, replaced shocks, helped clean the weapons systems, and trouble-shot problems with Echo's mechanics as much as we could. The work was somewhat complex, and took a lot of physical effort.

Working on the track treads and pads required the removal of several pieces of armor called 'skirts,' each weighing upwards of one-hundred pounds, fastened to the Bradley's hull with large bolts. Thankfully, each Bradley was equipped with an impact wrench. It took one soldier holding the armor piece and another working the impact wrench to remove them. Once the top of the track was exposed, we could unfasten the track shoes themselves. Each shoe was connected to the other by pin running lengthwise through bushings. To detach them, a nut was removed and a metal pin had to be pushed through with the use of a metal spike and a sledgehammer. Some came apart easier than others, and the moon dust of the motorpool made it tricky. We often had to dig out a space in which to work, and dropping a bolt or tool in the deep stuff meant it was lost forever. Once detached, we drove the Bradley off of the treads and were left with thirty feet of track. We had to perform that entire procedure to change a single track shoe, and had done so countless times throughout the tour.

Sometimes we had to change out the entire track system, which required taking the whole thing apart in sections of seven track shoes each and replacing them. (They came in slabs of seven, and we had to turn in old ones in the same way.) Each shoe weighed ten pounds or more. The track sections were laid flat, hammered into place with a sledge, and a pin was driven through to attach it all together. Once it assembled, a soldier got in the front of the Bradley, lifted up an end, and draped over the sprocket while a driver was moving the Bradley backwards. Once the teeth of the sprocket caught the track, the soldier continued to guide it rearward until it was laid over the entire suspension and the ends met up. To attach it, we had clamps that pulled the shoes together by tightening them, and again a track pin was driven through and a nut was affixed to hold it in place. To say the least, it was back-breaking work.

Maintaining the Humvees wasn't nearly as bad. Their main source of trouble was engine wear. Although they'd been outfitted with larger engines to sustain the extra weight of the armor their constant use still wore them out. At any given time, a quarter of our vehicles were inoperable for one reason or another. This fact complicated the planning of patrols and raids more than any other contingency, and it ensured that any time we had on the FOB would be devoted in large part to working in the motorpool. Still, doing that kind of work was preferable to braving the IED-laden roads. At least we could take breaks and eat in the dining facility, and at the end of the day we could lounge in our air conditioned tent. It was hard to believe that kind of life was all that was known for many soldiers on Kalsu. When we were back on the FOB, we lived as they did.

That meant that our PT and training continued when we weren't busy with other tasks. That October, the time to take our PT test finally arrived. I was glad to be getting it out of the way. I informed my soldiers that I didn't mind if their performance wasn't exactly shining on this one. We would have another opportunity to do better in the US. I would run a pace that was above passing, and all I expected was that they keep up with me. As a combat leader, I was more worried about them exhausting themselves than achieving a high score. The next day we would be patrolling, and keeping them healthy and sharp for that was my top priority. Everyone did well with the sit-ups and push-ups included in the test, but I worried about the run. The dust had been severe for the past few weeks, and it affected my breathing. I was worried about the wrong things, it turned out.

We had charted out a two-mile course for the run that ran almost to the FOB's front gate before turning down the road where the interpreters and laundry service were situated. From there, it was another turn to a road leading past Kalsu's secondary, or northern gate, and then another turn putting us on a road back towards our tents. Two laps of this course would comprise the two miles required of the PT test.

Early in the morning (we at least timed it so that the run wouldn't be during the heat of the day), we set out. I kept a decent pace with Graham and McFarland behind me. We had gone nearly a half-mile when a huge explosion went off a few hundred meters away. Luckily there was a bunker just off the road, and we dived into it for cover. That all-too-familiar pang of fear overcame me, and I felt helpless and vulnerable without my weapon or gear. I had no ICOM to call in our status, and as far as I knew the platoon was scattered along the two-mile course.

The explosion came from the secondary gate towards which we'd been running, only a couple hundred meters away. After pausing in the bunker for a minute or two I couldn't resist wanting to help. That was no mortar or rocket. It was a car bomb that we heard, and undoubtedly there would be scores of wounded that needed help. The soldiers with me agreed. We got out of the small bunker and ran towards the thickening plume of smoke, the sickening dread in my stomach growing all the while. We didn't get far before 1LT Kelley caught up with us.

"Hey! You guys okay?" he asked as he got closer.

"We're good! Sir, we're going to help out," I yelled out to him.

"Negative, get back to the tent and get your gear, there's nothing we can do like this. I came out to get you guys," he said.

He was right. There was nothing we could do in our PT shorts and t-shirt. It was adrenaline that had sent us toward it in the first place. The smell of burning fuel and debris mingled with burning flesh wafted towards us. Without another word, we sprinted back to our tents, where everyone was putting on gear and rushing outside. The whole FOB was rushing around frantically. I scrambled to put my body armor on and turn on my ICOM. I was trembling; the adrenaline was hitting hard. I got out of the tent dressed in my PT uniform, helmet, and body armor, ready for whatever. That wouldn't do, someone passed down the line, get changed into our DCUs.

As we gathered by our tents, our first step was to ensure that we had accountability for all of our soldiers, just like we had to do after any attack. We got a head count just our platoon sergeant ran over.

"Okay men, here's the deal. A car bomb just hit the north gate. There are a lot of casualties. They're being helped, but we need to clear the FOB of any and all Iraqis. Stay in squads, stay on line. We've been assigned the motorpool area to clear. Simple, men, any Iraqi you see gets detained. Squad leaders, move out. Keep your ICOMs on, and be careful."

With that, we moved out. The motorpool area was directly to the north of us, and it took us close to the gate that had been hit. It was still early, and not many Iraqi laborers had arrived. We kept a close eye out, but did not see any of them lingering about. It only took us minutes to reach the perimeter, where we reported the area clear and turned around to cover the area again. We began to piece together what happened as we talked with other soldiers clearing the FOB.

A truck full of Iraqi laborers had exploded once it got inside the outer gate. It killed scores of Iraqis and wounded several of the soldiers on guard at the time. The carnage there was horrific, body parts everywhere and viscera splattered all over the concrete walls. I was glad I didn't have to see it in person. One of the wounded was my old team leader from my Fort Irwin OPFOR days. Word was that he may lose a leg. I hadn't seen him much during the tour, but I still knew him well enough to be disturbed by the news. Although guards in the towers at Kalsu had taken sniper fire on occasion, this was the first time we'd been hit with a car bomb there.

I kept it to myself, because there was really no need to voice it, but I was incensed about being so close to that danger without any means of protection. We had nothing with us and were hundreds of meters from our equipment. The purpose of the regulation of having a weapon, thirty rounds of ammunition, and a field dressing at all times was clear that morning. There were no areas in Iraq in which we could expect to be completely safe. It's why I was dumbfounded by the idea to start PT like we were back in the US. Incidentally, after that day I never heard a word about plans to re-schedule the PT test or to even continue training for it. I was pissed off that it had even been thought of in the first place, and glad that someone had finally realized we were at war.

The war was indeed raging in our sector. Nothing slowed

down. Actually, the seriousness of our situation grew that October. Iraq was poised to hold its second elections, this time to ratify the constitution that the delegates elected in January had written. It was expected that violence would soar in the weeks and days leading up to the polling, a repeat of the veritable insurgent offensive that occurred in January. This time, as a demonstration of the progress towards sovereignty towards which Iraq was striving, no US forces were to take part in security operations on the day of voting. We were tasked with preparing the polling sites in addition to increased patrols, though. The idea was to funnel pedestrian and vehicle traffic into a few routes which the Iraqi Army could easily manage. In Diyara this was fairly simple.

There were only three or four ways to enter the village of Diyara, and our mission was to narrow this down to one. To do so, we were to seal off roads with concrete barriers and barbed wire – not an easy task given that we had to help engineers maneuver heavy equipment through the narrow canal roads around the village. So for a couple of weeks that's what we did outside the wire. Usually, two concrete T-barriers and a few strands of concertina wire were enough to block off a road. Any kind of wire was tricky material, though, as we'd learned offloading the Bradleys our first night in Kalsu and on a couple of patrols. It had a tendency to become hopelessly entangled in the tracks and suspension of our vehicles if it was run over, and a Bradley driver's field of vision, restricted as it was, made such a scenario almost inevitable when driving in close proximity to it.

Toward the end of the work, we had to take CPT Ramirez out to Diyara to inspect the progress. It was an impromptu sort of mission in that we threw together a few people in two Bradleys without paying attention to section assignments. I ended up riding in SFC Torgerson's Bradley with CPT Ramirez and one of my soldiers, Cervantes. I didn't know him all that well on a personal level since he was one of the quietest guys in the platoon. He did what he was told without question, always paid attention, and despite his small stature humped a SAW around without complaint. He was a tough, young soldier, and I liked having him around. I took some pleasure in sharing the sweltering heat back of the Bradley with the CO. Any time our superiors roughed it out with us was comforting.

The mission was simple. We just travelled to a location at which we'd placed obstacles, dropped ramp, hopped out, and took a look around. The CO was satisfied with our work. He nearly always was, and had a cheery demeanor about him regardless of the conditions. After inspecting a few obstacles, we were navigating a narrow canal road on our way to the next. The Bradley came to an abrupt halt and I heard the crew yelling into their microphones about concertina wire. When the ramp dropped I knew exactly why.

I hopped out of the back, taking Cervantes with me. The CO followed. SFC Torgerson yelled down from the turret that we were stuck in the wire, and that I needed to get us out of it quickly – being immobilized was a serious security risk. I took a brief survey of the situation. The wire was old stuff, slightly rusted and more brittle than the newer strands. It was tangled in the top of the track by the sprocket on the right side, the driver's blind spot. The wire was still attached to a picket driven into the ground just off the road, and it had pulled it enough to create tension all along its length. It appeared that the only way to loosen it would be to remove the picket first. The Bradley couldn't move; doing so would only entangle it further and risk damaging the suspension system. When I reached through a small opening in the tangle of rusty razor wire and tried to wiggle the picket out of its hole, it held fast. It might as well have been in cement. I asked Cervantes for the sledge hammer.

Carefully, I got the sledge into the open space and started

swinging it lightly, hoping to tap the picket and loosen the ground around it. I felt a sharp sting on my left hand. When I swung the hammer again I saw a splatter of blood on the ground.

"You fucking idiot," I said aloud to myself. Blood was pouring from a gash on my left pinky knuckle.

"SGT Ervin's hurt,"Cervantes told SFC Torgerson. He quickly dismounted the turret to have a look.

"Hey, get his field dressing and wrap this thing up. It looks deep." Somewhat white in the face, Cervantes grabbed the field dressing from my pouch. "Yeah," continued SFC Torgerson, "That looks pretty bad. We need to get you to the aid station."

As Cervantes began wrapping the field dressing around the wound the pain began. It throbbed badly once it was fully wrapped and tightened. I put my hand on top of my helmet to keep the wound elevated and climbed back into the Bradley. Cervantes and SFC Torgerson continued the process of clearing the wire from the tracks. Within a few minutes, we were free of the entanglement and headed back to Kalsu. Back in the troop compartment before we took off, CPT Ramirez grimaced at me.

"It's all good, SGT Ervin, no big deal. Loosen up your body armor, undo your pants from your boots, and try to relax." I did as he told me, keeping my hand on my helmet. The blood had begun to seep through the dressing by now, and I was feeling faint from the heat and maybe the loss of blood. When the ramp closed I saw the spots of blood drying on it. In fact, there was blood everywhere. I didn't realize how much had been flowing out of me.

In spite of my alarm, I wondered if I would be reprimanded. We weren't supposed to work with concertina wire with bare hands. Every vehicle had at least one pair of tough gauntlets designed to protect us from the wire. I hadn't bothered to don them before getting out and wrestling with the stuff. I hoped I wouldn't get in any serious trouble. The Army frowned upon injuries that could be prevented, and this was a good example of one.

The patrol made its way back to Kalsu quickly. Even though the injury wasn't incredibly serious, it was still an injury. When we arrived at the gate the CO asked if I'd be able to walk to the aid station on my own, since the patrol had to turn right around to continue their inspection of the obstacles. I assured him that it wouldn't be a problem, but I silently hoped that someone on the FOB would give me a ride. They dropped me off and turned around, leaving me to my short walk to the squadron aid station.

I felt embarrassed. Yes, I was injured and in need of medical attention, but I felt like I'd brought it upon myself. What did I expect would happen attempting to free the vehicle from rusty concertina wire with my bare hands? Uniform and gear in disarray I trudged through the dust until some NCO, not realizing I was hurt, told me to "fix myself." I shamefully made the trek to the aid station.

When I arrived a female medic told me to get all of my gear off and place it in the corner. It felt great to be in air conditioning, and even better to be under the care of a girl. She was exceptionally nice to me; her tone conveyed a compassion that I hadn't heard since being back home. She recorded essential information on the medical form.

"Okay, SGT Ervin, I'm going to have to take this field dressing off so we can have a look, okay? Don't look at it if you don't think you can handle it," she said calmly. I chuckled at how sensitive she thought I must be to the sights of an injury.

"Go ahead, just be careful, okay?" My voice was surprisingly shaky. I was interested to see the extent of the damage, though.

"Don't worry. Just relax, and we'll get this cleaned up." When she'd finished removing the bandage, I saw why Cervantes had a shocked look on his face. The gash on my pinky knuckle extended halfway around my hand, almost to the palm.

It was about an inch-and-half long, and was gaping open at least three-fourths of an inch wide. It was deep. It had stopped bleeding, so I was able to see the layers of flesh and the exposed tendons of my knuckle. It looked mangled. The medic called the doctor on duty over so he could have a look.

He ran a finger along my pinky finger and asked if I could feel it. I couldn't. All I felt was the sting of air on my exposed knuckle. He picked up a syringe filled with an anesthetic and injected it all around the wound. My skin puffed, and once I assured them I couldn't feel anything, he had the medic begin cleaning it up. I didn't look this time, because I knew she was basically digging around in there trying to find all the bits of dirt and debris inside. When it was clean the doctor came over and sewed me up. It took twelve stitches not counting the three or four inside the wound itself. I remembered because it was October 12.

Once finished, the doctor wrote me a prescription for a narcotic painkiller, an anti-inflammatory pill, and an antibiotic, then gave me some instructions. As the medic applied a clean dressing and splint on my finger, she told me to keep it clean and immobilized. I laughed at the 'keeping it clean' part. That would probably be easier said than done in that cesspool. The gash needed to heal before I would be able to move it. I was told to report back to the aid station the next day so they could take a look. With that, I made my way back to Echo Troop's tents, chagrined at the thought of having to tell my squad leader that I'd be out of action for the foreseeable future.

"Ervin, what in the hell did you do to yourself, man," asked SSG Lutz when I walked through the entrance of the squad leader tent. SSG Moon and a few of the other NCOs came around to take a look at my bandaged hand.

"Fucking concertina wire got me," I replied. I was sure that he'd already been told what happened by our platoon sergeant, who had returned by now.

"You're gonna be out of the picture for a little while I reckon."

"Yeah, you could say that. It's deep – I can see my knuckle. Twelve stitches plus some on the inside." I handed him the profile the doctor had written, ordering me to light duty until the laceration healed. This essentially meant that I couldn't go on any missions. It also precluded me from doing any heavy lifting or manual labor that would require the use of my left hand.

"Do you think I'll get in trouble for not wearing gloves?" I asked hesitantly. He looked at me somewhat puzzled. It didn't seem like the thought had ever occurred to him, and he cracked a grin. He always had a way of being light-hearted regardless of the circumstances.

"No, man, don't be silly. You were doing your job. Shit happens, dude."

"On that note, what am I supposed to do now?"

"Well, I'll get with SFC Torgerson and figure something out. I'm sure you can find plenty of ways to be useful in the meantime. Just keep me posted and take care of yourself."

"Roger, sergeant, will do." With that I went back to my tent. There were only a few guys milling around inside. Steppe was one of them. He'd heard what happened and was dying to see the extent of the damage. I undid the bandage and showed him. By now the pain medicine I'd taken was kicking in, so I worried less about exposing the wound. It looked pretty gross.

"Wow, dude, you really fucked yourself up," he said as he contemplated the stitched mess. "Let me take a couple of pictures so you can show your girlfriend." He laughed a little.

"Yeah man, they'll be happy to hear that I won't be out there in the boonies, at least. I won't lie to you. It will be a nice break." In other wars they'd called such an injury a 'million dollar wound.' It wasn't serious enough to do anything but put you out

234

of action. I had a talk with McFarland to let him know he would be in charge of the team for a while. It was only one soldier besides him, but when we changed up the organization for raids and other missions he'd probably have to lead a full team. I had confidence that he would do a good job. He was a knowledgeable soldier; for the most part he was virtually on auto-pilot. We were looking to send him to the promotion board for sergeant soon anyway.

For the rest of the day I took stock of what happened. I made phone calls to Karen and my parents, informing them that I was okay, for the most part, and that I wouldn't be in the line of danger for a good while. I could hear the relief in their voices as we spoke. Although they knew about the mortars and rockets on the FOB, they also knew that the real danger came from being out on patrol. As such, they considered this injury a blessing in disguise. I did not quite see it that way.

That night, in spite of the effects of the Loritabs, which were powerful, my mind was swirling. A complex set of feelings was emerging as the realization of the impact of this injury began to take shape. A lot of it was guilt. My soldiers and friends would be going about their dangerous business without me. It felt wrong that I had a ticket out of the perils of patrolling and raiding, and worse still; I'd been injured in a silly accident – one that I felt was easily preventable and entirely my fault. I did not feel that I should be granted the privilege of relative safety in return for an error on my part. None of it seemed right. Many of my comrades had children, some had already been to Iraq or Afghanistan, and at the time it didn't seem fair that I was the one to be sitting out for a while.

Part of that guilt stemmed from the immense relief I felt, also. I would not have to climb into the back of a Bradley and fight off panic anymore. I didn't have to gaze into the IED craters on the sides of the roads, worry about traffic around me, or wonder if I'd be shot in the face when I kicked down a door. The only danger I'd find myself in for a while was the slim chance of being hurt by a mortar or rocket. That didn't compare to the rest of it. For the first time in more than a year I allowed myself to think about surviving the entire ordeal that had been my time Iraq. My chances of coming home alive increased dramatically when the concertina wire sliced open my hand. It was difficult to be comfortable with that concept knowing my peers did not share in my relatively good fortune. Regardless of how I felt about my current situation, there was little I could do about it besides making myself useful, and in the next few days I found that I could still be of help to my platoon.

I couldn't use my left hand at all. It was splinted, stitched, and it hurt like hell. It felt more like bruise than a laceration for some reason. I talked with my platoon sergeant within the first few days of my injury. I explained that I did not want to be dead weight I wanted to do all I could to keep the platoon running, so I volunteered to take over maintenance duties. Instead of the guys finishing a patrol and spending an hour or more in the motorpool area working on vehicles, I'd take whoever else didn't have to patrol that day and do the work. I just asked the drivers to let me know of any issues they'd found and I'd take care of the rest. It was pretty difficult for me to do something as simple as checking the oil on a Humvee with one hand, but I had the time to muddle through it. I still kept the radios filled with the proper frequencies. I cleaned the tent. I replenished ammo in the vehicles and cleaned the machine guns. And, of course, there was still a lot of paperwork to do, a task for which I'd always been chosen, anyway.

An example of this was writing up requests for medals. Towards the end of the tour the NCOs had to write award recommendations for their soldiers. Everyone was put in for an Army

Commendation Medal, and everyone would get it, but the paperwork involved was tedious. (Platoon sergeants and above received the Bronze Star Medal.) The awards were intended to be a tangible bonus for a soldier's overseas service in addition to the Combat Infantry Badge, which we had all earned back in March. A few had been promoted, too. Steppe finally got his sergeant stripes that summer. The award citations were difficult to write – not because there wasn't anything good to say about the recipients, but because they had to be worded in an exact manner and completely free of errors. At the best of times, it was a difficult task. In Iraq, there simply wasn't enough time for devote to achieve the level of perfection headquarters required. I helped edit a lot of the awards in my newly found free time, and was glad to do it. I began to realize that keeping busy was essential for me.

Although having a break wasn't bad most of the time, it turned out that it could be the worst thing in the world. When the guys in my section went out on patrol or the platoon headed to Diyara I was alone. Bravo section was usually sleeping while Alpha was patrolling. I felt their absence heavily. I'd spent so much time with those men that I'd taken for granted how close we'd become. They were more than family at that point. Unlike being on leave with plenty of distractions, waiting on their return from operations was hell. I'd listen for IEDs in their general direction and hang out near Echo's CP waiting for any bad news. It was miserable with worry, and I wanted nothing more than to be out there with them. But my injury had me going other places as well. When I saw the doctor for the second or third time since being injured, I figured out where I would be going, and where I might end up.

"Well soldier," the doctor looked up from my hand, "it looks like we're going to have to send you up to Baghdad to have an orthopedic specialist look at this. I don't think you'll lose your finger, but we need to make sure you'll be able to use it later on. The orderly will square away your travel orders. Just take these papers to your first sergeant." I was shocked. I knew that I'd cut it pretty deep, but being medevaced to Baghdad for it seemed far-fetched.

"If it requires surgery," he continued, "you'll have to go to Germany." Again I looked at him in disbelief.

"You mean it's that bad, sir?" My heart sunk. I didn't want to leave my unit at all.

"You've cut deep into your knuckle. They may have to re-attach tendons. I'm not sure, that's why we're going to have a specialist look at it. Don't worry, you'll be okay. Just keep it dry and clean and it should heal up within a couple of months."

It dawned on me that my war might very well be over. Germany was where seriously wounded or sick soldiers were evacuated to, and more often than not they did not come back to Iraq. Usually from there they went home to continue being treated or be discharged.

After informing SSG Lutz and SFC Torgerson of the latest development, I went to the CP and handed the paperwork to the first sergeant. He was not surprised. The look he gave me was hard to explain. It was a look that held full knowledge that I was going to be out of danger, and he was happy for me. I brought up the fact that I'd rather be patrolling, and he rolled his eyes. Get healed up, was the gist of what he said. An injury was an injury, and it was my duty to recuperate as quickly as possible – and correctly – so I could get back to the work of leading soldiers. He echoed what my leaders had been trying to tell me since I'd gotten hurt: take care of yourself. You've done what's expected of you, and now it's your duty to convalesce. When I got back to my tent and told everyone that I might be going away for a little while, they weren't surprised, either. I began thinking of what Baghdad would be like. Although we'd been within a day's drive of the place for nearly a year, not many of us had been there. It was pretty exciting at first, but I should have known better by then.

Flying to Baghdad on a routine medevac was similar to flying to Balad on leave. I turned in my weapon, stripped my body armor of most of its pouches besides the first aid kit, and reported to the aid station. Another soldier and I were then directed to wait in a tent until the medevac helicopter arrived to take us north. He was from the HHT mortar section and had twisted his knee badly while doing a fire mission. We joked about how little the mortars had been used, and he was surprised to hear that we wanted to use them more often but for one reason or another were not allowed. There wasn't anything else to do but talk. The next morning our medevac chopper arrived. When it touched down, we clambered aboard and a flight medic helped us with our seatbelts. The flight into the city was nothing remarkable, although I was surprised at the sight of Baghdad as we approached it.

I expected a more modernized city instead of the sprawling, wretched slum that extended beyond the horizon. There were no skyscrapers and very few tall buildings. In fact, it just looked like a larger version of any other city in Iraq. The clusters of tan brick and stucco buildings were interspersed with narrow streets and alleys, above them a contorted mass of power lines. It looked crowded and dilapidated. It was big, though. The Tigris River meandered through the city, bisecting it. Everything smelled the same as well. The rotors of the helicopter wafted the scent of sewage and decay into the cabin. As famous as Baghdad was, seeing it for the first time was anticlimactic. It was just another Iraqi shithole to me.

We'd been flying low the entire way, and we skimmed over the city quickly, reaching the helipad in the Green Zone mere seconds after passing the outskirts of the city. Then I was intro-duced to a Blackhawk's agility, much to my stomach's dismay. While waiting to land, the aircraft flew in tight circles around the landing zone, banked at about forty-five degrees. It felt like being in a centrifuge. When we touched down, the mortarman and I staggered out of the chopper. Neither of us could walk straight. The combined effects of pain medication and the mo-tion had us staggering and wobbling off of the helipad. An or-derly awaited us at its edge, just short of a three-story building that I assumed was the hospital. When I reached the concrete barrier I put a hand on it to steady myself and began throwing up. The mortarman did the same, and the orderly chuckled.

"Welcome to 86th CSH. Don't worry guys, that landing gets everyone," he said.

I wasn't laughing; I felt like hell. He waited a moment for us to finish throwing up and led us into the hospital to be checked in at the reception area. I walked through a sliding glass door into a surprising modern and immaculately clean hospital. We signed our names on a sheet of paper and went our separate ways, each given directions to the department where we were to be seen. It was a busy place. Nurses, doctors, and orderlies hur-ried through the corridors wearing DCU pants and hospital-green scrub tops. I felt out of place in my filthy body armor, longer hair, and stained and frayed uniform. It was also strange to see Iraqi civilians being treated there. As I tried to find my way to the orthopedics department I got a reminder of where I was.

I walked down a wrong corridor and found myself on the trauma ward. Peering inside the rooms as I passed them, I saw shattered men. The white bandages, some with blood seeping through, did not hide the fact that several of them were ampu-tees. Others were burned horribly, and I was glad their bandages covered what must have been the worst of it. It was eerily quiet in that hallway, and I picked up the pace to get out of there. I'd never seen so many wounded men and did not relish the sight at all. I felt ashamed for being in the same place as these soldiers with my silly, cut-up hand. I also realized I was in the same hospital in which many of my friends had died after being evacuated. It floored me, and I was glad when a soldier saw that I looked bewildered and guided me to the orthopedics department.

Two men sat lounging in a room when I got there. I handed the junior looking of the two a few slips of paper the doctor at Kalsu had sent with me. He nodded in understanding and motioned me to have a seat on an examination table. The doctor came over, and I explained how I'd hurt myself and how it felt.

"You allergic to anything, buddy? We're going to be moving your hand around a lot so I'm going to give you something for the pain," said the orderly as he readied a syringe.

"No, I'm not allergic to anything. Maybe helicopter rides," I said weakly. I must have been a sorry sight. Between the motion sickness and the sight of the wounded guys I was not feeling well. With that he gave me a shot. Everything got fuzzy immediately, but I thought I heard someone say something to the effect that it was a pretty generous dose of dilaudid they'd just given me. They wiggled my fingers around for a little while, recorded some notes to hand to me, and showed me to the door. In the hallway I saw a soldier and asked for directions to the temporary barracks. After stumbling my way there, I fell into a cot and was fast asleep.

I awoke to a nearly empty room. I could tell it was evening by the waning light. Attempting to gather my senses, I went out to the helipad to have a cigarette. I was groggy, to say the least. I wondered why they'd given me so much pain medication. My thoughts were interrupted by a Humvee that came screeching up to the entrance of the hospital. It was riddled with shrapnel holes. The gunner on top looked panicked. The occupants burst out of the doors, and shell casings came tumbling to the ground. Two frantic soldiers rushed to the back door, opened it and, reached inside. I heard the soldier inside screaming in agony. As they pulled him out, I saw that one of his legs was covered in blood and hanging limply. His buddies carried him into the hospital, and when the sliding glass doors closed the screaming stopped. I looked at the gunner, still in the turret. He'd taken off his Kevlar and sunglasses. Eyes wide open, he stared into the space in front of the Humvee, his face a mask of shock, horror, and frustration. He slammed his Kevlar on the roof of the vehicle and, barely intelligibly, cussed a few times.

My cigarette began burning my fingertips. I hadn't noticed that I was still smoking. My eyes were riveted to the scene in front of me. When the gunner started getting out of the turret, I snubbed the cigarette out and walked past his vehicle. We exchanged glances and nods. There wasn't anything I could say to him. Skirting the pools of blood that led into the hospital, I walked inside and back to the temporary barracks.

I felt sorry for the soldiers who had just brought their buddy inside. I knew the frustration on the gunner's face intimately. The sense of utter helplessness that IEDs inspired went against every grain of our training. It was a sad moment to realize that soldiers all across Iraq were dealing with the exact same demons. I was glad that I was going back to my corner of it the next day, where I could at least be around familiar faces.

13

My birthday present on October 21st came in the form of staples in my hand. Other than that, it was a non-event. It hardly crossed my mind. The doctor had removed the stitches a few days earlier and applied liquid stitch. It was still hot enough that I sweat through the bandages, though, and the gash kept coming apart. The dead, white skin that surrounded it smelled horrible despite my best attempts to keep it clean, and the doctor had decided that staples would keep the wound closed and prevent infection. It ended up being a painful, gross-looking mess. I wondered if the doctor had taken the stitches out too early. Either way it was healing slowly and painfully. I probably didn't help its healing by working as hard as I did, but it didn't much matter. I was doing more for it than I thought.

Turning a year older didn't matter much, but I began feeling differently all the same. I was able to keep relatively clean. For most of the year I'd had to go for a week or more without a shower at a time. I'd dry-shaved with water bottles and fought off the worst of the filth with baby wipes and worn a rank, nasty uniform under my equally filthy, smelly body armor and helmet. Now that I wasn't patrolling, though, I was able to take a shower each night and wear clean uniforms. I didn't take it for granted. I got dirty working in the motorpool, of course, and the dusty, hot FOB wasn't exactly the cleanest place, but it was nothing like being outside the wire all the time. The shower, the three good meals each day, plus spending more time in air conditioning was a stark contrast to the life I'd been living for the better part of a year. It was an entirely different world.

When the first sergeant eventually wrangled me up to work in Echo's CP I was introduced to another world, too. I still helped the platoon the best I could, but each morning I'd report to the first sergeant and serve as one of his orderlies. The bright side was that I'd still be around familiar faces. CPT Capps had been assigned as Echo's XO, and we had some interesting conversations in the CP. Becker was in there with me, too. In his characteristically wry sense of humor, he showed me what we had to do in there. A lot of it was just being a gopher. I'd pick up intelligence briefings from Task Force HQ, and run all sorts of paperwork from one place to another. We handled the mail for the Troop, and distributing it to all the soldiers I got to see a lot more of the other platoons and hang out with them some. I also monitored the radios during the day as patrols called in SITREPs. It got boring. Becker and I joked around a lot about the first sergeant to pass the time. It was a different world, though. Knowing the dangerous spots on the roads was replaced by knowing how to work a copy machine.

Sometimes, though, the platoon brought elements of the world out there back with them. One of the things I always managed to help them with was processing and turning in detainees. Bringing in captured Iraqis to turn in was always a pain. Two sworn statements had to accompany each of the detainees, and each had to include the following: why the individual was detained, the date, time, and location of their capture, a summary of the circumstances leading to their capture, and their physical condition at the time of apprehension. Getting the paperwork right was essential.

It wasn't hard to figure out that the sworn statements were the means by which we legitimized what we did beyond the wire. It held us accountable for our actions. Furthermore, it contributed to intelligence gathering and informed whoever eventually ended up with the detainees why they'd been captured. I presumed the statements of soldiers would eventually be used in the detainee's trial, and they could also be used as evidence in a court-martial. In other words, it kept the way we fought the war legal. But the paperwork wasn't the entire process.

One night in November, 1st platoon came back with five or six detainees from a raid. It was a pitch black night, so dark that the guys had attached chemlites to the detainees to keep track of them in the darkness. They'd corralled them into a bunker situated between our tents and the squadron CP. When I met up with them, I told the lieutenant I could take over guarding them while they squared away all the paperwork. We had our own processing to do before turning them in, and I knew it pretty well. I had the interpreter get their identification documents from the Ziploc bags slung around each detainee's neck and tell me the names. I recorded them as best as I could, but it was always a bit of guesswork as to the English spelling. Even so, by now their names had become more familiar to me. After that, I got a flashlight out and got our platoon's digital camera. Going in the same order as their listed names, I removed their blindfolds and took pictures of each of them. This information went into a database Echo kept wherein the names and mug shots of every Iraqi we captured were stored. When this was done, all I had to do was guard them. A lot of times this entailed helping them out to a degree.

Detainees were most often terrified. They rarely spoke unless spoken to, and even then they kept conversation to a minimum. Many of them trembled uncontrollably and muttered prayers to Allah. These particular detainees were stoic in their captivity compared to others I'd been around. When the lieutenant left me with the lot of them, the first thing I did was offer them water. They spoke enough English to know what I was talking about. I just lifted a bottle of water to their lips and let them drink. Shortly after I'd lit a cigarette, one of them asked me for one. I gave him the one I'd lit. Soon the rest followed suit, and all of them were smoking without their hands. We may have been in Iraq for a long time, and I may have lost several close friends, but I was still a human being. Being rough with them at the time of their capture was one thing, but after that it was doctrine to prevent mistreatment. Pretty soon the lieutenant and my squad leader returned with all of the paperwork completed, and I volunteered to take them to Kalsu's detention center on the corner of the FOB.

Like I'd learned to do before, I had them all line up. I held the front man's shirt and had the interpreter instruct them to hold the man's shirt behind them. It may have been easier to take their blindfolds off, but giving captured Iraqis an accurate mental picture of the layout of our FOB was ludicrous. We did still get mortared regularly, after all. It was slow progress to the detention area. When I arrived, I lined them up on a wall and they squatted down. I informed the guard at the entrance that I had prisoners to hand over, and called the lieutenant on my ICOM to let him know I'd made it. For some reason, it took the MPs a while to come outside. While I waited, someone approached me out of the darkness from the direction of the Special Forces compound.

"These your hajjis?" he asked when he came up beside me. I smelled alcohol. Unfamiliar as it was at that point, it stood out.

"Yeah," I replied. I couldn't make him out too well in the darkness, but he didn't look like a regular grunt at all. He looked sort of shaggy and was a big guy.

"Fuck these people. I hate them." He approached the first Iraqi in the line and continued, slurring a little. "How many fucking Americans did you kill today, you camel fucker? Huh?! Huh?! I know you can understand me you piece of shit." With

246

that he smacked the detainee, hitting him hard enough that his head bounced off the wall.

"Hey! What the fuck man? I'm guarding these guys!" I was startled, and not a little scared. I had no idea who this man was. It was my duty to safeguard the prisoners. He slapped the Iraqi again. I adjusted my grip on the shotgun I was carrying. "Dude, seriously Cut it out."

"Whoa buddy, whoa. You're not going to shoot me over a fucking hajji are you? You've got to be kidding me." He staggered back a few steps from the Iraqi.

"Listen man, I've got no love for these people. Either way, I can't let you hurt them. C'mon man, you know how it is. My guys captured them. If I turn them in all beaten up who do you think is going to catch the flack?" My voice was shaky. Maybe he noticed it, maybe not. He was right; I didn't want to shoot someone over an Iraqi. I didn't want to get into any kind of fight at all with this guy. He was a good deal bigger than me, and I was injured.

"Dude, just do us both a favor and get the fuck out here," I tried my best to sound authoritative, but wished the MPs would hurry up and get outside their compound.

"Yeah, these fucking people aren't worth my time," he said with a snicker. He turned around and walked back into the darkness as I sighed with relief. My heart was pounding out of my chest. Part of it was narrowly avoiding a scrape, but part of it was worrying about whether I'd get into trouble. As the soldier guarding these prisoners I was legally bound to protect them. I hadn't anticipated the situation in the least, and I wondered whether or not I'd reacted in an appropriate way. When the MP guard came out and told me they were ready for me, I helped get the Iraqis back on their feet and guided them into the compound. I didn't breathe a word of what had just happened. After their duty NCO had checked over the paperwork I was free to go. On the way back to the tents, I tried to think through the dilemma in which I'd found myself.

On the one hand, I could keep quiet about what had happened and more than likely the incident would be over. On the other hand, if the Iraqis told the MPs what happened, however unlikely, Echo troopers could get in trouble for prisoner abuse. If I told my chain of command what happened, and the guy who'd done the beating got in trouble, I could have a very dangerous enemy on the FOB. I was pretty sure the guy was Special Forces judging by his hair and slightly different uniform. Among soldiers, there's an unspoken rule that we didn't get one another in trouble if it could be avoided. I didn't relish the thought of being labeled a rat who had gotten soldiers in trouble for the sake of an Iraqi.

Yet the more I thought about the incident, the more the answer seemed to make itself clear. If anyone was going to be prosecuted for prisoner abuse, I had to make sure it wasn't my buddies. I owed them my loyalty first and foremost. They hadn't done anything wrong. Perhaps I had. Either way, the guys who had detained these prisoners had done it by the book. I resolved to tell my chain of command, knowing full well that I was about to be involved in a sticky situation. I got to Echo's tents just as my squad leader was settling in for the night.

"SSG Lutz, you have a minute? It's pretty serious."

"Oh shit man, what now?" He was dog tired, and I had a tendency to take things more seriously than I needed to at times. He probably expected more of the same. I told him all of what had just happened, adding that I didn't want anyone to get in trouble, but that I couldn't let it slide, either.

"No man, you've done the right thing. Let's go get SFC T." With that he got up, put his blouse on, and we walked over to the next tent to inform him. I explained the incident again, and the look on SFC Torgerson's face told me that I'd done the right

248

thing by telling my superiors. He told me not to worry about it tonight, and that in the morning we'd have to talk with Echo's CO. My heart nearly dropped. No one wants to have the CO's attention unless he was pinning a medal or a promotion on you. It didn't matter now, having set this thing in motion I had to see it through. That night I took an extra pain pill in the hopes of being able to sleep. I didn't tell the guys in the tent what had happened. Steppe could tell something was bugging me, but I'd been told to keep it quiet. I popped in a DVD and lay on my cot, dreading the morning.

After breakfast, I met up with SFC Torgerson and went to the Troop CP. The first sergeant and CO had already been informed of the gist of what had happened, but had me tell them in specific detail. As they printed a sworn statement for me to fill out CPT Ramirez spoke:

"Well, you did the right thing. It sounds like one of the SF guys drank too much and fucked up. We'll go over later this afternoon and talk with their CO. I know him pretty well, he's a decent man. Look," he said, looking me in the eyes as I glanced up from the paperwork, "there's no reason to be nervous." Like always, he was pretty upbeat and positive. CPT Capps added his agreement. I had a lot of respect and trust for him, but I still had my misgivings.

"Sir, like I've told my squad leader and platoon sergeant, I just don't want to get anyone in trouble. My soldiers shouldn't suffer from someone else's bad call, though."

"You're right. None of my soldiers are going to get hemmed up for this. Honestly, the SF guy probably won't either. We're just going to do this formally so everything is squared away properly."

"Roger that, sir." He'd said that to relieve some of my worry, but it really didn't. I was less worried about UCMJ than being targeted by a pissed off Green Beret. He probably knew that was one of my concerns, but like many other things in the Army, it was unspoken.

Later that morning I found myself in front of a Special Forces Captain. He had me and my CO take a seat in their CP. It didn't look much different than ours except that they had different weapons lying about. He told me to have a cigarette, since they smoked in their tents, and he lit a cigar.

"SGT Ervin, you've just made my day," he said. I'm certain my eyes got as round as saucers when he said this, because my heart was in my throat. "We're pretty sure we figured out who did this. I have to tell you, he's a shitbag and we've been trying to get him out of our team for a long time. He's a liaison, not really one of us, and he's been causing us a lot of problems. Finally we can kick his ass out. I don't blame you one bit for doing what you did. I sure as shit wouldn't want one of my guys to take a round for some idiot's mistake. There won't be anything official, but he's definitely out of our team."

I felt somewhat relieved immediately. CPT Ramirez thanked him for his understanding, and we left. It was over. I was thankful to get back to my tent and wait on the tumult in my stomach to go away. Although I'd been reassured repeatedly that I'd made the right decision, the incident was haunting. Luckily we were on the home stretch, even if that didn't quite mean things were settling down.

There were significant changes that November. It got cold at night, and stayed fairly cool during the day. We broke out our cold weather again and were all relieved that the days of maddening heat were behind us. Operationally speaking, 2-11 stepped it up, with security on MSR Tampa becoming a top priority. CP 18 was fortified with bunkers and sandbag emplacements. Each of the four overpasses on the highway were manned with Bradley sections, their optics trained up and down the thoroughfare in an effort to keep it clear of IEDs. The tactic worked. Several would-be IED planters were shot up in the course of the first few weeks that the additional security was in place. It seemed at long last the Bradley's long range capabilities were brought to the fore. I listened to some of the engagements on the radio, and heard about more from my buddies. Steppe told me it almost seemed too easy.

The insurgents did not seem aware of the fact that a Bradley could see them at night as they dug holes on the side of the road. They thought even less of the fact that the 25mm AP rounds could reach out well past a thousand meters. It was one of the few times during the tour when our superior technology and firepower made a significant difference. Steppe told me a few times that he was glad to be hitting back at the Iraqis. They were racking up a lot of kills, and I was happy about it. I was also happy to hear Bradleys shooting at night instead of the rumbling of IEDs all the time.

However, there were setbacks. Echo had finally handed over responsibility for securing Diyara patrol base to another unit in the squadron, but within a few weeks of doing so the base suffered a devastating attack. Insurgents mortared the hell out of the small base, followed by small-arms fire, and the Americans and Iraqis stationed there were forced to abandon the untenable position for a while. It was re-occupied within a few days, but the structure itself was in sorry shape and would take a while to repair.

It was a strange feeling to hear that. We'd sacrificed a lot to gain a toehold in that dangerous place, and had planned out reactions to attacks often in our training classes. I wondered what would have happened if we'd been there when it was attacked in such force. After the mind-numbing, endless hours pulling guard there, we felt cheated out of the opportunity to get in a fight there.

The FOB itself changed a bit. An additional internet café was put in place. Internet connection, albeit unreliable, was introduced into the tents to make it easier to keep in touch with family and friends back home. Then there was the expanded Iraqi store and a coffee shop in our squadron area. You could buy sodas and food and get patches sewed onto your uniform at the store in addition to the pirated movies. The coffee shop was strange. They'd built a small building with a large deck covered by camouflage netting. On the deck were wooden benches and plastic tables and chairs in which soldiers could relax. It even stayed dimly lit at night. At some point in the tour the chow hall had begun operating on regular, state-side hours, so the Iraqi store and coffee shop were the only places to grab a bite after hours. We wondered how much money there were making.

Kalsu was changing in other ways. Small trailers to house soldiers were placed in an empty field, although the grunts knew we'd never seen them. More soldiers were trickling in that November, too. A contingent of Puerto Rican National Guard soldiers arrived to take over guard duties on the perimeter and gates of Kalsu. Soldier from the 4th Infantry Division, our replacements, also appeared in small numbers. They stood out in the new uniforms the Army had adopted that year, Army Combat Uniforms (ACUs), which were more compatible with body armor and had a grey-green digital camouflage pattern. The new guys were also distinguishable by the immaculate cleanliness of their uniforms and equipment. We looked raggedy in comparison. They were a welcome sight, even though I knew it would be some time before enough of them arrived to make a difference. Still, the feeling in the air that the tour was ending was growing by the day.

My hand was proving reluctant to heal properly. It caused enough concern among the doctors and medics on Kalsu to get me sent to Baghdad. The trip and the sights in the Green Zone had lost their luster by then. Their chow hall may have been immaculate, there may have been civilians and mercenaries walking around, but it was still Iraq. The doctor there x-rayed my hand and told me that although I could expect some arthritis, everything seemed to be intact and would heal eventually. He didn't expect that I'd be in working condition anytime soon, though, and gave me orders for light duty until for a few weeks after the staples came out. I didn't know what to think of the news. I felt terrible being back inside the wire all the time when my platoon was busting their ass out there and dealing with all the danger, and now it was virtually certain that I wouldn't be back out there with them. I was still anxious to get back to Kalsu, although this time the return journey would be different.

I departed Baghdad just a few days short of Thanksgiving and was dropped off in Balad. There I would await a Catfish Air flight back to Kalsu. There, I would also experience detoxification from narcotic pain medicine. I did not expect it. During my journey, though, my prescription for pain meds was due to expire. After taking the last one at night, alone in a temporary barracks building, I awoke the next morning feeling awful. I was in a cold sweat, my stomach lurched, and I had the runs. I was irritable beyond belief and angry for no reason. It dawned on me that I'd been on the medication long enough to be experiencing withdrawal symptoms. It was altogether a terrible feeling. I hid in that holding area on Balad for my whole time there, venturing out only when I needed to check in to see if I was flying that day or not. It was a long couple of days, but towards the end of the second day I began to feel better physically. Mentally was another story. It was a strange time, perhaps owing to the holiday.

Although not separated by a great distance, the circuitous route I flew back had me in the air all of Thanksgiving Day. Strapped into a Blackhawk and shivering against the cold blast of wind, I flew over Fallujah, Baghdad again, our sister FOB in

Iskandariyah, and finally back to Kalsu. I'll never forget passing through Fallujah. We briefly touched down in a tiny, sandy FOB on the outskirts of the city. I thought about the fact that every Thanksgiving after this one would be absolutely grand because I wouldn't be flying over Fallujah. When the helicopter finally touched down in Kalsu, I was pretty glad to be back. I knew the next time I would be leaving the place would be permanently. I reported in to the Echo's CP, where the first sergeant greeted me and suggested we go get our Thanksgiving dinner in the chow hall.

I didn't end up sitting with him, though. I went through the line and got my turkey, dressing, mashed potatoes, rolls, and still-frozen pumpkin pie. It tasted okay. I believe the cooks did the best they could for us over there, which wasn't much sometimes. The food wasn't my issue though. I had a lot on my mind. I'd spent the previous Thanksgiving in the Box at Fort Irwin, wrapping up our training rotation with the 155th. I had eaten that meal with Smitty, and despite our longing to be back in our barracks and clean, I realized now that we had it good. We were all together; Prince, Smitty, Steppe, Maida, and CPT Harting had all shared that meal with me. It seemed like ages ago.

A lot had changed since then. Now we were wrapping up our entire deployment. Echo had gained a few soldiers along the way, but we'd lost several, and those losses affected me deeply that Thanksgiving. It may have been the holiday that put everything into a murky perspective, or even the lingering withdrawal symptoms, but I felt like I'd had quite enough of Iraq. Everything had lost what little luster it had to begin with, and I was just tired of it. The constant threat of mortars and rockets, the startling, noisy bouts outgoing artillery fire, the dusty tents, port-a-johns, the incessant noise of helicopter engines, the infrequent calls home – all that I'd glossed over through most of the tour hit me hard. There had been no real privacy (besides a port-a-john, in which everything that required privacy was attended to), and in reality no real break in the danger and stress for most of a year. I was ready to go home, and there were several signs that everyone felt the same way.

One thing I'd noticed more in the last couple of months of being there was everyone spending more time in relative solitude. When my section was on the FOB, there were hours of silence in the tent. Soldiers read, watched their DVDs, or piddled around without as much conversation as before. Guys went to the gym alone, didn't care to eat their meals with others as often, and in general just became more withdrawn. Everyone was friendly to one another like before; an individual's seclusion was more a symptom of their own growing impatience to leave Iraq more than impatience with each other. In that sense it was strange. One would think that several men sharing extremely close quarters for so long would grow tired of the company, but no fights ever broke out and there were scarcely ever any arguments. Given the stress everyone was under this surprised me.

The signs that we were ready to go home were apparent outside the wire, too. Steppe kept me abreast of what was going on out there. He'd said that gunners were shooting warning shots more than ever before. They were being careful in the last month or so that we were there, and as a result the Iraqis were getting shot at more often. They had good reason to still be wary. The IEDs were still abundant. I still heard their distinct rumble on the FOB frequently, and they were still causing casualties. At least one soldier was killed in November. The mortars and rockets had decreased to the point of being sporadic on the FOB, but the mortar attack on Diyara earlier had everyone wondering about the same happening while they were on CP 18. No one wanted to be the last one to die in Iraq. With the goal of coming home so tantalizingly close, who could blame them? It wasn't likely that I'd ever do a combat mission again, be it a patrol, raid, or whatever, but I felt the same way. It wasn't worth taking chances anymore. Home was closer than it had ever been, and it was the topic of a lot of speculation.

"Home by Christmas" was the latest word that December. I was enough of a history buff to take it with a large grain of salt, and my three and a half years in the Army had taught me to be a pessimist when it came to any such forecasts. It was an awful month. The feelings that pervaded our minds were an anxious mixture of impatience, boredom, and annoyance. The men of 1st platoon were still out there doing the job, even though I believe they were more than over it. They were sick of it. This late in the game, any notion of novelty and excitement was long gone, the means of distracting oneself played out, and – to put it bluntly – we were fed up with it in its entirety. I spent each day listening for minute clues from the CO and first sergeant of when we would get the hell out of there. That's how I knew that the latest projections. There was still a lot to do, though. Our tour wasn't over until we were packed up, our sector was handed over the 4th ID, and we were on a plane home. Beginning some of the packing that month was a good sign, but it had its downside.

In the months since Prince and Smith had gotten killed I hadn't thought about them often. No one really talked about them much, either. The platoon had signed a copy of *Where the Wild Things Are* to send home to Smitty's family, and we'd had memorial bracelets made and sent to us, but I did my best not to think about them a lot. It was better to block out the darkness as best I could and focus on the tasks at hand. As we started packing away non-essential items into connex containers for shipment home, to include some of our personal gear in foot lockers that we didn't need any more, we all got a stark reminder of who wasn't coming back with us.

After a soldier was killed or wounded their foot lockers and the rest of their belongings had been stored in the connex. Just like our stuff, it had to be laid out and inventoried exactly so that it could be inspected for US Customs' purposes. When we emptied the connex, there it all was; their rucksacks, extra boots, ammo pouches, laptop computers, and everything else that our fallen friends had when they died was in there. It was up to one of us to go through it all and write up an inventory. I volunteered to do it, and SFC Torgerson helped me. It was just one of those unpleasant things that needed to be done. What I remember most from that day was standing there, our lockers and duffel bags lined up in a formation. Not every locker had a soldier beside it. 3rd platoon had to do the same with Maida's gear. I remember thinking that it would be hard on their families to receive their personal belongings that long after their deaths.

Then one day during a 1st platoon NCO meeting I got the best news I'd ever received in Iraq. It was official, and we could pass it along to our soldiers. A lot of us would indeed be going home that December. The plan was to redeploy the Task Force in four groups, or chalks, each to leave within a week or two weeks of each other. Everyone had already been assigned a chalk, and I was elated to learn that my name was on the first flight out. On December 16, 2005, I would leave Kalsu for the last time. As welcome as the news was, I still had my doubts. An adage that I'd come to live by in Iraq was to expect the worst, that way there were no nasty surprises. But as far as anyone knew, we at least weren't going to be extended beyond our tour. The exact dates could change, but not by enough to matter that much.

I don't remember much of my last week at Kalsu. Soldiers were still patrolling non-stop until our replacements arrived in force, and even after they'd arrived guys would have to do right seat rides like the Marines had done for us. The men on the last flights out would mainly be doing this, so it was business as usual right up until the day prior to departure. There were many more ACU-clad, fresh soldiers at Kalsu by this point, though, and it was their presence that allowed me to finally understand the appearance and demeanor of the Marines we had replaced eleven months ago. They had been over it, too. They'd lost friends, patrolled endlessly, had been mortared, rocketed, shot at, and blown up. That they didn't greet us with enthusiasm was understandable. They knew several of us wouldn't make it back. I also understood their disregard for Iraqi lives. I couldn't relate to their disgust at having taken casualties as late in the tour as they did, but I understood how it could seem a maddening, futile waste of lives. When we had arrived in January, they were played out after their seven months. After nearly a year, we were, too.

On December 16, those of us who were leaving first turned in our weapons and ammunition. We were done. I said my good-byes to the men remaining, like Steppe and McFarland, and wished them luck. I told them I was anxious for their return. I took a final look at our tent. Cleared of everything but a duffel bag and rucksack for each of the soldiers, it reverted back to what it was – a dusty, cramped tent. I could hardly believe that I had been so comfortable living there. In fact, I had longed to be back within its confines for days on end. I didn't know exactly what kind of living arrangements I would have when I returned to Irwin, but I could guarantee it would be a giant leap above a filthy tent. This last look at my home was one of the first of many instances where I began to feel a sense of perspective of what I'd been through in the last year. Confused by a strange sort of sentimentalism, I turned my back on it and headed out towards the helipad, where I would board a helicopter to take me away from Kalsu.

My last Blackhawk helicopter ride took me to Al-Taqqadum Airbase (or TQ) west of Baghdad. It was a sprawling base in the middle of the desert. The first chalk of 2-11 troopers was held in a transient area, where we slept in large circus tents and did our best to pass the time. The PX and recreation areas didn't hold any attraction for us with home and the United States so close. Mostly, we read books and joked with one another. The tension that had blunted our conversations and spirits was slowly going away, although in truth we were there for a few days in a state of limbo that reminded me of how purgatory had been described. Still in Iraq, but done with our mission, we had nothing to do but wait on the C-130 flight that would take us to Kuwait. In an MWR tent, I found a book that brought about some powerful homesickness. It was called *At Home in the Heart of Appalachia*, written by a native West Virginian who, after spending several years away from his home state, returned with a renewed appreciation for the place. It was ironically prescient.

After a couple of days, we piled into a bus and were driven to the airstrip. It was a cold, windy, and dusty night. Stepping onto the ramp of the aircraft, I said goodbye to Iraq. "Good fucking riddance," was about all the sentiment I could muster. I may have been happier if we were flying directly to California, but we still had to make a stop in Kuwait. There, our bags would be inspected by customs and we would wait, once again, for our flight home. I don't remember much about Kuwait. Between leaving Kalsu and arriving there I had come down with a tremendous cold, and so I slept most of the time. It was a nice place compared to some of the locations and temporary homes to which I'd been accustomed. We were billeted in buildings of sorts, had access to all the usual KBR amenities, and most importantly, we were safe. That's more than likely the reason I slept so long and so well there. I didn't have to keep an ear out for incoming.

On Christmas Eve, a bus ride on the Kuwaiti highways took us to an airfield where our MAC flight awaited us to take us all the way home. Soldiers coming into country for Operation Iraqi Freedom IV were all over the place in their ACUs. We looked tired and raggedy compared to them, and our appearance re-minded me of the soldiers I'd seen upon arriving in Kuwait that were departing. Taking the last step off of the Asian continent, I felt an immense relief. It was over. I was leaving the Middle East for good. Sick as I was, I wasn't buoyant, just relieved. A tired-ness had overcome me while in Kuwait that I really couldn't shake, despite the fact that I should have been elated. I felt like hell, really. Still, when the plane's landing gear lifted off the tar-mac I smiled, and content with the knowledge that I'd be at Fort Irwin soon enough, I settled down to get some sleep. I was still excited, so for the first leg of the trip I wasn't able to sleep, but I did relax.

Our first stop was Shannon, Ireland, where the plane would refuel and we would be able to get out and stretch our legs. As the plane descended I recognized instantly why Ireland was called the Emerald Isle. Everything there was a bright, vibrant green. It may have only been the stark contrast from the brown world that I had just departed, but even in the cold drizzle and waning light of evening the place looked immaculate. The smok-ers among us filed past a busy airport bar and down to the smok-ing area. Shivering against the cold, I noticed a large number of half-empty pint glasses of dark, Irish beer. It was strange to see alcohol. There was also a duty-free store stocked with European liquors to which my desert-camouflaged comrades flocked. The rule was that every soldier was allowed to buy two bottles, but we were strictly forbidden to drink any of it on the flight. I didn't really have booze on my mind, so limited my shopping to some cold medicine and a few small souvenirs for my family.

When the plane took off to cross the Atlantic, the smell of liquor appeared in the cabin shortly afterwards. I was too sick to partake, but I suspect that a good sized portion of the couple of hundred soldiers on the flight did. It certainly smelled like it. One could hardly blame them. Apparently some of the guys got a little too friendly with one of the flight attendants, who then felt it necessary to inform Echo Troop's first sergeant of the transgression. Being in charge of the chalk, he came out to the front of the plane and got everyone's attention.

He threatened to hold us over when we arrived in the states in order to give everyone a breathalyzer and drug test. It rankled me a little until I mulled it over. It was a hollow threat. Many of the soldiers' families would be there to greet them, and although he said that wouldn't stop him, I knew he wanted to be free just as much as the rest of us. It was a reminder that we were returning to the different world that was the stateside Army. Discipline would be measured in behaving ourselves and looking sharp in our uniforms instead of making the right call of whether or not to shoot someone.

Our next stop in Bangor, Maine, was memorable. We landed there on the evening of Christmas Eve. (A plane travelling from east to west across such a large distance seemed to stand still in time as it passed successive time zones.) Again, we were allowed to get out and stretch our legs. As we stepped into the terminal, much to my shock, we were greeted by an applauding crowd. A lot of Maine residents, including more than a few Vietnam veterans, turned out to welcome returning soldiers to the states. They didn't let the fact that it was Christmas Eve stop them. I was exhausted, and my cold hadn't abated, but I was deeply touched. Here were average people doing something as simple as expressing their gratitude for our service overseas.

As the smokers stepped outside, the US greeted us with its weather. It was snowing, and a biting wind went right through our light desert uniforms. A man walked up to me, noticing my obvious discomfort, and handed me the coat off his back. I was blown away. I muttered my thanks, and he mentioned something about how it was the least he could do. I disagreed. It was one of the nicest gestures I'd ever experienced. That stop in

Maine demonstrated to us that our service was appreciated. I'll never forget the warmth of their welcome in that biting cold place. It began to feel like we were home. We still had a country to traverse, though.

There was no sleep on that last leg, which took about five hours. Inundated with cold medicine, I attempted to read. It was to no avail. I was excited. Also, I was ready to get off of the plane, take a hot shower, and sleep in a bed – a real bed. We received a short briefing consisting of information the first sergeant had received when he called Fort Irwin from Maine. We were landing at the same airfield from which we had departed and would take a bus back to Irwin. There, we'd have a small ceremony in the post recreation center where families would welcome us home. After being dismissed, we would have a few days off. Single soldiers, we were told, had a welcome basket in their pre-assigned barracks rooms. A few days off sounded wonderful considering my last bit of freedom had happened nearly six months ago.

After what seemed like an eternity we landed. Erickson was there with some other rear detachment soldiers to help us with our bags and such. It was good to see him, and he looked healthy. He asked how the rest of the platoon was doing. I could only tell him that we were glad to be coming home. Seeing him brought back some bad memories, but there was still a lot to be happy about. I got on the bus, excited at the prospect of seeing Fort Irwin for the first time in my life. Before Iraq, there wasn't anything about the place to be excited about. It was much different now. When the lights of the base appeared over the horizon, I could hardly believe it. We were back.

With a strange, dazed feeling, I filed into the recreation center with the rest of the chalk and got into formation. We must have looked a little worse for wear, with wrinkled uniforms and exhausted faces. It didn't matter to the crowd on the bleachers that greeted us. They clapped, yelled, and whistled for us. I couldn't see them for the tears in my eyes. It was powerfully emotional, but how exactly to describe those feelings of relief, gratitude, and finality escapes me. The first sergeant didn't even try for a grand speech. He simply saluted the officer that welcomed us and reported that the first chalk was accounted for. He turned around to address the formation.

"Welcome home, men," he said, as choked up as I felt. "Dismissed."

With that the crowd on the bleachers descended upon us. Families were reunited. There were a lot of tears, and more smiles. No one was there to greet me since my family lived far away, and I was due out of the Army soon anyway so didn't want them to make the trip. I made my exit to retrieve my bags. I ran into a sergeant on rear detachment that was out there to hand us the keys to our barracks rooms, now in a different building. I shouldered my rucksack, grabbed my duffel bag, and walked the short distance to the barracks alone the same as I'd done that January day nearly a year ago. This time was much different.

It was early morning, Christmas Day, 2005 – the merriest Christmas I'd ever had. My war was over.

Afterword

I suppose this is where you would expect me to expound upon the meanings of that experience and reveal some hidden truths regarding it. I don't think I can. I came home with more questions about that war than I took with me. I didn't know who we had really faced, how we really fared against them, or if we had made a difference. I didn't know if it was worth it or not. The war got worse before it got better, and in the end claimed around 4,500 American lives and wounded tens of thousands more. Even after our withdrawal, the future of that country is uncertain. The fact that in September 2013 car bombs still ravaged central Iraq in a continuance of sectarian violence tells me that it may be some time before I have those answers. Even at that, there are some things I do understand.

I considered myself fortunate in that it wasn't any worse than it was. I knew I was lucky to have survived while sixteen Soldiers of Task Force 2-11 did not. I was thankful that I never had to go back. I am enriched in that I have a multitude of friends gained from my time serving that I can call brothers. I miss the men we lost, but I still recognize the value in having known them. The memory of them has shaped a part of my character and has influenced quite a few steps I've taken in my life. And, of course, I'm still haunted by a lot of what I saw and sometimes did. The Ghosts of Babylon reside in many of us. Beyond those very personal meanings, though, I believe I lack the proper perspective to discuss the broader definitions of what I witnessed and did. It doesn't mean the perspective I have isn't useful in terms of informing others, though.

I was also fortunate enough to study history after returning home. It was then that I grasped the importance of this experience and the value of the endurance of my memories. Posterity is informed of its past only through the voices of the people who lived through events. The study of any historical event or process begins right there, and the more plentiful those voices the more accurate and enhanced that study will be. The interpretations and meanings may evolve as the intellectual filters of our society change, but those voices do not. Each generation has the raw material from which to glean its own understanding and meaning. I may not understand these broader definitions, and maybe I never will. But I and my brothers will never forget what happened there. It is my hope that by recording that knowledge, others may know and remember as well.